ALSO BY JONATHAN SCHELL

The Village of Ben Suc (1967)
The Military Half (1968)
The Time of Illusion (1976)

THESE ARE BORZOI BOOKS
PUBLISHED IN NEW YORK BY ALFRED A. KNOPF

THE
FATE OF
THE EARTH

THE
FATE OF
THE EARTH

Jonathan Schell

ALFRED A. KNOPF · NEW YORK
1982

THIS IS A BORZOI BOOK
PUBLISHED BY ALFRED A. KNOPF, INC.

Copyright © 1982 by Jonathan Schell
All rights reserved under
International and Pan-American Copyright Conventions.
Published in the United States by
Alfred A. Knopf, Inc., New York,
and simultaneously in Canada by
Random House of Canada Limited, Toronto.
Distributed by Random House, Inc., New York.

This book originally appeared in *The New Yorker*.

Library of Congress Cataloging in Publication Data

Schell, Jonathan [date]
The fate of the earth.

Includes index.
1. Atomic warfare. I. Title.
UF767.S2365   1982   355'.0217   81–48610
ISBN 0–394–52559–0   AACR2

Manufactured in the United States of America
First Edition

*I dedicate this book
with love to my sister, Suzy.*

CONTENTS

I.
A REPUBLIC OF
INSECTS AND GRASS

Since July 16, 1945, when the first atomic bomb was detonated, at the Trinity test site, near Alamogordo, New Mexico, mankind has lived with nuclear weapons in its midst. Each year, the number of bombs has grown, until now there are some fifty thousand warheads in the world, possessing the explosive yield of roughly twenty billion tons of TNT, or one million six hundred thousand times the yield of the bomb that was dropped by the United States on the city of Hiroshima, in Japan, less than a month after the Trinity explosion. These bombs were built as "weapons" for "war," but their significance greatly transcends war and all its causes and outcomes. They grew out of history, yet they threaten to end history. They were made by men, yet they threaten to annihilate man. They are a pit into which the whole world can fall—a nemesis of all human intentions, actions, and hopes. Only life itself, which they threaten to swallow up, can give the measure of their significance. Yet in spite of the immeasurable importance of nuclear weapons, the world has declined, on the whole, to think about them very much. We have thus far failed to fashion, or to discover within ourselves, an emotional or intellectual or political response to them. This peculiar failure of response, in which hundreds of millions of people acknowledge the presence of an immediate, unremitting threat to their existence and to the existence of the world they live in but do nothing about it—a failure in which both self-interest and fellow-feeling seem to have died—has itself been such a striking phenomenon that it has to be regarded as an extremely important part of the nuclear predicament as this has existed so far. Only very recently have there been signs, in Europe and in the United States, that public opinion has been stirring awake, and that ordinary people may be beginning to ask themselves how they should respond to the nuclear peril.

In what follows, I shall offer some thoughts on the origin and the significance of this predicament, on why we have so long resisted attempts to think about it (we even call a nuclear holocaust "unthinkable") or deal with it, and on the shape and magnitude of the choice that it forces upon us. But first I wish to describe the consequences for the world, insofar as these can be known, of a full-scale nuclear holocaust at the current level of global armament. We have lived in the shadow of nuclear arms for more than thirty-six years, so it does not seem too soon for us to familiarize ourselves with them—to acquaint ourselves with such matters as the "thermal pulse," the "blast wave," and the "three stages of radiation sickness." A description of a full-scale holocaust seems to be made necessary by the simple but basic rule that in order to discuss something one should first know what it is. A considerable number of excellent studies concentrating on various aspects of the damage that can be done by nuclear arms do exist, many of them written only in the last few years. These include a report entitled "The Effects of Nuclear War," which was published in 1979 by the Congressional Office of Technology Assessment, and which deals chiefly with the consequences of a holocaust for the societies of the United States and the Soviet Union; the latest (1977) edition of the indispensable

4

classic textbook "The Effects of Nuclear Weapons," which is edited by Samuel Glasstone and Philip J. Dolan (hereafter I shall refer to it as "Glasstone") and was published jointly by the Department of Defense and the Energy Research and Development Administration, and which makes use of the government's findings from the bombing of Hiroshima and Nagasaki and from the American nuclear-test program to describe the characteristics and the destructive effects of nuclear explosions of all kinds; "Hiroshima and Nagasaki," a comprehensive study, carried out by a group of distinguished Japanese scientists and published here in 1981, of the consequences of the bombing of those two cities; "Long-Term Worldwide Effects of Multiple Nuclear-Weapons Detonations," a report on the global ecological consequences of a nuclear holocaust which was published in 1975 by the National Academy of Sciences (hereafter referred to as the N.A.S. report); a report of research conducted in 1974 and 1975 for the Department of Transportation's Climatic Impact Assessment Program on the consequences of man-made perturbances —including the explosion of nuclear weapons—of the earth's atmosphere; and "Survival of Food Crops and Livestock in the Event of Nuclear War," proceedings of a 1970 symposium held at Brookhaven National Laboratory, on Long Island, and sponsored by the Office of Civil Defense, the Atomic Energy Commission, and the Department of Agriculture, at which the effects of radiation from fallout on both domesticated and natural ecosystems were discussed. Drawing on these and other printed sources, and also on interviews that I conducted recently with a number of scientists, I have attempted to piece together an account of the principal consequences of a full-scale holocaust. Such an account, which in its nature must be both technical and gruesome, cannot be other than hateful to dwell on, yet it may be only by descending into this hell in imagination now that we can hope to escape descending into it in reality at some later time. The knowledge we thus gain cannot in itself protect us from nuclear annihilation, but without it we cannot begin to take the measures that can actually protect us—or, for that matter, even begin to think in an appropriate way about our plight.

The widespread belief that a nuclear holocaust would in some sense bring about the end of the world has been reflected in the pronouncements of both American and Soviet leaders in the years since the invention of nuclear weapons. For example, President Dwight Eisenhower wrote in a letter in 1956 that one day both sides would have to "meet at the conference table with the understanding that the era of armaments has ended, and the human race must conform its actions to this truth or die." More recently—at a press conference in 1974—Secretary of State Henry Kissinger said that "the accumulation of nuclear arms has to be constrained if mankind is not to destroy itself." And President Jimmy Carter said in his farewell address a year ago that after a nuclear holocaust "the survivors, if any, would live in despair amid the poisoned ruins of a civilization that had committed suicide." Soviet leaders have been no less categorical in their remarks. In late 1981, for example, the Soviet government printed a booklet in which it stated, "The Soviet Union holds that nuclear war would be a universal disaster, and that it would most probably mean the end of civilization. It may lead to the destruction of all mankind." In these and other statements, examples of which could be multiplied indefinitely, Soviet and American leaders have acknowledged the supreme importance of the nuclear peril. However, they have not been precise about what level of catastrophe they were speaking of, and a variety of different outcomes, including the annihilation of the belligerent nations, the destruction of "human civilization," the extinction of mankind, and the extinction of life on earth, have been mentioned, in loose rhetorical fashion, more or less interchangeably. No doubt, the leaders have been vague in part because of the difficulty of making reliable predictions about an event that has no precedent. Yet it seems important to arrive, on the basis of available information, at some judgment concerning the likelihood of these outcomes, for they are not the same. Nor, presumably, would the appropriate political response to all of them be the same. The annihilation of the belligerent nations would be a catastrophe beyond anything in history, but it would not be the end of the world. The destruction of human civilization, even without the biological destruction of the human species, may perhaps rightly be called the end of the world, since it would be the end of that sum of cultural achievements and human relationships which constitutes what many people mean when they speak of "the world." The biological destruction of mankind would, of course, be the end of the world in a stricter sense. As for the destruction of all life on the planet, it would be not merely a human but a planetary end—the death of the earth. And although the annihilation of other forms of life could hardly be of concern to human beings once they themselves had been annihilated, this more comprehensive, planetary termination is nevertheless full of sorrowful meaning for us as we reflect on the possibility now, while we still exist. We not only live on the earth but also are of the earth, and the thought of its death, or even of its mutilation, touches a deep chord in our nature. Finally, it must be noted that a number of observers have, especially in recent years, denied that a holocaust would obliterate even the societies directly attacked. If this were so, then nuclear weapons, while remaining fearsome, would be qualitatively no different from other weapons of war, and the greater part of the nuclear predicament would melt away. (In the discussions of some analysts, nuclear attacks are made to sound almost beneficial. For example, one official of the Office of Civil Defense wrote a few years back that although it might be "verging on the macabre" to say so, "a nuclear war could alleviate some of the factors leading to today's ecological disturbances that are due to current high-population concentrations and heavy industrial production." According to a different, less sanguine view of things, this observation and other cheerful asides of the kind which crop up from time to time in the literature go well over the verge of the macabre.)

Anyone who inquires into the effects of a nuclear holocaust is bound to be assailed by powerful and conflicting emotions. Preëminent among these, almost certainly, will be an overwhelming revulsion at the tremendous scene of devastation, suffering, and death which is opened to view. And accompanying the revulsion there may be a sense of helplessness and defeat, brought about by an awareness of the incapacity of the human soul to take in so much

7

horror. A nuclear holocaust, widely regarded as "unthinkable" but never as undoable, appears to confront us with an action that we can perform but cannot quite conceive. Following upon these first responses, there may come a recoil, and a decision, whether conscious or unconscious, not to think any longer about the possibility of a nuclear holocaust. (Since a holocaust is a wholly prospective rather than a present calamity, the act of thinking about it is voluntary, and the choice of not thinking about it is always available.) When one tries to face the nuclear predicament, one feels sick, whereas when one pushes it out of mind, as apparently one must do most of the time in order to carry on with life, one feels well again. But this feeling of well-being is based on a denial of the most important reality of our time, and therefore is itself a kind of sickness. A society that systematically shuts its eyes to an urgent peril to its physical survival and fails to take any steps to save itself cannot be called psychologically well. In effect, whether we think about nuclear weapons or avoid thinking about them, their presence among us makes us sick, and there seems to be little of a purely mental or emotional nature that we can do about it.

A part of our quandary may lie in the fact that even a denial of the reality stems from what is, in a sense, a refusal to accept nuclear annihilation; that is, a refusal to accept even in imagination what Dr. Robert Jay Lifton, the author of pioneering studies of the psychology of the nuclear predicament, has appropriately called an "immersion in death." As such, the denial may have intermixed in it something that is valuable and worthy of respect. Like active revulsion and protest against nuclear weapons, a denial of their reality may spring—in part, at least—from a love of life, and since a love of life may ultimately be all that we have to pit against our doom. we cannot afford thoughtlessly to tear aside any of its manifestations. Because denial is a form of self-protection, if only against anguishing thoughts and feelings, and because it contains something useful, and perhaps even, in its way, necessary to life, anyone who invites people to draw aside the veil and look at the peril face to face is at risk of trespassing on inhibitions that are a part of our humanity. I hope in these reflections to proceed with the utmost possible respect for all forms of refusal to accept the unnatural and horrifying prospect of a nuclear holocaust.

When men split the nucleus of the atom, they unleashed into terrestrial nature a basic energy of the cosmos—the energy latent in mass—which had never before been active in any major way on earth. Until then, this energy had been kept largely within the nucleus by a force known to physicists as the strong force, which is the glue that holds the nucleus of an atom together, and is by far the strongest of the four basic forces that determine the behavior of all matter in the universe. The strong force and what is called the weak force are chiefly responsible for the static properties of nuclei. The two others, which, being outside the nucleus, had until the explosion of nuclear weapons been responsible for virtually all life and motion on earth since the earth's formation, four and a half billion years ago, are the electromagnetic force, which is responsible for, among other things, all chemical bonds, and the gravitational force, which is a force of attraction between masses. It is largely because strong-force reactions, in which the energy in mass is released, were almost entirely excluded from terrestrial affairs (one of the few exceptions is a spontaneous nuclear chain reaction that once broke out in a West African uranium deposit) and because weak-force reactions (manifested in the decay of radioactive materials) were inconspicuous enough to go mostly unnoticed that the two great conservation laws of nineteenth-century physics —the law of the conservation of energy and the law of the conservation of mass—appeared to physicists of that time to hold true. Nineteenth-century science believed that mass and energy constituted separate, closed systems, in which the amount of each remained forever constant, no matter what transformations each might undergo. It was not until twentieth-century physicists, pursuing their investigations into the realms of the irreducibly small and the unexceedably large, examined the properties of energy, mass, time, and space in the subatomic realm and the cosmic realm that mass and energy were discovered to be interchangeable entities. The new relationship was governed by Albert Einstein's laws of relativity and by quantum theory, and these—not to go deeply into theoretical matters—can be described as general physical laws of the universe, of which the Newtonian laws proved to be limiting cases. (It is because the limits included almost all the middle-sized phenomena readily available to human inspection that the need for more encompassing laws was not felt until our century.)

Broadly speaking, Newtonian physics emerged as a human-scale or earthly-scale physics, valid for velocities and sizes commonly encountered by human senses, while relativity together with quantum theory was recognized as a universal physics, valid for all phenomena. (Something of the uncanny quality of modern physics' violation of common sense—by, for instance, the concept of "curved space"—inheres in the seemingly ungraspable, and therefore "unreal," power of nuclear weapons, whose construction is based on the new principles.) Likewise, the laws of conservation of mass and energy held, to a high degree of approximation, for most then observable earthly energies, masses, and velocities but broke down for the energies, masses, and velocities in the subatomic realm. Einstein noted, "It turned out that the inertia of a system necessarily depends on its energy content, and this led straight to the notion that inert mass is simply latent energy. The principle of the conservation of mass lost its independence and became fused with that of the conservation of energy." Of mass in its slow-moving, relatively unenergetic terrestrial state, Einstein remarked, "It is as though a man who is fabulously rich [i.e., mass] should never spend or give away a cent [i.e., of its energy]; no one could tell how rich he was," and on that ground Einstein excused his nineteenth-century predecessors for failing to notice what he called the "tremendous energy" in mass. By comparison with the forms of energy active on earth during its first four and a half billion years, the amount of energy latent in mass was indeed tremendous. The rate of conversion of mass into energy is given by Einstein's formula $E = mc^2$, or energy equals mass times the speed of light squared—a formula that has won what is, considering the fateful importance it has assumed for the survival of human life, a well-justified place in popular folklore. Since the speed of light is over a hundred and eighty-six thousand miles per second—the greatest velocity attainable by anything in the universe—the value in energy obtained from the transformation of even small quantities of mass is extremely high. For example, the amount of mass expended in the destruction of Hiroshima was about a gram—or one-thirtieth of an ounce. (The bomb itself, a complex machine, weighed four tons.) It would have required twelve thousand five hundred tons of TNT to release the same amount of energy. You might say that the energy yielded by application of the universal physics of the twentieth century exceeds the energy yielded by that of the terrestrial, or planetary, physics of the nineteenth century as the cosmos exceeds the earth. Yet it was within the earth's comparatively tiny, frail ecosphere that mankind released the newly tapped cosmic energy. In view of this scientific background, President Harry Truman was speaking to the point when, in his announcement that the United States had dropped an atomic bomb on Hiroshima, he told the world that "the basic power of the universe" had been harnessed for war by the United States, and added that "the force from which the sun draws its powers has been loosed against those who brought war to the Far East." The huge—the monstrous—disproportion between "the basic power of the universe" and the merely terrestrial creatures by which and against which it was aimed in anger defined the dread predicament that the world has tried, and failed, to come to terms with ever since.

It was fortunate for earthly life that it grew up sheltered from strong-force reactions and from the nuclear energies that they release; in fact, it is doubtful whether life could have developed at all on earth if it had somehow been conditioned by continuous strong-force reactions. These release enormous bursts of energy themselves, but they also set the stage for the protracted release of energy by the other nuclear force—the weak force—in the form of nuclear radiation. When an atomic nucleus is split, releasing energy, various unstable isotopes are produced, and these new nuclei, acting under the influence of the weak force, decay, emitting radioactivity into the environment. Most of the radioactivity that occurs naturally on earth is emitted by radioactive isotopes created in strong-force reactions that occurred before the formation of the earth—in early supernovae or at the beginning of the universe, when atoms were taking shape—and by new unstable isotopes that are the products of this radioactivity. (A smaller amount of radioactivity is being continually created by the bombardment of the earth with cosmic rays.) The original radioactive isotopes are like clocks that were wound up once and have been running down ever since. Their numbers have been decreasing as their nuclei have decayed and become stable, with each species dwindling at a precise and different rate. Left to itself, the planet's supply of radioactivity would, over billions of years, have gradually declined. But when man began to split the nuclei of atoms, in bombs and in nuclear reactors, he began to create fresh batches of radioactive materials and these, like new clocks set ticking, emitted new radiation as they also began to dwindle away toward stability. (Testing in the atmosphere was banned by treaty in 1963—France and China did not concur and have since held atmospheric tests—but before that it increased the background radiation of the earth. As a result, the present annual per-capita radiation dose in the United States is four and a half per cent above the natural background level for this country.) In general magnitude, the energy of radioactive emissions greatly overmatches the strength of the chemical bonds that hold living things together. The vulnerability to radioactivity of genetic material, in particular, is well known. It is perhaps not surprising that when cosmic energies are turned loose on a small planet overwhelming destruction is the result. Einstein was only one among many farseeing people to express an understanding of this fundamental mismatch of strengths when he stated, in 1950, as he contemplated the likely detonation of a hydrogen—or thermonuclear—bomb (the first one was actually exploded, by the United States, in the fall of 1952), that "radioactive poisoning of the atmosphere and hence

12

annihilation of any life on earth has been brought within the range of technical possibilities."

The path of scientific discovery from Einstein's formulation, in 1905, for the conversion of mass into energy to the actual release by man of nuclear energy—a path in which the principles of quantum mechanics had to be developed and the basic structure of matter had to be unfolded—took several decades to travel. As late as the early nineteen-thirties, many of the best-qualified scientists had no notion that the nucleus of the atom could be fissioned. But in 1938 two Austrian physicists, Lise Meitner and Otto Frisch, correctly interpreting the results of some earlier experiments, announced that if uranium atoms were bombarded with neutrons they would split— or fission—into nearly equal parts, forming new elements and releasing some of their mass as energy, the amount being calculable by Einstein's renowned equation. The next step in obtaining usable energy from matter would be to bring about a chain reaction of fissioning uranium atoms, and this was undertaken in 1939 by the United States government, first under the auspices of an Advisory Committee on Uranium and later by the secret, multi-billion-dollar program known as the Manhattan Project, whose aim was to build an atomic bomb for use by the Allies in the Second World War. When a uranium nucleus is split, it releases several neutrons at high velocity. In a chain reaction, the neutrons released split other nuclei, which, in turn, release other neutrons, and these neutrons split still further nuclei, and so on—in a series that ends only when the available material is used up or dispersed. In some substances, such as uranium-235 or plutonium-239, a spontaneous chain reaction will start when enough of the material—a quantity known as a critical mass—is assembled in one place. But a chain reaction does not necessarily make a bomb. For an explosion to occur, the reaction has to go on long enough for explosive energies to build up before the immensely rapid expansion of the fissionable material brought about by the energy released in the chain reaction terminates the reaction. The required prolongation can be produced by sudden compression of the fissionable material to a very high density. Then the neutrons, flying about among the more tightly packed atoms, will spawn a larger number of "generations" of fissioned nuclei before the chain reaction is halted by dispersion. Since the number of fissions increases exponentially with each new generation, a huge amount of energy is created very rapidly in the late generations of the reaction. According to Glasstone, the release of energy equivalent to one hundred thousand tons of TNT would require the creation of fifty-eight generations before the reaction ended, and ninety-nine and nine-tenths per cent of the energy would be released in the last seven generations. Since each generation would require no more than a hundred-millionth of a second, this energy would be released in less than a tenth of a millionth of a second. ("Clearly," Glasstone remarks, "most of the fission energy is released in an extremely short period.")

In a fission reaction, energy is released in an expenditure of mass. Each atom contains a balance of forces and energies. Within the nucleus, the "tremendous energy" latent in mass is kept out of general circulation by the binding action of the strong force, holding the particles of the nucleus—its protons and neutrons—together. The strong force, however, is opposed by positive electrical charges that are carried by the protons in the nucleus and tend to drive the protons apart. The nuclei of the heaviest atoms, such as uranium and plutonium, are the least tightly bound together, because they contain the largest numbers of protons and so the electrical repulsion is greatest in them. (In fact, the presence of the disintegrative pressure of the electrical force within nuclei, which increases with the number of protons, forms an upper limit to the size of nuclei; there is a point beyond which they cannot cohere for any length of time.) Because of the relative weakness of the binding force in the heaviest nuclei, they are the best for fissioning. When the nucleus of an atom of uranium-235 is struck by a neutron, the binding grip of the strong force is loosed, electrical repulsion takes over, the nucleus divides, and its fragments are driven apart with an energy of motion which, in obedience to Einstein's equation, is equal to the amount of the mass lost times the speed of light squared.

14

Energy can also be released by fusion, which is the basis for the hydrogen bomb. To cause fusion, nuclei must be driven against one another with such velocity that the electrical repulsion between their respective protons is overcome and the strong force can act to bind them together into new nuclei. The best nuclei for fusion are the lightest—those of hydrogen and its isotopes and the elements nearest them in mass, because, having the fewest protons, they have the smallest amount of electrical repulsion to overcome. Dr. Henry Kendall, who teaches physics at the Massachusetts Institute of Technology and guides research in particle physics there, and who, as chairman of the Union of Concerned Scientists, has for many years devoted much of his time and attention to the nuclear question in all its aspects, recently described to me what happens in a fusion reaction. "Let a small rounded depression—or 'well,' to use the proper physical term—in a level board stand for a nucleus, and let a much smaller steel ball stand for a particle," he said. "If you roll the ball along the board at the well, it will travel down one side of the well, up the other, and out again. On the other hand, if you start the ball rolling at a point partway down one side of the well, it will rise to an equal height on the other side, then return to its starting point, and, barring other influences, continue to oscillate like that forever. This is a good representation of the bound state of the particle in the nucleus. The problem of fusion is to introduce the steel ball into the well from the outside and have it remain there in the bound state instead of shooting out the other side. It can do this only by somehow *giving up* energy. In fusion, we give the name 'binding energy' to the amount that must be given up for the outside particle to become bound in the well. A good example of this loss of energy occurs in the fusion of deuterium and tritium, two isotopes of hydrogen. The tritium nucleus contains one proton and two neutrons, and the deuterium nucleus contains one proton and one neutron, for a total of five particles. In the fusion of these isotopes, four of the particles—two neutrons and two protons—hang together very tightly, and are able to swat out the remaining neutron with incredible violence, thus getting rid of the necessary amount of energy. And this is the energy that a fusion reaction releases.

Once the four other particles have done that, they can run around in their hole undisturbed. But in order for this or any fusion reaction to take place the nuclei have to be driven very close together. Only then can the strong force reach out its stubby but powerful arms in the giant handshake that fuses the nuclei together and unleashes the explosive energy of the hydrogen bomb."

Fission and fusion can occur in a great many forms, but in all of them mass is lost, the grip of the strong force is tightened on the products of the reaction, and energy is released. A typical hydrogen bomb is a four-stage device. In the first stage, a conventional explosion is set off; in the second stage, the conventional explosion initiates a fission reaction, which is, in fact, an atomic bomb; in the third stage, the heat from the atomic bomb initiates a fusion reaction; and in the fourth stage neutrons from the fusion reaction initiate additional fission, on a scale vastly greater than the first, in a surrounding blanket of fissionable material. In my conversation with Dr. Kendall, he described the explosion of an average hydrogen bomb to me in somewhat more detail. "The trigger," he said, "consists of a carefully fashioned, subcritical, spherical piece of plutonium, with a neutron-initiator device in its interior and a high-explosive jacket surrounding it. Things begin when detonators all over the sphere of the high-explosive jacket go off—as nearly simultaneously as the design permits. Now the high-explosive jacket explodes and sends a shock wave travelling inward in a shrinking concentric sphere, and gaining in force and temperature as it proceeds. When its leading edge reaches the plutonium core, there is an abrupt jump in pressure, which squeezes the plutonium in on all sides with great precision. The pressure makes the plutonium go from subcritical to supercritical. At this point, the neutron initiator fires, and the chain reaction begins. The trick is to compress the plutonium as much as possible as quickly as possible because then more generations of nuclei will be fissioned, and more energy will be released, before the explosion, in effect, blows itself out. When that happens, all the energy from the plutonium trigger will have been released, and particles whose atomic identity has been lost will be boiling and surging in an expanded sphere whose temperature exceeds stellar levels. In all the universe, temperatures of equal heat are to be found only in such transient phenomena as exploding supernovae. Now the fusion—otherwise known as the thermonuclear reaction, because of the extreme heat needed to initiate it—can begin. The fusion fuels—lithium and isotopes of hydrogen—fly around with such velocity that they can simply coast right into one another, spitting out nuclear particles as they fuse. This is not a chain reaction, but again the explosion is stopped by the expansion caused by its own heat. By the time that happens, however, the last stage—the fissioning, by neutrons released both by the fission trigger and by the fusion reaction, of the surrounding blanket of material, which might be uranium-238—is under way. There is basically no limit to the size or yield of a thermonuclear weapon. The only limits on a bomb's destructive effect are the earth's capacity to absorb the blast."

Whereas most conventional bombs produce only one destructive effect—the shock wave—nuclear weapons produce many destructive effects. At the moment of the explosion, when the temperature of the weapon material, instantly gasified, is at the superstellar level, the pressure is millions of times the normal atmospheric pressure. Immediately, radiation, consisting mainly of gamma rays, which are a very high-energy form of electromagnetic radiation, begins to stream outward into the environment. This is called the "initial nuclear radiation," and is the first of the destructive effects of a nuclear explosion. In an air burst of a one-megaton bomb—a bomb with the explosive yield of a million tons of TNT, which is a medium-sized weapon in present-day nuclear arsenals—the initial nuclear radiation can kill unprotected human beings in an area of some six square miles. Virtually simultaneously with the initial nuclear radiation, in a second destructive effect of the explosion, an electromagnetic pulse is generated by the intense gamma radiation acting on the air. In a high-altitude detonation, the pulse can knock out electrical equipment over a wide area by inducing a powerful surge of voltage through various conductors, such as antennas, overhead power lines, pipes, and railroad tracks. The Defense Department's Civil Preparedness Agency reported in 1977 that a single multi-kiloton nuclear weapon detonated one hundred and twenty-five miles over Omaha, Nebraska, could generate an electromagnetic pulse strong enough to damage solid-state electrical circuits throughout the entire continental United States and in parts of Canada and Mexico, and thus threaten to bring the economies of these countries to a halt. When the fusion and fission reactions have blown themselves out, a fireball takes shape. As it expands, energy is absorbed in the form of X rays by the surrounding air, and then the air re-radiates a portion of that energy into the environment in the form of the thermal pulse—a wave of blinding light and intense heat—which is the third of the destructive effects of a nuclear explosion. (If the burst is low enough, the fireball touches the ground, vaporizing or incinerating almost everything within it.) The thermal pulse of a one-megaton bomb lasts for about ten seconds and can cause second-degree burns in exposed human beings at a distance of nine and a half miles, or in an area of more than two hundred and eighty square miles, and that of a twenty-megaton bomb (a large weapon by modern standards) lasts for about twenty seconds and can produce the same consequences at a distance of twenty-eight miles, or in an area of two thousand four hundred and sixty square miles. As the fireball expands, it also sends out a blast wave in all directions, and this is the fourth destructive effect of the explosion. The blast wave of an air-burst one-megaton bomb can flatten or severely damage all but the strongest buildings within a radius of four and a half miles, and that of a twenty-megaton bomb can do the same within a radius of twelve miles. As the fireball burns, it rises, condensing water from the surrounding atmosphere to form the characteristic mushroom cloud. If the bomb has been set off on the ground or close enough to it so that the fireball touches the surface, in a so-called ground burst, a crater will be formed, and tons of dust and debris will be fused with the intensely radioactive fission products and sucked up into the mushroom cloud. This mixture will return to earth as radioactive fallout, most of it in the form of fine ash, in the fifth destructive effect of the explosion. Depending upon the composition of the surface, from forty to seventy per cent of this fallout—often called the "early" or "local" fallout—descends to earth within about a day of the explosion, in the vicinity of the blast and downwind from it, exposing human beings to radiation disease, an illness that is fatal when exposure is intense. Air bursts may also produce local fallout, but in much smaller quantities. The lethal range of the local fallout depends on a number of circumstances, including the weather, but under average conditions a one-megaton ground burst would, according to the report by the Office of Technology Assessment, lethally contaminate over a thousand square miles. (A lethal dose, by convention, is considered to be the amount of radiation that, if delivered over a short period of time, would kill half the able-bodied young adult population.)

The initial nuclear radiation, the electromagnetic pulse, the thermal pulse, the blast wave, and the local fallout may be described as the local primary effects of nuclear weapons. Naturally, when many bombs are exploded the scope of these effects is increased accordingly. But in addition these primary effects produce innumerable secondary effects on societies and natural environments, some of which may be even more harmful than the primary ones. To give just one example, nuclear weapons, by flattening and setting fire to huge, heavily built-up areas, generate mass fires, and in some cases these may kill more people than the original thermal pulses and blast waves. Moreover, there are—quite distinct from both the local primary effects of individual bombs and their secondary effects—global primary effects, which do not become significant unless thousands of bombs are detonated all around the earth. And these global primary effects produce innumerable secondary effects of their own throughout the ecosystem of the earth as a whole. For a full-scale holocaust is more than the sum of its local parts; it is also a powerful direct blow to the ecosphere. In that sense, a holocaust is to the earth what a single bomb is to a city. Three grave direct global effects have been discovered so far. The first is the "delayed," or "worldwide," fallout. In detonations greater than one hundred kilotons, part of the fallout does not fall to the ground in the vicinity of the explosion but rises high into the troposphere and into the stratosphere, circulates around the earth, and then, over months or years, descends, contaminating the whole surface of the globe—although with doses of radiation far weaker than those delivered by the local fallout. Nuclear-fission products comprise some three hundred radioactive isotopes, and though some of them decay to relatively harmless levels of radioactivity within a few hours, minutes, or even seconds, others persist to emit radiation for up to millions of years. The short-lived isotopes are the ones most responsible for the lethal effects of the local fallout, and the long-lived ones are responsible for the contamination of the earth by stratospheric fallout. The energy released by all fallout from a thermonuclear explosion is about five per cent of the total. By convention, this energy is not calculated in the stated yield of a weapon, yet in a ten-thousand-megaton attack the equivalent of five hundred megatons of explosive energy, or forty thousand times the yield of the Hiroshima bomb, would be released in the form of radioactivity. This release may be considered a protracted afterburst, which is dispersed into the land, air, and sea, and into the tissues, bones, roots, stems, and leaves of living things, and goes on detonating there almost indefinitely after the explosion. The second of the global effects that have been discovered so far is the lofting, from ground bursts, of millions of tons of dust into the stratosphere; this is likely to produce general cooling of the earth's surface. The third of the global effects is a predicted partial destruction of the layer of ozone that surrounds the entire earth in the stratosphere. A nuclear fireball, by burning nitrogen in the air, produces large quantities of oxides of nitrogen. These are carried by the heat of the blast into the stratosphere, where, through a series of chemical reactions, they bring about a depletion of the ozone layer. Such a depletion may persist for years. The 1975 N.A.S. report has estimated that in a holocaust in which ten thousand megatons were detonated in the Northern Hemisphere the reduction of ozone in this hemisphere could be as high as seventy per cent and in the Southern Hemisphere as high as forty per cent, and that it could take as long as thirty years for the ozone level to return to normal. The ozone layer is crucial to life on earth, because it shields the surface of the earth from lethal levels of ultraviolet radiation, which is present in sunlight. Glasstone remarks simply, "If it were not for the absorption of much of the solar ultraviolet radiation by the ozone, life as currently known could not exist except possibly in the ocean." Without the ozone shield, sunlight, the life-giver, would become a life-extinguisher. In judging the global effects of a holocaust, therefore, the primary question is not how many people would be irradiated, burned, or crushed to death by the immediate effects of the bombs but how well the ecosphere, regarded as a single living entity, on which all forms of life depend for their continued existence, would hold up. The issue is the habitability of the earth, and it is in this context, not in the context of the direct slaughter of hundreds of millions of people by the local effects, that the question of human survival arises.

Usually, people wait for things to occur before trying to describe them. (Futurology has never been a very respectable field of inquiry.) But since we cannot afford under any circumstances to let a holocaust occur, we are forced in this one case to become the historians of the future—to chronicle and commit to memory an event that we have never experienced and must never experience. This unique endeavor, in which foresight is asked to perform a task usually reserved for hindsight, raises a host of special difficulties. There is a categorical difference, often overlooked, between trying to describe an event that has already happened (whether it is Napoleon's invasion of Russia or the pollution of the environment by acid rain) and trying to describe one that has yet to happen—and one, in addition, for which there is no precedent, or even near-precedent, in history. Lacking experience to guide our thoughts and impress itself on our feelings, we resort to speculation. But speculation, however brilliantly it may be carried out, is at best only a poor substitute for experience. Experience gives us facts, whereas in pure speculation we are thrown back on theory, which has never been a very reliable guide to future events. Moreover, experience engraves its lessons in our hearts through suffering and the other consequences that it has for our lives; but speculation leaves our lives untouched, and so gives us leeway to reject its conclusions, no matter how well argued they may be. (In the world of strategic theory, in particular, where strategists labor to simulate actual situations on the far side of the nuclear abyss, so that generals and statesmen can prepare to make their decisions in case the worst happens, there is sometimes an unfortunate tendency to mistake pure ratiocination for reality, and to pretend to a knowledge of the future that it is not given to human beings to have.) Our knowledge of the local primary effects of the bombs, which is based both on the physical principles that made their construction possible and on experience gathered from the bombings of Hiroshima and Nagasaki and from testing, is quite solid. And our knowledge of the extent of the local primary effects of many weapons used together, which is obtained simply by using the multiplication table, is also solid: knowing that the thermal pulse of a twenty-megaton bomb can give people at least second-degree burns in an area of two thousand four hundred and sixty square miles, we can easily figure out that the pulses of a hundred twenty-megaton bombs can give people at least second-degree burns in an area of two hundred and forty-six thousand square miles. Nevertheless, it may be that our knowledge even of the primary effects is still incomplete, for during our test program new ones kept being discovered. One example is the electromagnetic pulse, whose importance was not recognized until around 1960, when, after more than a decade of tests, scientists realized that this effect accounted for unexpected electrical failures that had been occurring all along in equipment around the test sites. And it is only in recent years that the Defense Department has been trying to take account strategically of this startling capacity of just one bomb to put the technical equipment of a whole continent out of action.

When we proceed from the local effects of single explosions to the effects of thousands of them on societies and environments, the picture clouds considerably, because then we go beyond both the certainties of physics and our slender base of experience, and speculatively encounter the full complexity of human affairs and of the biosphere. Looked at in its entirety, a nuclear holocaust can be said to assail human life at three levels: the level of individual life, the level of human society, and the level of the natural environment—including the environment of the earth as a whole. At none of these levels can the destructiveness of nuclear weapons be measured in terms of firepower alone. At each level, life has both considerable recuperative powers, which might restore it even after devastating injury, and points of exceptional vulnerability, which leave it open to sudden, wholesale, and permanent collapse, even when comparatively little violence has been applied. Just as a machine may break down if one small part is removed, and a person may die if a single artery or vein is blocked, a modern technological society may come to a standstill if its fuel supply is cut off, and an ecosystem may collapse if its ozone shield is depleted. Nuclear weapons thus do not only kill directly, with their tremendous violence, but also kill indirectly, by breaking down the man-made and the natural systems on which individual lives collectively depend. Human beings require constant provision and care, supplied both by their societies and by the natural environment, and if these are suddenly removed people will die just as surely as if they had been struck by a bullet. Nuclear weapons are unique in that they attack the support systems of life at every level. And these systems, of course, are not isolated from each other but are parts of a single whole: ecological collapse, if it goes far enough, will bring about social collapse, and social collapse will bring about individual deaths. Furthermore, the destructive consequences of a nuclear attack are immeasurably compounded by the likelihood that all or most of the bombs will be detonated within the space of a few hours, in a single huge concussion. Normally, a locality devastated by a catastrophe, whether natural or man-made, will sooner or later receive help from untouched outside areas, as Hiroshima and Nagasaki did after they were bombed; but a nuclear holocaust would devastate the "outside" areas as well, leaving the victims to fend for themselves in a shattered society and natural environment. And what is true for each city is also true for the earth as a whole: a devastated earth can hardly expect "outside" help. The earth is the largest of the support systems for life, and the impairment of the earth is the largest of the perils posed by nuclear weapons.

The incredible complexity of all these effects, acting, interacting, and interacting again, precludes confident detailed representation of the events in a holocaust. We deal inevitably with approximations, probabilities, even guesses. However, it is important to point out that our uncertainty pertains not to *whether* the effects will interact, multiplying their destructive power as they do so, but only to *how*. It follows that our almost built-in bias, determined by the limitations of the human mind in judging future events, is to underestimate the harm. To fear interactive consequences that we cannot predict, or even imagine, may not be impossible, but it is very difficult. Let us consider, for example, some of the possible ways in which a person in a targeted country might die. He might be incinerated by the fireball or the thermal pulse. He might be lethally irradiated by the initial nuclear radiation. He might be crushed to death or hurled to his death by the blast wave or its debris. He might be lethally irradiated by the local fallout. He might be burned to death in a firestorm. He might be injured by one or another of these effects and then die of his wounds before he was able to make his way out of the devastated zone in which he found himself. He might die of starvation, because the economy had collapsed and no food was being grown or delivered, or because existing local crops had been killed by radiation, or because the local ecosystem had been ruined, or because the ecosphere of the earth as a whole was collapsing. He might die of cold, for lack of heat and clothing, or of exposure, for lack of shelter. He might be killed by people seeking food or shelter that he had obtained. He might die of an illness spread in an epidemic. He might be killed by exposure to the sun if he stayed outside too long following serious ozone depletion. Or he might be killed by any combination of these perils. But while there is almost no end to the ways to die in and after a holocaust, each person has only one life to lose: someone who has been killed by the thermal pulse can't be killed again in an epidemic. Therefore, anyone who wishes to describe a holocaust is always at risk of depicting scenes of devastation that in reality would never take place, because the people in them would already have been killed off in some earlier scene of devastation. The task is made all the more confusing by the fact that causes of death and destruction do not exist side by side in the world but often encompass one another, in widening rings. Thus, if it turned out that a holocaust rendered the earth uninhabitable by human beings, then all the more immediate forms of death would be nothing more than redundant preliminaries, leading up to the extinction of the whole species by a hostile environment. Or if a continental ecosystem was so thoroughly destroyed by a direct attack that it could no longer sustain a significant human population, the more immediate causes of death would again decline in importance. In much the same way, if an airplane is hit by gunfire, and thereby caused to crash, dooming all the passengers, it makes little difference whether the shots also killed a few of the passengers in advance of the crash. On the other hand, if the larger consequences, which are less predictable than the local ones, failed to occur, then the local ones would have their full importance again.

Faced with uncertainties of this kind, some analysts of nuclear destruction have resorted to fiction, assigning to the imagination the work that investigation is unable to do. But then the results are just what one would expect: fiction. An approach more appropriate to our intellectual circumstances would be to acknowledge a high degree of uncertainty as an intrinsic and extremely important part of dealing with a possible holocaust. A nuclear holocaust is an event that is obscure because it is future, and uncertainty, while it has to be recognized in all calculations of future events, has a special place in calculations of a nuclear holocaust, because a holocaust is something that we aspire to keep in the future forever, and never to permit into the present. You might say that uncertainty, like the thermal pulses or the blast waves, is one of the features of a holocaust. Our procedure, then, should be not to insist on a precision that is beyond our grasp but to inquire into the rough probabilities of various results insofar as we can judge them, and then to ask ourselves what our political responsibilities are in the light of these probabilities. This embrace of investigative modesty—this acceptance of our limited ability to predict the consequences of a holocaust—would itself be a token of our reluctance to extinguish ourselves.

There are two further aspects of a holocaust which, though

they do not further obscure the factual picture, nevertheless vex our understanding of this event. The first is that although in imagination we can try to survey the whole prospective scene of destruction, inquiring into how many would live and how many would die and how far the collapse of the environment would go under attacks of different sizes, and piling up statistics on how many square miles would be lethally contaminated, or what percentage of the population would receive first-, second-, or third-degree burns, or be trapped in the rubble of its burning houses, or be irradiated to death, no one actually experiencing a holocaust would have any such overview. The news of other parts necessary to put together that picture would be one of the things that were immediately lost, and each surviving person, his vision drastically foreshortened by the collapse of his world, and his impressions clouded by his pain, shock, bewilderment, and grief, would see only as far as whatever scene of chaos and agony happened to lie at hand. For it would not be only such abstractions as "industry" and "society" and "the environment" that would be destroyed in a nuclear holocaust; it would also be, over and over again, the small collections of cherished things, known landscapes, and beloved people that made up the immediate contents of individual lives.

The other obstacle to our understanding is that when we strain to picture what the scene would be like after a holocaust we tend to forget that for most people, and perhaps for all, it wouldn't be *like* anything, because they would be dead. To depict the scene as it would appear to the living is to that extent a falsification, and the greater the number killed, the greater the falsification. The right vantage point from which to view a holocaust is that of a corpse, but from that vantage point, of course, there is nothing to report.

The specific train of events that might lead up to an attack is, obviously, among the unpredictables, but a few general possibilities can be outlined. One would be a wholly accidental attack, triggered by human error or mechanical failure. On three occasions in the last couple of years, American nuclear forces were placed on the early stages of alert: twice because of the malfunctioning of a computer chip in the North American Air Defense Command's warning system, and once when a test tape depicting a missile attack was inadvertently inserted in the system. The greatest danger in computer-generated misinformation and other mechanical errors may be that one error might start a chain reaction of escalating responses between command centers, leading, eventually, to an attack. If in the midst of a crisis Country A was misled by its computers into thinking that Country B was getting ready to attack, and went on alert, Country B might notice this and go on alert in response. Then Country A, observing the now indubitably real alert of Country B, might conclude that its computers had been right after all, and increase its alert. This move would then be noticed by Country B, which would, in turn, increase its alert, and so on, until either the mistake was straightened out or an attack was launched. A holocaust might also be touched off by conventional or nuclear hostilities between smaller powers, which could draw in the superpowers. Another possibility would be a deliberate, unprovoked preëmptive strike by one side against the other. Most observers regard an attack of this kind as exceedingly unlikely in either direction, but the logic of present nuclear strategy drives both sides to prepare to respond to one, for the central tenet of nuclear strategy is that each side will refrain from launching an all-out first strike against the other only if it knows that even after it has done so the other side will retain forces sufficient to launch an utterly devastating counterblow. What is more likely, in the opinion of many, is a preëmptive strike launched in the midst of an international crisis. Neither quite planned (in the sense of being a cold-blooded, premeditated strike, out of the blue) nor quite accidental (in the sense of being caused by technical failure), such an attack would be precipitated by a combination on one side or both sides of belligerency, reckless actions, miscalculation, and fear of a first strike by the other side. Each side's possible fear of a first strike by the other side has become an element of increasing danger in recent years. Modern weapons, such as the Soviet SS-18 and SS-19 and the improved American Minuteman III missile and planned MX missile, have a greatly increased ability to destroy enemy missiles in their silos, thus adding to the incentive on both sides to strike first. The peril is that in a crisis either side, fearful of losing the preëmptive advantage, would go ahead and order a first strike.

It was during an international crisis—the Cuban missile crisis, in 1962—that the world apparently came as close as it has yet come to a nuclear holocaust. On that occasion, and perhaps on that occasion alone, a dread of nuclear doom became palpable not only in the councils of power but among ordinary people around the world. At the height of the crisis, it is reported, President John Kennedy believed that the odds on the occurrence of a holocaust were between one out of three and even. In the memoir "Thirteen Days," Robert Kennedy, the President's brother, who was Attorney General at the time, and who advised the President in the crisis, offered a recollection of the moments of greatest peril. President Kennedy had ordered a blockade of all shipping to Cuba, where, American intelligence had found, the Soviet Union was emplacing missiles capable of carrying nuclear warheads. Missile crews in the United States had been placed on maximum alert. Now, at a few minutes after ten o'clock on the morning of October 24th, two Russian ships, accompanied by a Russian submarine, had approached to within a few miles of the blockade. Robert Kennedy wrote in his memoir:

> I think these few minutes were the time of gravest concern for the President. Was the world on the brink of a holocaust? Was it our error? A mistake? Was there something further that should have been done? Or not done? His hand went up to his face and covered his mouth. He opened and closed his fist. His face seemed drawn, his eyes pained, almost gray. We stared at each other across the table. For a few fleeting seconds, it was almost as though no one else was there and he was no longer the President.
>
> Inexplicably, I thought of when he was ill and almost died; when he lost his child; when we learned that our oldest brother had been killed; of personal times of strain and

hurt. . . . We had come to the time of final decision. . . .
I felt we were on the edge of a precipice with no way off.
This time, the moment was now—not next week—not tomorrow, "so we can have another meeting and decide";
not in eight hours, "so we can send another message to
Khrushchev and perhaps he will finally understand." No,
none of that was possible. One thousand miles away in the
vast expanse of the Atlantic Ocean the final decisions were
going to be made in the next few minutes. President Kennedy had initiated the course of events, but he no longer
had control over them.

Any number of future crises that would lead to an attack can be
pictured, but I would like to mention one possible category that
seems particularly dangerous. In the theory of nuclear deterrence,
each side would ideally deter attacks at every level of violence
with a deterrent force at the same level. Thus, conventional attacks
would be deterred with conventional forces, tactical attacks would
be deterred with tactical forces, and strategic attacks would be
deterred with strategic forces. The theoretical advantage of match-
ing forces in this fashion would be that the opening moves in hypothetical hostilities would not automatically lead to escalation—for
example, by leading the side weaker in conventional forces to respond to a conventional attack with nuclear weapons. However,
the facts of geography make such ideal deterrent symmetry impracticable. The Soviet Union's proximity both to Western Europe and
to the Middle East gives it a heavy conventional preponderance in
those parts of the world. Therefore, throughout the postwar period
it has been American policy to deter a Soviet conventional attack
in Europe with tactical nuclear arms. And in January of 1980 President Carter, in effect, extended the policy to include protection of
the nations around the Persian Gulf. In his State of the Union
address for 1980, Carter said, "An attempt by any outside force to
gain control of the Persian Gulf region will be regarded as an assault
on the vital interests of the United States of America. And such an
assault will be repelled by any means necessary, including military

force." Since the United States clearly lacked the conventional power to repel a Soviet attack in a region near the borders of the Soviet Union, "any means" could refer to nothing but nuclear arms. The threat was spelled out explicitly shortly after the speech, in a story in the New York *Times*—thought to be a leak from the Administration—about a 1979 Defense Department "study," which, according to the *Times,* said that American conventional forces could not stop a Soviet thrust into northern Iran, and that "to prevail in an Iranian scenario, we might have to threaten or make use of tactical nuclear weapons." The words of this study put the world on notice that the use of nuclear arms not only was contemplated in past crises but will continue to be contemplated in future ones.

It is possible to picture a nuclear attack of any shape or size. An attack might use all the weapons at the attacker's disposal or any portion of them. It might be aimed at military targets, at industry, at the population, or at all or some combination of these. The attack might be mainly air-burst, and would increase the range of severe damage from the blast waves, or it might be mainly ground-burst, to destroy hard targets such as land-based nuclear missiles or command-and-control centers, or to deliver the largest possible amount of fallout, or it might combine air bursts and ground bursts in any proportion. It could be launched in the daytime or at night, in summer or in winter, with warning or without warning. The sequence of events once hostilities had begun also lies open. For example, it seems quite possible that the leaders of a nation that had just suffered a nuclear attack would be sparing in their response, tailoring it to political objectives rather than to the vengeful aim of wiping out the society whose leaders had launched the attack. On the other hand, they might retaliate with all the forces at their disposal, as they say they will do. Then again, the two sides might expend their forces gradually, in a series of ad-hoc "exchanges," launched in an atmosphere of misinformation and intellectual and moral disorientation. The state of mind of the decision-makers might be one of calm rationality, of hatred, of shock, of hysteria, or even of outright insanity. They might follow coldly reasoned scenarios of destruction to the letter, and exterminate one another in that way. Or, for all we are able to know now, having at first hardened their "resolve" to follow the scenarios through to the end, they might suddenly reverse themselves, and proceed to the negotiating table after only incompletely destroying one another. Lacking any experience of what decisions human beings make under full-scale nuclear attack, we simply do not know what they would do.

Not surprisingly, predictions of the course of an attack are subject to intellectual fashion (there being nothing in the way of experience to guide them). In the nineteen-sixties, for example, it was widely believed that the most important attack to deter was an all-out one, but in the last few years the idea that a "limited nuclear war" might be fought has come into vogue. (The concept of limited nuclear war also had an earlier vogue, in the late nineteen-fifties, when some strategists were seeking an alternative to Secretary of State John Foster Dulles's strategy of "massive retaliation.") The premise of the limited-war theory is that nuclear hostilities can be halted at some new equilibrium in the balance of forces, before all-out attacks have been launched. In particular, it has been argued recently by nuclear theorists that the Soviet Union is now able to launch a devastating first strike at American bombers and land-based missiles, leaving the United States in the unfavorable position of having to choose between using its less accurate submarine-based missiles to directly attack Soviet society—and thus risk a direct attack on its own society in return—and doing nothing. Rather than initiate the annihilation of both societies, it is argued, American leaders might acquiesce in the Soviet first strike. But there is something dreamlike and fantastic in this concept of a wholly one-way nuclear strike, which, while leaving intact the power of the assaulted country to devastate the society of the aggressor, would somehow allow the aggressor to dictate terms. What seems to have been forgotten is that, unless one assumes that the adversary has gone insane (in which case not even the most foolproof scenarios can save us), military actions are taken with some aim in mind—for example, the aim of conquering a particular territory. This imagined first strike would in itself achieve nothing, and the moment the Soviet Union might try to achieve some actual advantage—for example, by marching into the Middle East to seize its oil fields—two or three nuclear weapons from among the thousands remaining in American arsenals would suffice to put a quick end to the undertaking. Or if the United States retaliated with only ten bombs on Soviet cities, holding back the rest, the Soviet Union would suffer unprecedented losses while gaining nothing. In other words, in this scenario—and, indeed, in any number of other scenarios for "limited nuclear war" which could be mentioned—strategic theory seems to have taken on a weird life of its own, in which the weapons are pictured as having their own quarrel to settle, irrespective of mere human purposes. In general, in the theoretically sophisticated but often humanly deficient world of nuclear strategic theory it is likely to be overlooked that the outbreak of nuclear hostilities in itself assumes the collapse of every usual restraint of reason and humanity. Once the mass killing of a nuclear holocaust had begun, the scruples, and even the reckonings of self-interest, that normally keep the actions of nations within certain bounds would by definition have been trampled down, and would probably offer little further protection for anybody. In the unimaginable mental and spiritual climate of the world at that point it is hard to imagine what force could be counted on to hold the world back from all-out destruction.

However, it would be misleading to suggest that once one nuclear weapon had been used it would be inevitable for all of them to be used. Rather, the point is that once a catastrophe that we now find "unthinkable" actually commenced, people would act in ways that are unforeseeable by theorists—or, for that matter, by the future actors themselves. Predictions about the size and form of a nuclear holocaust are really predictions about human decisions, and these are notoriously incalculable in advance—especially when the decisions in question are going to be made in the midst of unimaginable mayhem. Secretary of Defense Robert McNamara probably said the last word on this subject when he remarked before the House Armed Services Committee in 1963, in regard to a possible defense of Europe, that once the first tactical nuclear weapon had been used the world would have been launched into "a vast unknown." Therefore, in picturing a Soviet attack on the United States I shall not venture any predictions concerning the shape and size of the attack, since to do so, it seems to me, would be to pretend to a kind of knowledge that we are incapable of. Instead, I shall simply choose two basic assumptions—using the word to mean not predictions but postulates. The first assumption is that most of the Soviet strategic forces are used in the attack, and the second is that the attack is aimed at military facilities, industry, and the population centers of the United States. I have chosen these assumptions not because I "predict" an attack of this kind, which is the most damaging of the attacks that appear to have a likely chance of occurring, but because, in the absence of any basis for confident prediction, and, in particular, of any reliable assurance that an attack would remain "limited," they are the only assumptions that represent the full measure of our peril. At the very least, they are not farfetched. The first assumption is supported by many statements by leaders on both sides. The Soviet government, which, of course, is one of the actors concerned, has frequently stated the view that nuclear hostilities cannot be limited, and Secretary of Defense Harold Brown also said, in 1977, that a nuclear conflict probably could not be limited. Concerning the second assumption, the significant point is that the fundamental logic of the strategy of both sides is, in McNamara's words, to hold not just the military forces of the other side hostage but also its "society as a whole." Just how the strategists on both sides achieve this is unknown, but it seems unwarranted to suppose that there will be much relief for either population in the merciful sentiments of targeters.

A further set of assumptions that influence one's judgment of the consequences of a holocaust concerns the possibility of civil defense. These assumptions also depend in part on certain circumstances that are unknowable in advance, such as whether the attack occurs in the daytime or at night, but they also depend on circumstances that are more or less built into the situation, and can therefore be predicted. The two main components of a conceivable civil defense against nuclear attack are evacuation and sheltering. In a protracted crisis, a country might seek to protect its population by evacuating its cities and towns before any attack had actually been launched; but, for a variety of reasons, such a strategy seems impracticable or useless. To begin with, an enemy that was bent on attacking one's population might retarget its missiles against people in the places to which they had fled. Also, during the days of evacuation people would be more vulnerable to attack than they were even in their cities. (Probably the worst assumption regarding evacuation would be that the attack came while evacuation was under way.) A further disadvantage of a policy of evacuation is that it would offer the foe a means of utterly disrupting the society by threats alone, since an evacuated society would be one that had stopped functioning for any other purpose. Shelters appear to be no more promising than evacuation. The Soviet missiles closest to the United States, which are stationed on submarines several hundred miles from our shores, can deliver their warheads on coastal targets about ten minutes after they are fired, and on inland targets a few minutes later. The intercontinental ballistic missiles, which are all launched from within the Soviet Union, would arrive fifteen or twenty minutes after that. The bombers would arrive in several hours. But, according to the Arms Control and Disarmament Agency, it requires fifteen minutes after missiles have been launched for the earliest warnings to be given to the population. Even assuming—very optimistically, I think—that it would take only another fifteen minutes or so for any significant number of people to become aware of the warnings and go to shelters, a surprise attack would indeed catch the great majority of people by surprise.

For most people, however, the lack of any opportunity to proceed to shelters would be without importance in any case, since shelters, even if they existed, would be of no use. It is now commonly acknowledged that economically feasible shelters cannot provide protection against the blast, heat, intense radiation, and mass fires that would probably occur in densely populated regions of the country—that such shelters could save lives only in places that were subjected to nothing worse than modest amounts of fallout. Furthermore, there is a very serious question whether many people would survive in the long run even if they did manage to save themselves in the short run by sealing themselves up in shelters for several weeks or months. Finally, it seems worth mentioning that, whatever the potential value of shelters might be, most existing ones either are situated in places where they are useless (in large cities, for example) or lack some or all of the following necessary equipment for an effective shelter: adequate shielding from radiation; air filters that would screen out radioactive particles; food and water to last as long as several months; an independent heating system, in places where winters are severe; medical supplies for the injured, sick, and dying, who might be in the majority in the shelters; radiation counters to measure levels of radiation outdoors, so that people could know when it was safe to leave the shelter and could determine whether food and drink were contaminated; and a burial system wholly contained within the shelter, in which to bury those who died of their injuries or illness during the shelter period.

Systems setting up evacuation procedures and shelters are often presented as humanitarian measures that would save lives in the event of a nuclear attack. In the last analysis, however, the civil-defense issue is a strategic, not a humanitarian, question. It is fundamental to the nuclear strategy of both the Soviet Union and the United States that each preserve the capacity to devastate the population of the other after itself absorbing the largest first strike that is within the other's capacity. Therefore, any serious attempt by either side to make its population safe from nuclear attack—assuming for the moment that this could be done—would be extremely likely to call forth a strategic countermove by the other side, probably taking the form of increased armament. Since the extraordinary power of modern weapons makes such compensation quite easy, it is safe

35

to assume that for the foreseeable future the population of each side is going to remain exactly as vulnerable as the other side wants it to be.

The yardsticks by which one can measure the destruction that will be caused by weapons of different sizes are provided by the bombings of Hiroshima and Nagasaki and American nuclear tests in which the effects of hydrogen bombs with up to sixteen hundred times the explosive yield of the Hiroshima bomb were determined. The data gathered from these experiences make it a straightforward matter to work out the distances from the explosion at which different intensities of the various effects of a bomb are likely to occur. In the back of the Glasstone book, the reader will find a small dial computer that places all this information at his fingertips. Thus, if one would like to know how deep a crater a twenty-megaton ground burst will leave in wet soil one has only to set a pointer at twenty megatons and look in a small window showing crater size to find that the depth would be six hundred feet—a hole deep enough to bury a fair-sized skyscraper. Yet this small circular computer, on which the downfall of every city on earth is distilled into a few lines and figures, can, of course, tell us nothing of the human reality of nuclear destruction. Part of the horror of thinking about a holocaust lies in the fact that it leads us to supplant the human world with a statistical world; we seek a human truth and come up with a handful of figures. The only source that gives us a glimpse of that human truth is the testimony of the survivors of the Hiroshima and Nagasaki bombings. Because the bombing of Hiroshima has been more thoroughly investigated than the bombing of Nagasaki, and therefore more information about it is available, I shall restrict myself to a brief description of that catastrophe.

On August 6, 1945, at 8:16 A.M., a fission bomb with a yield of twelve and a half kilotons was detonated about nineteen hundred feet above the central section of Hiroshima. By present-day standards, the bomb was a small one, and in today's arsenals it would be classed among the merely tactical weapons. Nevertheless, it was large enough to transform a city of some three hundred and forty thousand people into hell in the space of a few seconds. "It is no exaggeration," the authors of "Hiroshima and Nagasaki" tell us, "to say that the whole city was ruined instantaneously." In that instant, tens of thousands of people were burned, blasted, and crushed to death. Other tens of thousands suffered injuries of every description or were doomed to die of radiation sickness. The center of the city was flattened, and every part of the city was damaged. The trunks of bamboo trees as far away as five miles from ground zero—the point on the ground directly under the center of the explosion—were charred. Almost half the trees within a mile and a quarter were knocked down. Windows nearly seventeen miles away were broken. Half an hour after the blast, fires set by the thermal pulse and by the collapse of the buildings began to coalesce into a firestorm, which lasted for six hours. Starting about 9 A.M. and lasting until late afternoon, a "black rain" generated by the bomb (otherwise, the day was fair) fell on the western portions of the city, carrying radioactive fallout from the blast to the ground. For four hours at midday, a violent whirlwind, born of the strange meteorological conditions produced by the explosion, further devastated the city. The number of people who were killed outright or who died of their injuries over the next three months is estimated to be a hundred and thirty thousand. Sixty-eight per cent of the buildings in the city were either completely destroyed or damaged beyond repair, and the center of the city was turned into a flat, rubble-strewn plain dotted with the ruins of a few of the sturdier buildings.

In the minutes after the detonation, the day grew dark, as heavy clouds of dust and smoke filled the air. A whole city had fallen in a moment, and in and under its ruins were its people. Among those still living, most were injured, and of these most were burned or had in some way been battered or had suffered both kinds of injury. Those within a mile and a quarter of ground zero had also been subjected to intense nuclear radiation, often in lethal doses. When people revived enough from their unconsciousness or shock to see what was happening around them, they found that where a second before there had been a city getting ready to go

37

about its daily business on a peaceful, warm August morning, now there was a heap of debris and corpses and a stunned mass of injured humanity. But at first, as they awakened and tried to find their bearings in the gathering darkness, many felt cut off and alone. In a recent volume of recollections by survivors called "Unforgettable Fire," in which the effects of the bombing are rendered in drawings as well as in words, Mrs. Haruko Ogasawara, a young girl on that August morning, recalls that she was at first knocked unconscious. She goes on to write:

> How many seconds or minutes had passed I could not tell, but, regaining consciousness, I found myself lying on the ground covered with pieces of wood. When I stood up in a frantic effort to look around, there was darkness. Terribly frightened, I thought I was alone in a world of death, and groped for any light. My fear was so great I did not think anyone would truly understand. When I came to my senses, I found my clothes in shreds, and I was without my wooden sandals.

Soon cries of pain and cries for help from the wounded filled the air. Survivors heard the voices of their families and their friends calling out in the gloom. Mrs. Ogasawara writes:

> Suddenly, I wondered what had happened to my mother and sister. My mother was then forty-five, and my sister five years old. When the darkness began to fade, I found that there was nothing around me. My house, the next door neighbor's house, and the next had all vanished. I was standing amid the ruins of my house. No one was around. It was quiet, very quiet—an eerie moment. I discovered my mother in a water tank. She had fainted. Crying out, "Mama, Mama," I shook her to bring her back to her senses. After coming to, my mother began to shout madly for my sister: "Eiko! Eiko!"
>
> I wondered how much time had passed when there were cries of searchers. Children were calling their parents' names, and parents were calling the names of their chil-

dren. We were calling desperately for my sister and listening for her voice and looking to see her. Suddenly, Mother cried "Oh Eiko!" Four or five meters away, my sister's head was sticking out and was calling my mother. . . . Mother and I worked desperately to remove the plaster and pillars and pulled her out with great effort. Her body had turned purple from the bruises, and her arm was so badly wounded that we could have placed two fingers in the wound.

Others were less fortunate in their searches and rescue attempts. In "Unforgettable Fire," a housewife describes a scene she saw:

A mother, driven half-mad while looking for her child, was calling his name. At last she found him. His head looked like a boiled octopus. His eyes were half-closed, and his mouth was white, pursed, and swollen.

Throughout the city, parents were discovering their wounded or dead children, and children were discovering their wounded or dead parents. Kikuno Segawa recalls seeing a little girl with her dead mother:

A woman who looked like an expectant mother was dead. At her side, a girl of about three years of age brought some water in an empty can she had found. She was trying to let her mother drink from it.

The sight of people in extremities of suffering was ubiquitous. Kinzo Nishida recalls:

While taking my severely wounded wife out to the riverbank by the side of the hill of Nakahiro-machi, I was horrified, indeed, at the sight of a stark naked man standing in the rain with his eyeball in his palm. He looked to be in great pain, but there was nothing that I could do for him.

Many people were astonished by the sheer sudden absence of the known world. The writer Yoko Ota later wrote:

> I just could not understand why our surroundings had changed so greatly in one instant. . . . I thought it might have been something which had nothing to do with the war—the collapse of the earth, which it was said would take place at the end of the world, and which I had read about as a child.

And a history professor who looked back at the city after the explosion remarked later, "I saw that Hiroshima had disappeared."

As the fires sprang up in the ruins, many people, having found injured family members and friends, were now forced to abandon them to the flames or to lose their own lives in the firestorm. Those who left children, husbands, wives, friends, and strangers to burn often found these experiences the most awful of the entire ordeal. Mikio Inoue describes how one man, a professor, came to abandon his wife:

> It was when I crossed Miyuki Bridge that I saw Professor Takenaka, standing at the foot of the bridge. He was almost naked, wearing nothing but shorts, and he had a ball of rice in his right hand. Beyond the streetcar line, the northern area was covered by red fire burning against the sky. Far away from the line, Ote-machi was also a sea of fire.
>
> That day, Professor Takenaka had not gone to Hiroshima University, and the A-bomb exploded when he was at home. He tried to rescue his wife, who was trapped under a roofbeam, but all his efforts were in vain. The fire was threatening him also. His wife pleaded, "Run away, dear!" He was forced to desert his wife and escape from the fire. He was now at the foot of Miyuki Bridge.
>
> But I wonder how he came to hold that ball of rice in his hand. His naked figure, standing there before the flames with that ball of rice, looked to me as a symbol of the modest hopes of human beings.

In "Hiroshima," John Hersey describes the flight of a group of German priests and their Japanese colleagues through a burning section of the city:

> The street was cluttered with parts of houses that had slid into it, and with fallen telephone poles and wires. From every second or third house came the voices of people buried and abandoned, who invariably screamed, with formal politeness, *"Tasukete kure!* Help, if you please!" The priests recognized several ruins from which these cries came as the homes of friends, but because of the fire it was too late to help.

And thus it happened that throughout Hiroshima all the ties of affection and respect that join human beings to one another were being pulled and rent by the spreading firestorm. Soon processions of the injured—processions of a kind that had never been seen before in history—began to file away from the center of the city toward its outskirts. Most of the people suffered from burns, which had often blackened their skin or caused it to sag off them. A grocer who joined one of these processions has described them in an interview with Robert Jay Lifton which appears in his book "Death in Life":

> They held their arms bent [forward] . . . and their skin—not only on their hands but on their faces and bodies, too—hung down. . . . If there had been only one or two such people . . . perhaps I would not have had such a strong impression. But wherever I walked, I met these people. . . . Many of them died along the road. I can still picture them in my mind—like walking ghosts. They didn't look like people of this world.

The grocer also recalls that because of people's injuries "you couldn't tell whether you were looking at them from in front or in back." People found it impossible to recognize one another. A woman who at the time was a girl of thirteen, and suffered disfiguring burns on her face, has recalled, "My face was so distorted and changed that people couldn't tell who I was. After a while I could call others' names but they couldn't recognize me." In addition to being injured, many people were vomiting—an early symptom of radiation sickness. For many, horrifying and unreal events occurred in a chaotic jumble. In "Unforgettable Fire," Torako Hironaka enumerates some of the things that she remembers:

1. Some burned work-clothes.
2. People crying for help with their heads, shoulders, or the soles of their feet injured by fragments of broken window glass. Glass fragments were scattered everywhere.
3. [A woman] crying, saying "Aigo! Aigo!" (a Korean expression of sorrow).
4. A burning pine tree.
5. A naked woman.
6. Naked girls crying, "Stupid America!"
7. I was crouching in a puddle, for fear of being shot by a machine gun. My breasts were torn.
8. Burned down electric power lines.
9. A telephone pole had burned and fallen down.
10. A field of watermelons.
11. A dead horse.
12. What with dead cats, pigs, and people, it was just a hell on earth.

Physical collapse brought emotional and spiritual collapse with it. The survivors were, on the whole, listless and stupefied. After the escapes, and the failures to escape, from the firestorm, a silence fell over the city and its remaining population. People suffered and died without speaking or otherwise making a sound. The processions of the injured, too, were soundless. Dr. Michihiko Hachiya has written in his book "Hiroshima Diary":

Those who were able walked silently toward the suburbs in the distant hills, their spirits broken, their initiative gone. When asked whence they had come, they pointed to the city and said, "That way," and when asked where they were going, pointed away from the city and said, "This way." They were so broken and confused that they moved and behaved like automatons.

Their reactions had astonished outsiders, who reported with amazement the spectacle of long files of people holding stolidly to a narrow, rough path when close by was a smooth, easy road going in the same direction. The outsiders could not grasp the fact that they were witnessing the exodus of a people who walked in the realm of dreams.

Those who were still capable of action often acted in an absurd or an insane way. Some of them energetically pursued tasks that had made sense in the intact Hiroshima of a few minutes before but were now utterly inappropriate. Hersey relates that the German priests were bent on bringing to safety a suitcase, containing diocesan accounts and a sum of money, that they had rescued from the fire and were carrying around with them through the burning city. And Dr. Lifton describes a young soldier's punctilious efforts to find and preserve the ashes of a burned military code book while people around him were screaming for help. Other people simply lost their minds. For example, when the German priests were escaping from the firestorm, one of them, Father Wilhelm Kleinsorge, carried on his back a Mr. Fukai, who kept saying that he wanted to remain where he was. When Father Kleinsorge finally put Mr. Fukai down, he started running. Hersey writes:

> Father Kleinsorge shouted to a dozen soldiers, who were standing by the bridge, to stop him. As Father Kleinsorge started back to get Mr. Fukai, Father LaSalle called out, "Hurry! Don't waste time!" So Father Kleinsorge just requested the soldiers to take care of Mr. Fukai. They said they would, but the little, broken man got away from them, and the last the priests could see of him, he was running back toward the fire.

In the weeks after the bombing, many survivors began to notice the appearance of petechiae—small spots caused by hemorrhages—on their skin. These usually signalled the onset of the critical stage of radiation sickness. In the first stage, the victims characteristically vomited repeatedly, ran a fever, and developed an abnormal thirst. (The cry "Water! Water!" was one of the few sounds often heard in Hiroshima on the day of the bombing.) Then, after a few hours or days, there was a deceptively hopeful period of remission of symptoms, called the latency period, which lasted from about a week to about four weeks. Radiation attacks the reproductive function of cells, and those that reproduce most frequently are therefore the most vulnerable. Among these are the bone-marrow cells, which are responsible for the production of blood cells. During the latency period, the count of white blood cells, which are instrumental in fighting infections, and the count of platelets, which are instrumental in clotting, drop precipitously, so the body is poorly defended against infection and is liable to hemorrhaging. In the third, and final, stage, which may last for several weeks, the victim's hair may fall out and he may suffer from diarrhea and may bleed from the intestines, the mouth, or other parts of the body, and in the end he will either recover or die. Because the fireball of the Hiroshima bomb did not touch the ground, very little ground material was mixed with the fission products of the bomb, and therefore very little local fallout was generated. (What fallout there was descended in the black rain.) Therefore, the fatalities from radiation sickness were probably all caused by the initial nuclear radiation, and since this affected only people within a radius of a mile and a quarter of ground zero, most of the people who received lethal doses were killed more quickly by the thermal pulse and the blast wave. Thus, Hiroshima did not experience the mass radiation sickness that can be expected if a weapon is ground-burst. Since the Nagasaki bomb was also burst in the air, the effect of widespread lethal fallout on large areas, causing the death by radiation sickness of whole populations in the hours, days, and weeks after the blast, is a form of nuclear horror that the world has not experienced.

In the months and years following the bombing of Hiroshima, after radiation sickness had run its course and most of the injured had either died of their wounds or recovered from them, the inhabitants of the city began to learn that the exposure to radiation they had experienced would bring about a wide variety of illnesses, many of them lethal, throughout the lifetimes of those who had been exposed. An early sign that the harm from radiation was not restricted to radiation sickness came in the months immediately following the bombing, when people found that their reproductive organs had been temporarily harmed, with men experiencing sterility and women experiencing abnormalities in their menstrual cycles. Then, over the years, other illnesses, including cataracts of the eye and leukemia and other forms of cancer, began to appear in larger than normally expected numbers among the exposed population. In all these illnesses, correlations have been found between nearness to the explosion and incidence of the disease. Also, fetuses exposed to the bomb's radiation in utero exhibited abnormalities and developmental retardation. Those exposed within the mile-and-a-quarter radius were seven times as likely as unexposed fetuses to die in utero, and were also seven times as likely to die at birth or in infancy. Surviving children who were exposed in utero tended to be shorter and lighter than other children, and were more often mentally retarded. One of the most serious abnormalities caused by exposure to the bomb's radiation was microcephaly—abnormal smallness of the head, which is often accompanied by mental retardation. In one study, thirty-three cases of microcephaly were found among a hundred and sixty-nine children exposed in utero.

What happened at Hiroshima was less than a millionth part of a holocaust at present levels of world nuclear armament. The more than millionfold difference amounts to more than a difference in magnitude; it is also a difference in kind. The authors of "Hiroshima and Nagasaki" observe that "an atomic bomb's massive destruction and indiscriminate slaughter involves the sweeping breakdown of all order and existence—in a word, the collapse of society itself," and that therefore "the essence of atomic destruction lies in the totality of its impact on man and society." This is true also of a holocaust, of course, except that the totalities in question are now not single cities but nations, ecosystems, and the earth's ecosphere.

Yet with the exception of fallout, which was relatively light at Hiroshima and Nagasaki (because both the bombs were air-burst), the immediate devastation caused by today's bombs would be of a sort similar to the devastation in those cities. The immediate effects of a twenty-megaton bomb are not different in kind from those of a twelve-and-a-half-kiloton bomb; they are only more extensive. (The proportions of the effects do change greatly with yield, however. In small bombs, the effects of the initial nuclear radiation are important, because it strikes areas in which people might otherwise have remained alive, but in larger bombs—ones in the megaton range— the consequences of the initial nuclear radiation, whose range does not increase very much with yield, are negligible, because it strikes areas in which everyone will have already been burned or blasted to death.) In bursts of both weapons, for instance, there is a radius within which the thermal pulse can ignite newspapers: for the twelve-and-a-half-kiloton weapon, it is a little over two miles; for the twenty-megaton weapon, it is twenty-five miles. (Since there is no inherent limit on the size of a nuclear weapon, these figures can be increased indefinitely, subject only to the limitations imposed by the technical capacities of the bomb builder—and of the earth's capacity to absorb the blast. The Soviet Union, which has shown a liking for sheer size in so many of its undertakings, once detonated a sixty-megaton bomb.) Therefore, while the total effect of a holocaust is qualitatively different from the total effect of a single bomb, the experience of individual people in a holocaust would be, in the short term (and again excepting the presence of lethal fallout wherever the bombs were ground-burst), very much like the experience of individual people in Hiroshima. The Hiroshima people's experience, accordingly, is of much more than historical interest. It is a picture of what our whole world is always poised to become—a backdrop of scarcely imaginable horror lying just behind the surface of our normal life, and capable of breaking through into that normal life at any second. Whether we choose to think about it or not, it is an omnipresent, inescapable truth about our lives today that at every single moment each one of us may suddenly become the deranged mother looking for her burned child; the professor with the ball of rice in his hand whose wife has just told him "Run away, dear!" and died in the fires; Mr. Fukai running back into the firestorm; the naked man standing on the blasted plain that was his city, holding his eyeball in his hand; or, more likely, one of millions of corpses. For whatever our "modest hopes" as human beings may be, every one of them can be nullified by a nuclear holocaust.

One way to begin to grasp the destructive power of present-day nuclear weapons is to describe the consequences of the detonation of a one-megaton bomb, which possesses eighty times the explosive power of the Hiroshima bomb, on a large city, such as New York. Burst some eighty-five hundred feet above the Empire State Building, a one-megaton bomb would gut or flatten almost every building between Battery Park and 125th Street, or within a radius of four and four-tenths miles, or in an area of sixty-one square miles, and would heavily damage buildings between the northern tip of Staten Island and the George Washington Bridge, or within a radius of about eight miles, or in an area of about two hundred square miles. A conventional explosive delivers a swift shock, like a slap, to whatever it hits, but the blast wave of a sizable nuclear weapon endures for several seconds and "can surround and destroy whole buildings" (Glasstone). People, of course, would be picked up and hurled away from the blast along with the rest of the debris. Within the sixty-one square miles, the walls, roofs, and floors of any buildings that had not been flattened would be collapsed, and the people and furniture inside would be swept down onto the street. (Technically, this zone would be hit by various overpressures of at least five pounds per square inch. Overpressure is defined as the pressure in excess of normal atmospheric pressure.) As far away as ten miles from ground zero, pieces of glass and other sharp objects would be hurled about by the blast wave at lethal velocities. In Hiroshima, where buildings were low and, outside the center of the city, were often constructed of light materials, injuries from falling buildings were often minor. But in New York, where the buildings are tall and are constructed of heavy materials, the physical collapse of the city would certainly kill millions of people. The streets of New York are narrow ravines running between the high walls of the city's buildings. In a nuclear attack, the walls would fall and the ravines would fill up. The people in the buildings would fall to the street with the debris of the buildings, and the people in the street would be crushed by this avalanche of people and buildings. At a distance of two miles or so from ground zero, winds would reach four hundred miles an hour, and another two miles away they would reach a hundred and eighty miles an hour. Meanwhile, the fireball would be growing, until it was more than a mile wide, and rocketing upward, to a height of over six miles. For ten seconds, it would broil the city below. Anyone caught in the open within nine miles of ground zero would receive third-degree burns and would probably be killed; closer to the explosion, people would be charred and killed instantly. From Greenwich Village up to Central Park, the heat would be great enough to melt metal and glass. Readily inflammable materials, such as newspapers and dry leaves, would ignite in all five boroughs (though in only a small part of Staten Island) and west to the Passaic River, in New Jersey, within a radius of about nine and a half miles from ground zero, thereby creating an area of more than two hundred and eighty square miles in which mass fires were likely to break out.

If it were possible (as it would not be) for someone to stand at Fifth Avenue and Seventy-second Street (about two miles from ground zero) without being instantly killed, he would see the following sequence of events. A dazzling white light from the fireball would illumine the scene, continuing for perhaps thirty seconds. Simultaneously, searing heat would ignite everything flammable and start to melt windows, cars, buses, lampposts, and everything else made of metal or glass. People in the street would immediately catch fire, and would shortly be reduced to heavily charred corpses. About five seconds after the light appeared, the blast wave would strike, laden with the debris of a now nonexistent midtown. Some buildings might be crushed, as though a giant fist had squeezed them on all sides, and others might be picked up off their foundations and whirled uptown with the other debris. On the far side of Central Park, the West Side skyline would fall from south to north. The four-hundred-mile-an-hour wind would blow from south to north, die down after a few seconds, and then blow in the reverse direction with diminished intensity. While these things were happening, the fireball would be burning in the sky for the ten seconds of the thermal pulse. Soon huge, thick clouds of dust and smoke would envelop the scene, and as the mushroom cloud rushed overhead (it would have a diameter of about twelve miles) the light from the sun would be blotted out, and day would turn to night. Within minutes, fires, ignited both by the thermal pulse and by broken gas mains, tanks of gas and oil, and the like, would begin to spread in the darkness, and a strong, steady wind would begin to blow in the direction of the blast. As at Hiroshima, a whirlwind might be produced, which would sweep through the ruins, and radioactive rain, generated under the meteorological conditions created by the blast, might fall. Before long, the individual fires would coalesce into a mass fire, which, depending largely on the winds, would become either a conflagration or a firestorm. In a conflagration, prevailing winds spread a wall of fire as far as there is any combustible material to sustain it; in a firestorm, a vertical updraft caused by the fire itself sucks the surrounding air in toward a central point, and the fires therefore converge in a single fire of extreme heat. A mass fire of either kind renders shelters useless by burning up all the oxygen in the air and creating toxic gases, so that anyone inside the shelters is asphyxiated, and also by heating the ground to such high temperatures that the shelters turn, in effect, into ovens, cremating the people inside them. In Dresden, several days after the firestorm raised there by Allied conventional bombing, the interiors of some bomb shelters were still so hot that when they were opened the inrushing air caused the contents to burst into flame. Only those who had fled their shelters when the bombing started had any chance of surviving. (It is difficult to predict in a particular situation which form the fires will take. In actual experience, Hiroshima suffered a firestorm and Nagasaki suffered a conflagration.)

In this vast theatre of physical effects, all the scenes of agony and death that took place at Hiroshima would again take place, but now involving millions of people rather than hundreds of thousands.

Like the people of Hiroshima, the people of New York would be burned, battered, crushed, and irradiated in every conceivable way. The city and its people would be mingled in a smoldering heap. And then, as the fires started, the survivors (most of whom would be on the periphery of the explosion) would be driven to abandon to the flames those family members and other people who were unable to flee, or else to die with them. Before long, while the ruins burned, the processions of injured, mute people would begin their slow progress out of the outskirts of the devastated zone. However, this time a much smaller proportion of the population than at Hiroshima would have a chance of escaping. In general, as the size of the area of devastation increases, the possibilities for escape decrease. When the devastated area is relatively small, as it was at Hiroshima, people who are not incapacitated will have a good chance of escaping to safety before the fires coalesce into a mass fire. But when the devastated area is great, as it would be after the detonation of a megaton bomb, and fires are springing up at a distance of nine and a half miles from ground zero, and when what used to be the streets are piled high with burning rubble, and the day (if the attack occurs in the daytime) has grown impenetrably dark, there is little chance that anyone who is not on the very edge of the devastated area will be able to make his way to safety. In New York, most people would die wherever the blast found them, or not very far from there.

If instead of being burst in the air the bomb were burst on or near the ground in the vicinity of the Empire State Building, the overpressure would be very much greater near the center of the blast area but the range hit by a minimum of five pounds per square inch of overpressure would be less. The range of the thermal pulse would be about the same as that of the air burst. The fireball would be almost two miles across, and would engulf midtown Manhattan from Greenwich Village nearly to Central Park. Very little is known about what would happen to a city that was inside a fireball, but one would expect a good deal of what was there to be first pulverized and then melted or vaporized. Any human beings in the area would be reduced to smoke and ashes; they would simply disappear. A crater roughly three blocks in diameter and two hundred feet deep would open up. In addition, heavy radioactive fallout would be created as dust and debris from the city rose with the mushroom cloud and then fell back to the ground. Fallout would begin to drop almost immediately, contaminating the ground beneath the cloud with levels of radiation many times lethal doses, and quickly killing anyone who might have survived the blast wave and the thermal pulse and might now be attempting an escape; it is difficult to believe that there would be appreciable survival of the people of the city after a megaton ground burst. And for the next twenty-four hours or so more fallout would descend downwind from the blast, in a plume whose direction and length would depend on the speed and the direction of the wind that happened to be blowing at the time of the attack. If the wind was blowing at fifteen miles an hour, fallout of lethal intensity would descend in a plume about a hundred and fifty miles long and as much as fifteen miles wide. Fallout that was sublethal but could still cause serious illness would extend another hundred and fifty miles downwind. Exposure to radioactivity in human beings is measured in units called rems—an acronym for "roentgen equivalent in man." The roentgen is a standard measurement of gamma- and X-ray radiation, and the expression "equivalent in man" indicates that an adjustment has been made to take into account the differences in the degree of biological damage that is caused by radiation of different types. Many of the kinds of harm done to human beings by radiation—for example, the incidence of cancer and of genetic damage—depend on the dose accumulated over many years; but radiation sickness, capable of causing death, results from an "acute" dose, received in a period of anything from a few seconds to several days. Because almost ninety per cent of the so-called "infinite-time dose" of radiation from fallout—that is, the dose from a given quantity of fallout that one would receive if one lived for many thousands of years—is emitted in the first week, the one-week accumulated dose is often used as a convenient measure for calculating the immediate harm from fallout. Doses in the thousands of rems, which could be expected throughout the city, would attack the central nervous system and would bring about death within a few hours. Doses of around a thousand rems, which would be delivered some tens of miles downwind from the blast, would kill within two weeks everyone who was exposed to them. Doses of around five hundred rems, which would be delivered as far as a hundred and fifty miles downwind (given a wind speed of fifteen miles per hour), would kill half of all exposed able-bodied young adults. At this level of exposure, radiation sickness proceeds in the three stages observed at Hiroshima. The plume of lethal fallout could descend, depending on the direction of the wind, on other parts of New York State and parts of New Jersey, Pennsylvania, Delaware, Maryland, Connecticut, Massachusetts, Rhode Island, Vermont, and New Hampshire, killing additional millions of people. The circumstances in heavily contaminated areas, in which millions of people were all declining together, over a period of weeks, toward painful deaths, are ones that, like so many of the consequences of nuclear explosions, have never been experienced.

A description of the effects of a one-megaton bomb on New York City gives some notion of the meaning in human terms of a megaton of nuclear explosive power, but a weapon that is more likely to be used against New York is the twenty-megaton bomb, which has one thousand six hundred times the yield of the Hiroshima bomb. The Soviet Union is estimated to have at least a hundred and thirteen twenty-megaton bombs in its nuclear arsenal, carried by Bear intercontinental bombers. In addition, some of the Soviet SS-18 missiles are capable of carrying bombs of this size, although the actual yields are not known. Since the explosive power of the twenty-megaton bombs greatly exceeds the amount necessary to destroy most military targets, it is reasonable to suppose that they are meant for use against large cities. If a twenty-megaton bomb were air-burst over the Empire State Building at an altitude of thirty thousand feet, the zone gutted or flattened by the blast wave would have a radius of twelve miles and an area of more than four hundred and fifty square miles, reaching from the middle of Staten Island to the northern edge of the Bronx, the eastern edge of Queens, and well into New Jersey, and the zone of heavy damage from the blast wave (the zone hit by a minimum of two pounds of overpressure per square inch) would have a radius of twenty-one and a half miles, or an area of one thousand four hundred and fifty square miles, reaching to the southernmost tip of Staten Island, north as far as southern Rockland County, east into Nassau County, and west to Morris County, New Jersey. The fireball would be about four and a half miles in diameter and would radiate the thermal pulse for some twenty seconds. People caught in the open twenty-three miles away from ground zero, in Long Island, New Jersey, and southern New York State, would be burned to death. People hundreds of miles away who looked at the burst would be temporarily blinded and would risk permanent eye injury. (After the test of a fifteen-megaton bomb on Bikini Atoll, in the South Pacific, in March of 1954, small animals were found to have suffered retinal burns at a distance of three hundred and forty-five miles.) The mushroom cloud would be seventy miles in diameter. New York City and its suburbs would be transformed into a lifeless, flat, scorched desert in a few seconds.

If a twenty-megaton bomb were ground-burst on the Empire State Building, the range of severe blast damage would, as with the one-megaton ground blast, be reduced, but the fireball, which would be almost six miles in diameter, would cover Manhattan from Wall Street to northern Central Park and also parts of New Jersey, Brooklyn, and Queens, and everyone within it would be instantly killed, with most of them physically disappearing. Fallout would again be generated, this time covering thousands of square miles with lethal intensities of radiation. A fair portion of New York City and its incinerated population, now radioactive dust, would have risen into the mushroom cloud and would now be descending on the surrounding territory. On one of the few occasions when local fallout was generated by a test explosion in the multi-megaton range, the fifteen-megaton bomb tested on Bikini Atoll, which was exploded seven feet above the surface of a coral reef, "caused substantial contamination over an area of more than seven thousand square miles," according to Glasstone. If, as seems likely, a twenty-megaton bomb ground-burst on New York would produce at least a comparable amount of fallout, and if the wind carried the fallout onto populated areas, then this one bomb would probably doom upward of twenty million people, or almost ten per cent of the population of the United States.

The "strategic" forces of the Soviet Union—those that can deliver nuclear warheads to the United States—are so far capable of carrying seven thousand warheads with an estimated maximum yield of more than seventeen thousand megatons of explosive power, and, barring unexpected developments in arms-control talks, the number of warheads is expected to rise in the coming years. The actual megatonnage of the Soviet strategic forces is not known, and, for a number of reasons, including the fact that smaller warheads can be delivered more accurately, it is very likely that the actual megatonnage is lower than the maximum possible; however, it is reasonable to suppose that the actual megatonnage is as much as two-thirds of the maximum, which would be about eleven and a half thousand megatons. If we assume that in a first strike the Soviets held back about a thousand megatons (itself an immense force), then the attack would amount to about ten thousand megatons, or the equivalent of eight hundred thousand Hiroshima bombs. American strategic forces comprise about nine thousand warheads with a yield of some three thousand five hundred megatons. The total yield of these American forces was made comparatively low for strategic reasons. American planners discovered that smaller warheads can be delivered more accurately than larger ones, and are therefore more useful for attacking strategic forces on the other side. And, in fact, American missiles are substantially more accurate than Soviet ones. However, in the last year or so, in spite of this advantage in numbers of warheads and in accuracy, American leaders have come to believe that the American forces are inadequate, and, again barring unexpected developments in arms-control talks, both the yield of the American arsenal and the number of warheads in it are likely to rise dramatically. (Neither the United States nor the Soviet Union reveals the total explosive yield of its own forces. The public is left to turn to private organizations, which, by making use of hundreds of pieces of information that *have* been released by the two governments, piece together an over-all picture. The figures I have used to estimate the maximum capacities of the two sides are taken for the most part from tables provided in the latest edition of "The Military Balance," a standard yearly reference work on the strength of military forces around the world, which is published by a research institute in London called the International Institute for Strategic Studies.) The territory of the United States, including Alaska and Hawaii, is three million six hundred and fifteen thousand one hundred and twenty-two square miles. It contains approximately two hundred and twenty-five million people, of whom sixty per cent, or about a hundred and thirty-five million, live in various urban centers with a total area of only eighteen thousand square miles. I asked Dr. Kendall, who has done considerable research on the consequences of nuclear attacks, to sketch out in rough terms what the actual distribution of bombs might be in a ten-thousand-megaton Soviet attack in the early nineteen-eighties on all targets in the United States, military and civilian.

"Without serious distortion," he said, "we can begin by imagining that we would be dealing with ten thousand weapons of one megaton each, although in fact the yields would, of course, vary considerably. Let us also make the assumption, based on common knowledge of weapons design, that on average the yield would be one-half fission and one-half fusion. This proportion is important, because it is the fission products—a virtual museum of about three hundred radioactive isotopes, decaying at different rates—that give off radioactivity in fallout. Fusion can add to the total in ground bursts by radioactivation of ground material by neutrons, but the quantity added is comparatively small. Targets can be divided into two categories—hard and soft. Hard targets, of which there are about a thousand in the United States, are mostly missile silos. The majority of them can be destroyed only by huge, blunt overpressures, ranging anywhere from many hundreds to a few thousand pounds per square inch, and we can expect that two weapons might be devoted to each one to assure destruction. That would use up two thousand megatons. Because other strategic military targets—such as Strategic Air Command bases—are near centers of population, an attack on them as well, perhaps using another couple of hundred megatons, could cause a total of more than twenty million casualties, according to studies by the Arms Control and Disarmament Agency. If the nearly eight thousand weapons remaining were then devoted to the cities and towns of the United States in order of population, every community down to the level of fifteen hundred inhabitants would be hit with a megaton bomb—which is, of course, many, many times what would be necessary to annihilate a town that size. For obvious reasons, industry is highly correlated with population density, so an attack on the one necessarily hits the other, especially when an attack of this magnitude is considered. Ten thousand targets would include everything worth hitting in the country and much more; it would simply *be* the United States. The targeters would run out of targets and victims long before they ran out of bombs. If you imagine that the bombs were distributed according to population, then, allowing for the fact that the attack on the military installations would have already killed about twenty million people, you would have about forty megatons to devote to each remaining million people in the country. For the seven and a half million people in New York City, that would come to three hundred megatons. Bearing in mind what one megaton can do, you can see that this would be preposterous overkill. In practice, one might expect the New York metropolitan area to be hit with some dozens of one-megaton weapons."

In the first moments of a ten-thousand-megaton attack on the United States, I learned from Dr. Kendall and from other sources, flashes of white light would suddenly illumine large areas of the country as thousands of suns, each one brighter than the sun itself, blossomed over cities, suburbs, and towns. In those same moments, when the first wave of missiles arrived, the vast majority of the people in the regions first targeted would be irradiated, crushed, or burned to death. The thermal pulses could subject more than six hundred thousand square miles, or one-sixth of the total land mass of the nation, to a minimum level of forty calories per centimetre squared—a level of heat that chars human beings. (At Hiroshima, charred remains in the rough shape of human beings were a common sight.) Tens of millions of people would go up in smoke. As the attack proceeded, as much as three-quarters of the country could be subjected to incendiary levels of heat, and so, wherever there was inflammable material, could be set ablaze. In the ten seconds or so after each bomb hit, as blast waves swept outward from thousands of ground zeros, the physical plant of the United States would be swept away like leaves in a gust of wind. The six hundred thousand square miles already scorched by the forty or more calories of heat per centimetre squared would now be hit by blast waves of a minimum of five pounds per square inch, and virtually all the habitations, places of work, and other man-made things there—substantially the whole human construct in the United States—would be vaporized, blasted, or otherwise pulverized out of existence. Then, as clouds of dust rose from the earth, and mushroom clouds spread overhead, often linking to form vast canopies, day would turn to night. (These clouds could blanket as much as a third of the nation.) Shortly, fires would spring up in the debris of the cities and in every forest dry enough to burn. These fires would simply burn down the United States. When one pictures a full-scale attack on the United States, or on any other country, therefore, the picture of a single city being flattened by a single bomb—an image firmly engraved in the public imagination, probably because of the bombings of Hiroshima and Nagasaki—must give way to a picture of substantial sections of the country being turned by a sort of nuclear carpet-bombing into immense infernal regions, literally tens of thousands of square miles in area, from which escape is impossible. In Hiroshima and Nagasaki, those who had not been killed or injured so severely that they could not move were able to flee to the undevastated world around them, where they found help, but in any city where three or four bombs had been used—not to mention fifty, or a hundred—flight from one blast would only be flight toward another, and no one could escape alive. Within these regions, each of three of the immediate effects of nuclear weapons—initial radiation, thermal pulse, and blast wave—would alone be enough to kill most people: the initial nuclear radiation would subject tens of thousands of square miles to lethal doses; the blast waves, coming from all sides, would nowhere fall below the overpressure necessary to destroy almost all buildings; and the thermal pulses, also coming from all sides, would always be great enough to kill exposed people and, in addition, to set on fire everything that would burn. The ease with which virtually the whole population of the country could be trapped in these zones of universal death is suggested by the fact that the sixty per cent of the population that lives in an area of eighteen thousand square miles could be annihilated with only three hundred one-megaton bombs—the number necessary to cover the area with a minimum of five pounds per square inch of overpressure and forty calories per centimetre squared of heat. That would leave nine thousand seven hundred megatons, or ninety-seven per cent of the megatonnage in the attacking force, available for other targets. (It is hard to imagine what a targeter would do with all his bombs in these circumstances. Above several thousand megatons, it would almost become a matter of trying to hunt down individual people with nuclear warheads.)

The statistics on the initial nuclear radiation, the thermal pulses, and the blast waves in a nuclear holocaust can be presented in any number of ways, but all of them would be only variations on a simple theme—the annihilation of the United States and its people. Yet while the immediate nuclear effects are great enough in a ten-thousand-megaton attack to destroy the country many times over, they are not the most powerfully lethal of the local effects of nuclear weapons. The killing power of the local fallout is far greater. Therefore, if the Soviet Union was bent on producing the maximum over-kill—if, that is, its surviving leaders, whether out of calculation, rage, or madness, decided to eliminate the United States not merely as a political and social entity but as a biological one—they would burst their bombs on the ground rather than in the air. Although the scope of severe blast damage would then be reduced, the blast waves, fireballs, and thermal pulses would still be far more than enough to destroy the country, and, in addition, provided only that the bombs were dispersed widely enough, lethal fallout would spread throughout the nation. The amount of radiation delivered by the fallout from a ground burst of a given size is still uncertain—not least because, as Glasstone notes, there has never been a "true land surface burst" of a bomb with a yield of over one kiloton. (The Bikini burst was in part over the ocean.) Many factors make for uncertainty. To mention just a few: the relative amounts of the fallout that rises into the stratosphere and the fallout that descends to the ground near the blast are dependent on, among other things, the yield of the weapon, and, in any case, can be only guessed at; the composition of the fallout will vary with the composition of the material on the ground that is sucked up into the mushroom cloud; prediction of the distribution of fallout by winds of various speeds at various altitudes depends on a choice of several "models"; and the calculation of the arrival time of the fallout—an important calculation, since fallout cannot harm living things until it lands near them—is subject to similar speculative doubts. However, calculations on the basis of figures for a one-megaton ground burst which are given in the Office of Technology Assessment's report show that ten thousand megatons would yield one-week doses around the country averaging more than ten thousand rems. In actuality, of course, the bombs would almost certainly not be evenly spaced around the country but, rather, would be concentrated in populated areas and in missile fields; and the likelihood is that in most places where people lived or worked the doses would be many times the average, commonly reaching several tens of thousands of rems for the first week, while in remote areas they would be less, or, conceivably, even nonexistent. (The United States contains large tracts of empty desert, and to target them would be virtually meaningless from any point of view.)

These figures provide a context for judging the question of civil defense. With overwhelming immediate local effects striking the vast majority of the population, and with one-week doses of radiation then rising into the tens of thousands of rems, evacuation and shelters are a vain hope. Needless to say, in these circumstances evacuation before an attack would be an exercise in transporting

people from one death to another. In some depictions of a holocaust, various rescue operations are described, with unafflicted
survivors bringing food, clothes, and medical care to the afflicted,
and the afflicted making their way to thriving, untouched communities, where churches, school auditoriums, and the like would have
been set up for their care—as often happens after a bad snowstorm,
say. Obviously, none of this could come about. In the first place, in
a full-scale attack there would in all likelihood *be* no surviving
communities, and, in the second place, everyone who failed to seal
himself off from the outside environment for as long as several
months would soon die of radiation sickness. Hence, in the months
after a holocaust there would be no activity of any sort, as, in a
reversal of the normal state of things, the dead would lie on the
surface and the living, if there were any, would be buried underground.

To this description of radiation levels around the country, an
addition remains to be made. This is the fact that attacks on the
seventy-six nuclear power plants in the United States would produce fallout whose radiation had much greater longevity than that
of the weapons alone. The physicist Dr. Kosta Tsipis, of M.I.T., and
one of his students, Steven Fetter, recently published an article in
Scientific American called "Catastrophic Releases of Radioactivity,"
in which they calculate the damage from a one-megaton thermonuclear ground burst on a one-gigawatt nuclear power plant. In
such a ground burst, the facility's radioactive contents would be
vaporized along with everything nearby, and the remains would be
carried up into the mushroom cloud, from which they would descend to the earth with the rest of the fallout. But whereas the fission products of the weapon were newly made, and contained many
isotopes that would decay to insignificant levels very swiftly, the
fission products in a reactor would be a collection of longer-lived
isotopes (and this applies even more strongly to the spent fuel in
the reactor's holding pond), since the short-lived ones would, for
the most part, have had enough time to reduce themselves to harmless levels. The intense but comparatively short-lived radiation from
the weapon would kill people in the first few weeks and months, but

the long-lived radiation that was produced both by the weapon and by the power plant could prevent anyone from living on a vast area of land for decades after it fell. For example, after a year an area of some seventeen hundred square miles downwind of a power plant on which a one-megaton bomb had been ground-burst (again assuming a fifteen-mile-an-hour wind) would still be delivering more than fifty rems per year to anyone who tried to live there, and that is two hundred and fifty times the "safe" dose established by the E.P.A. The bomb by itself would produce this effect over an area of only twenty-six square miles. (In addition to offering an enemy a way of redoubling the effectiveness of his attacks in a full-scale holocaust, reactors provide targets of unparalleled danger in possible terrorist nuclear attacks. In an earlier paper, Tsipis and Fetter observe that "the destruction of a reactor with a nuclear weapon, even of relatively small yield, such as a crude terrorist nuclear device, would represent a national catastrophe of lasting consequences." It can be put down as one further alarming oddity of life in a nuclear world that in building nuclear power plants nations have opened themselves to catastrophic devastation and long-term contamination of their territories by enemies who manage to get hold of only a few nuclear weapons.)

If, in a nuclear holocaust, anyone hid himself deep enough under the earth and stayed there long enough to survive, he would emerge into a dying natural environment. The vulnerability of the environment is the last word in the argument against the usefulness of shelters: there is no hole big enough to hide all of nature in. Radioactivity penetrates the environment in many ways. The two most important components of radiation from fallout are gamma rays, which are electromagnetic radiation of the highest intensity, and beta particles, which are electrons fired at high speed from decaying nuclei. Gamma rays subject organisms to penetrating whole-body doses, and are responsible for most of the ill effects of radiation from fallout. Beta particles, which are less penetrating than gamma rays, act at short range, doing harm when they collect on the skin, or on the surface of a leaf. They are harmful to plants on whose foliage the fallout descends—producing "beta burn"—

and to grazing animals, which can suffer burns as well as gastro-intestinal damage from eating the foliage. Two of the most harmful radioactive isotopes present in fallout are strontium-90 (with a half-life of twenty-eight years) and cesium-137 (with a half-life of thirty years). They are taken up into the food chain through the roots of plants or through direct ingestion by animals, and contaminate the environment from within. Strontium-90 happens to resemble calcium in its chemical composition, and therefore finds its way into the human diet through dairy products and is eventually deposited by the body in the bones, where it is thought to cause bone cancer. (Every person in the world now has in his bones a measurable deposit of strontium-90 traceable to the fallout from atmospheric nuclear testing.)

Over the years, agencies and departments of the government have sponsored numerous research projects in which a large variety of plants and animals were irradiated in order to ascertain the lethal or sterilizing dose for each. These findings permit the prediction of many gross ecological consequences of a nuclear attack. According to "Survival of Food Crops and Livestock in the Event of Nuclear War," the proceedings of the 1970 symposium at Brookhaven National Laboratory, the lethal doses for most mammals lie between a few hundred rads and a thousand rads of gamma radiation; a rad—for "roentgen absorbed dose"—is a roentgen of radiation that has been absorbed by an organism, and is roughly equal to a rem. For example, the lethal doses of gamma radiation for animals in pasture, where fallout would be descending on them directly and they would be eating fallout that had fallen on the grass, and would thus suffer from doses of beta radiation as well, would be one hundred and eighty rads for cattle; two hundred and forty rads for sheep; five hundred and fifty rads for swine; three hundred and fifty rads for horses; and eight hundred rads for poultry. In a ten-thousand-megaton attack, which would create levels of radiation around the country averaging more than ten thousand rads, most of the mammals of the United States would be killed off. The lethal doses for birds are in roughly the same range as those for mammals, and birds, too, would be killed off. Fish are killed at doses of between one thousand one hundred rads and about five thousand six hundred rads, but their fate is less predictable. On the one hand, water is a shield from radiation, and would afford some protection; on the other hand, fallout might concentrate in bodies of water as it ran off from the land. (Because radiation causes no pain, animals, wandering at will through the environment, would not avoid it.) The one class of animals containing a number of species quite likely to survive, at least in the short run, is the insect class, for which in most known cases the lethal doses lie between about two thousand rads and about a hundred thousand rads. Insects, therefore, would be destroyed selectively. Unfortunately for the rest of the environment, many of the phytophagous species—insects that feed directly on vegetation—which "include some of the most ravaging species on earth" (according to Dr. Vernon M. Stern, an entomologist at the University of California at Riverside, writing in "Survival of Food Crops"), have very high tolerances, and so could be expected to survive disproportionately, and then to multiply greatly in the aftermath of an attack. The demise of their natural predators the birds would enhance their success.

Plants in general have a higher tolerance to radioactivity than animals do. Nevertheless, according to Dr. George M. Woodwell, who supervised the irradiation with gamma rays, over several years, of a small forest at Brookhaven Laboratory, a gamma-ray dose of ten thousand rads "would devastate most vegetation" in the United States, and, as in the case of the pastured animals, when one figures in the beta radiation that would also be delivered by fallout the estimates for the lethal doses of gamma rays must be reduced—in this case, cut in half. As a general rule, Dr. Woodwell and his colleagues at Brookhaven discovered, large plants are more vulnerable to radiation than small ones. Trees are among the first to die, grasses among the last. The most sensitive trees are pines and the other conifers, for which lethal doses are in roughly the same range as those for mammals. Any survivors coming out of their shelters a few months after the attack would find that all the pine trees that were still standing were already dead. The lethal doses for most deciduous trees range from about two thousand rads of gamma-ray radiation to about ten thousand rads, with the lethal doses for eighty per cent of deciduous species falling between two thousand and eight thousand rads. Since the addition of the beta-ray burden could lower these lethal doses for gamma rays by as much as fifty per cent, the actual lethal doses in gamma rays for these trees during an attack could be from one thousand to four thousand rads, and in a full-scale attack they would die. Then, after the trees had died, forest fires would break out around the United States. (Because as much as three-quarters of the country could be subjected to incendiary levels of the thermal pulses, the sheer scorching of the land could have killed off a substantial part of the plant life in the country in the first few seconds after the detonations, before radioactive poisoning set in.) Lethal doses for grasses on which tests have been done range between six thousand and thirty-three thousand rads, and a good deal of grass would therefore survive, except where the attacks had been heaviest. Most crops, on the other hand, are killed by doses below five thousands rads, and would be eliminated. (The lethal dose for spring barley seedlings, for example, is one thousand nine hundred and ninety rads, and that for spring wheat seedlings is three thousand and ninety rads.)

When vegetation is killed off, the land on which it grew is degraded. And as the land eroded after an attack life in lakes, rivers, and estuaries, already hard hit by radiation directly, would be further damaged by minerals flowing into the watercourses, causing eutrophication—a process in which an oversupply of nutrients in the water encourages the growth of algae and microscopic organisms, which, in turn, deplete the oxygen content of the water. When the soil loses its nutrients, it loses its ability to "sustain a mature community" (in Dr. Woodwell's words), and "gross simplification" of the environment occurs, in which "hardy species," such as moss and grass, replace vulnerable ones, such as trees; and "succession"—the process by which ecosystems recover lost diversity—is then "delayed or even arrested." In sum, a full-scale nuclear attack on the United States would devastate the natural environment on a scale unknown since early geological times, when, in response to natural catastrophes whose nature has not been determined, sudden mass extinctions of species and whole ecosystems occurred all over the earth. How far this "gross simplification" of the environment would go once virtually all animal life and the greater part of plant life had been destroyed and what patterns the surviving remnants of life would arrange themselves into over the long run are imponderables; but it appears that at the outset the United States would be a republic of insects and grass.

It has sometimes been claimed that the United States could survive a nuclear attack by the Soviet Union, but the bare figures on the extent of the blast waves, the thermal pulses, and the accumulated local fallout dash this hope irrevocably. They spell the doom of the United States. And if one imagines the reverse attack on the Soviet Union, its doom is spelled out in similar figures. (The greater land mass of the Soviet Union and the lower megatonnage of the American forces might reduce the factor of overkill somewhat.) Likewise, any country subjected to an attack of more than a few hundred megatons would be doomed. Japan, China, and the countries of Europe, where population densities are high, are especially vulnerable to damage, even at "low" levels of attack. There is no country in Europe in which survival of the population would be appreciable after the detonation of several hundred megatons; most European countries would be annihilated by tens of megatons. And these conclusions emerge even before one takes into account the global ecological consequences of a holocaust, which would be superimposed on the local consequences. As human life and the structure of human existence are seen in the light of each person's daily life and experience, they look impressively extensive and solid, but when human things are seen in the light of the universal power unleashed onto the earth by nuclear weapons they prove to be limited and fragile, as though they were nothing more than a mold or a lichen that appears in certain crevices of the landscape and can be burned off with relative ease by nuclear fire.

Many discussions of nuclear attacks on the United States devote considerable attention to their effect on the nation's economy, but if the population has been largely killed off and the natural environment is in a state of collapse "the economy" becomes a meaningless concept; for example, it makes no difference what percentage of "the automobile industry" has survived if all the producers and drivers of automobiles have died. Estimates of economic survival after a full-scale holocaust are, in fact, doubly unreal, because, as a number of government reports have shown, the nation's economy is so much more vulnerable to attack than the population that even at most levels of "limited" attack a greater proportion of the economy than of the population would be destroyed. An intact economic plant that goes to waste because there aren't enough people left to run it is one absurdity that a nuclear holocaust does not present us with. At relatively low levels of attack, however, the more or less complete destruction of the economy, accompanied by the survival of as much as twenty or thirty per cent of the population, is conceivable. Since the notion of "limited nuclear war" has recently become attractive to the American leadership, it may not be digressive to discuss what the consequences of smaller attacks would be. Our knowledge of nuclear effects is too imprecise to permit us to know at exactly what level of attack a given percentage of the population would survive, but the fact that sixty per cent of the population lives in eighteen thousand square miles and could be eliminated by the thermal pulses, blast waves, and mass fires produced by about three hundred one-megaton bombs suggests some rough magnitudes. The fallout that would be produced by the bombs if they were ground-burst would very likely kill ten or fifteen per cent of the remaining population (it could lethally contaminate some three hundred thousand square miles), and if several hundred additional megatons were used the percentage of the entire population killed in the short term might rise to something like eighty-five. Or, to put it differently, if the level of attack on civilian targets did not rise above the low hundreds of megatons tens of millions of people might survive in the short term. But that same level of attack would destroy so much of the physical plant of the economy, and, of course, so many of the laborers and managers who make it work, that in effect the economy would be nearly one hundred per cent destroyed. (There is a tendency when one is analyzing nuclear attacks to begin to accustom oneself to such expressions as "a thousand megatons," and therefore to begin to regard lower amounts as inconsequential. Yet even one megaton, which contains the explosive yield of eighty Hiroshimas, would, if it should be dropped in the United States in the form of a number of small bombs, be an unimaginable catastrophe. Ten megatons—eight hundred Hiroshimas—would leave any nation on earth devastated beyond anything in our historical experience. A hundred megatons— eight thousand Hiroshimas—is already outside comprehension.)

As soon as one assumes that many tens of millions of people might survive the early stages of an attack, what are often called the long-term effects of a holocaust come into view; in fact, it is only when the imagined attack is reduced to this level that it begins to make sense to talk about many of the long-term effects, because only then will there be people left living to suffer them. The most obvious of these is injury. In an attack that killed from fifty to seventy per cent of the population outright, the great majority of the survivors would be injured. In a limited attack, some people might try to make their way to shelters to escape the fallout, which would be less intense than in the larger attack but still lethal in most populated areas. (If we again assume ground bursts, and also assume that two thousand megatons have been used on military targets, then average levels of radiation around the country would be in the low thousands of rems. But in this case averages would have little or no meaning; actual levels would be very high in some places and very low or nonexistent in others, depending on targeting and weather patterns.) People who reached shelters and sealed themselves in in time might have a chance of survival in some areas, but a large number of people would have received lethal doses of radiation without knowing it (since exposure to radiation is painless) and would enter the shelters and die there, making life in the shelters unbearable for the others. With many people seeking to get into the shelters, attempts to decide who was to be allowed to enter and who was to be kept out would begin in bitterness and end in chaos. (In the nineteen-fifties, when Americans gave greater

67

thought to the matter of shelters than they do now, some communities began to prepare to defend their shelters against intruders by arming themselves.) Also, the withdrawal into shelters of the uninjured or lightly injured portion of the population would be more consequential for the survivors as a body, because in a limited attack there might be a considerable number of people on the surface who would have had a chance of surviving if they had not been abandoned. The widespread use of shelters would therefore mean additional deaths; the injured or sick people would die unattended on the surface while the uninjured and healthy people hid underground.

The injuries from the attack would very likely be compounded by epidemics. Dr. H. Jack Geiger, who teaches community medicine at the School of Biomedical Education of the City College of New York, recently described to me the likely medical conditions after a limited attack. "The landscape would be strewn with millions of corpses of human beings and animals," he pointed out. "This alone is a situation without precedent in history. There would be an immense source of pollution of water and food. If you read the literature concerning natural disasters such as floods and typhoons, you find that there is always an associated danger of cholera or typhoid. The corpses would also feed a fast-growing population of insects, and insects happen to be a prime vector of disease. Naturally, medical measures to fight disease would not be taken, since the blasts would have destroyed virtually all medical facilities. Nor, of course, would there be such elementary sanitary facilities as running water and garbage collection. Finally, the population's resistance to infection would have been weakened, since many would be suffering from sublethal radiation sickness and wounds. It would be impossible to devise circumstances more favorable to the spread of epidemics."

Strategists of nuclear conflict often speak of a period of "recovery" after a limited attack, but a likelier prospect is a long-term radical deterioration in the conditions of life. For a while, some supplies of food and clothing would be found in the rubble, but then these would give out. For a people, the economy—any kind of economy, whether primitive or modern—is the means of survival from day to day. So if you ruin the economy—if you suspend its functioning, even for a few months—you take away the means of survival. Eventually, if enough people do live, the economy will revive in one form or another, but in the meantime people will die: they will starve, because the supply of food has been cut off; they will freeze, because they have no fuel or shelter; they will perish of illness, because they have no medical care. If the economy in question is a modern technological one, the consequences will be particularly severe, for then the obstacles to restoring it will be greatest. Because a modern economy, like an ecosystem, is a single, interdependent whole, in which each part requires many other parts to keep functioning, its wholesale breakdown will leave people unable to perform the simplest, most essential tasks. Even agriculture —the immediate means of subsistence—is caught up in the operations of the interdependent machine, and breaks down when it breaks down. Modern agriculture depends on fertilizers to make crops grow, on machines to cultivate the crops, on transportation to carry the produce thousands of miles to the consumers, on fuel to run the means of transportation and the agricultural machinery, and on pesticides and drugs to increase production. If fertilizers, machines, transportation, fuel, pesticides, and drugs are taken away, agriculture will come to a halt, and people will starve. Also, because of the interdependence of the system, no sector of the economy can be repaired unless many of the other sectors are in good order.

But in a nuclear attack, of course, all sectors of the economy would be devastated at once. The task facing the survivors, therefore, would be not to restore the old economy but to invent a new one, on a far more primitive level. But the invention of a primitive economy would not be a simple matter. Even economies we think of as primitive depend on considerable knowledge accumulated through long experience, and in modern times this knowledge has been largely lost. The economy of the Middle Ages, for example, was far less productive than our own, but it was exceedingly complex, and it would not be within the capacity of people in our time suddenly to establish a medieval economic system in the ruins of their twentieth-century one. After a limited nuclear attack, the typical predicament of a survivor would be that of, say, a bus driver in a city who was used to shopping at a supermarket and found himself facing the question of how to grow his own food, or of a bookkeeper in a suburb who found that he must make his own clothing, not to mention the cloth for the clothing. Innumerable things that we now take for granted would abruptly be lacking. In addition to food and clothing, they would include: heating, electric lights, running water, telephones, mail, transportation of all kinds, all household appliances powered by electricity or gas, information other than by word of mouth, medical facilities, sanitary facilities, and basic social services, such as fire departments and police. To restore these essentials of life takes time; but there would be no time. Hunger, illness, and possibly cold would press in on the dazed, bewildered, disorganized, injured remnant of the population on the very day of the attack. They would have to start foraging immediately for their next meal. Sitting among the debris of the Space Age, they would find that the pieces of a shattered modern economy around them—here an automobile, there a washing machine—were mismatched to their elemental needs. Nor would life be made easier for them by the fact that their first need, once they left any shelters they might have found, would be to flee the heavily irradiated, burned-out territories where they used to live, and to start over in less irradiated, unburned territories, which would probably be in the wilderness. Facing these urgent requirements, they would not be worrying about rebuilding the automobile industry or the electronics industry; they would be worrying about how to find nonradioactive berries in the woods, or how to tell which trees had edible bark.

Lastly, over the decades not only would the survivors of a limited attack face a contaminated and degraded environment but they themselves—their flesh, bones, and genetic endowment—would be contaminated: the generations that would be trying to rebuild a human life would be sick and possibly deformed generations. The actual doses received by particular survivors would, of course, depend on their circumstances, but some notion of the extent of the contamination can perhaps be gathered from the fact that if people came out of shelters after three months into an area in which the fallout would in the long run deliver a dose of ten thousand rems they would still receive about three per cent of the total, or three hundred rems, over their lifetimes, with two hundred of those rems being received in the first year. I spoke to Dr. Edward Radford, who is a professor of environmental epidemiology at the University of Pittsburgh, and who was chairman from 1977 to 1980 of the National Academy of Sciences' Committee on the Biological Effects of Ionizing Radiations, about the medical consequences of such exposure. "The present incidence of cancer, exclusive of skin cancer, in the United States population is thirty per cent, and roughly seventeen per cent die of the disease," he told me. "Since the dose of radiation that doubles the cancer rate is about one hundred and fifty rems, we could expect that a dose of three hundred rems would cause just about everybody to get cancer of one kind or another, and perhaps half of them would die from it. In addition, the dose that is estimated to cause a doubling of the spontaneous-mutation rate—which now affects ten percent of all births—is also one hundred and fifty rems, and therefore we could also expect genetic abnormalities to increase dramatically." Whether a human community could survive bearing this burden of illness and mutation is at best questionable.

In considering the global consequences of a holocaust, the first question to be asked is how widespread the hostilities would be. It is often assumed that a holocaust, even if it were full-scale, would be restricted to the Northern Hemisphere, destroying the United States, the Soviet Union, Europe, China, and Japan, but in fact there is no assurance that hostilities would not spread to other parts of the world. Both Soviet and American leaders believe that the rivalry between their countries has worldwide ideological significance, and in the name of their causes they might well extend their attacks almost anywhere. Furthermore, it takes very little imagination to see that once the superpowers had absorbed several thousand megatons of nuclear explosives each they would no longer *be* superpowers; indeed, they would no longer exist as nations at all. At that point, any sizable nation that had been spared attack—for example, Vietnam, Mexico, Nigeria, Australia, or South Africa—might, in the minds of the leaders of the ex-superpowers, become tempting as a target. It might suddenly occur to them that on a devastated earth mere survival would be the stuff of global might, and either or both of the ex-superpowers might then set about destroying those surviving middle-ranking powers that seemed closest to sharing the ideology of the enemy. Again, it is impossible to know what thoughts would go through the minds of men in caves, or perhaps in airborne command posts, who had just carried out the slaughter of hundreds of millions of people and whose nations had been annihilated in a similar slaughter (and it should always be borne in mind that sheer insanity is one of the possibilities), but it could be that in some confused attempt to shape the political future of the post-holocaust world (if there is one) they would carry their struggle into the would-be-neutral world. It could be that even now the United States has a few dozen megatons reserved in one contingency plan or another for, say, Cuba, Vietnam, and North Korea, while the Soviet Union may have a similar fate in mind for, among others, Israel, South Africa, and Australia. We also have to ask ourselves what the Chinese, the French, and the British, who all possess nuclear arms, and the Israelis, the South Africans, and the Indians, who are all suspected of possessing them, would attempt once the mayhem began. And this list of nuclear-armed and possibly nuclear-armed countries shows every sign of being a growing one.

Although it may seem inappropriate to mention "civilization" in the same breath as the death of hundreds of millions of people, it should at least be pointed out that a full-scale holocaust would, if it extended throughout the Northern Hemisphere, eliminate the civilizations of Europe, China, Japan, Russia, and the United States from the earth.

As I have already mentioned, there are uncertainties inherent in any attempt to predict the consequences of a nuclear holocaust; but when we try to estimate those consequences for the targeted countries it turns out that the readily calculable local primary effects of the bombs are so overwhelming that we never arrive at the uncertainties. Obviously, there can be no tangled interplay of destructive influences in society if there is no society; and the local primary effects are more than enough to remove society from the picture. This is why those observers who speak of "recovery" after a holocaust or of "winning" a nuclear "war" are dreaming. They are living in a past that has been swept away forever by nuclear arms. However, when it comes to inquiring into the global ecological consequences of a holocaust and, with them, the risk of human extinction, the uncertainties, and the political questions they raise, move to the fore. To begin with, this inquiry requires us to concentrate our attention on the earth. The earth is a compound mystery, for it presents us with the mystery of life in its entirety, the mystery of every individual form of life, and the mystery of ourselves, and all our thoughts and works. (Since we are earth-made, investigation of the earth eventually becomes introspection.) The reason for our ignorance is not that our knowledge of the earth is slight—on the contrary, it is extensive, and has grown in this century more than in all other centuries put together—but that the amount to be known is demonstrably so much greater. There is a sense, of course, in which knowledge can increase ignorance. By leading to fresh discoveries, knowledge may open up new wonders to our view but not yet to our understanding. Our century's discoveries in the earth sciences have increased our ignorance in just this sense: they have given us a glimpse of how much there is still to find out. Dr. Lewis Thomas, the noted biologist and essayist, has defined this ignorance in categorical terms, saying, "We are ignorant about how we work, about where we fit in, and most of all about the enormous, imponderable system of life in which we are embedded as working parts. We do not really understand nature, at all." Of all the things to be said in a discussion of the global effects of a nuclear holocaust, this is by far the most important: that because of the extent of what we know that we don't know, we are simply debarred from making confident judgments.

Since an awareness of the boundaries of present knowledge is a necessary part of science's effort to achieve precision and clarity, it is not surprising that the literature on global nuclear effects is littered with reminders of the fallibility and, above all, of the incompleteness of our present understanding. This appropriately modest, tentative spirit has perhaps been best summed up in the opening comments of the Office of Technology Assessment report, which states that the most important thing to know about a holocaust is not anything that "is known" but "what is not known." A similar acknowledgment of the importance of the unknown is implicit in a remark in a 1977 "interim" report by the National Academy of Sciences on the peril to the stratosphere from man-made disturbances in general. "It is unfortunately true," the report says, "that, accompanying very substantial over-all progress, the recent development of our understanding of stratospheric chemistry has been dominated by major upheavals caused by the recognition of the importance of processes whose role either had not been properly appreciated . . . or whose rate coefficient had been grossly misjudged. . . . To say how many more major upheavals we should expect in the future is rather like trying to foresee the unforeseeable." The report goes on to note that as knowledge of the chemistry of the stratosphere has improved, it has turned out that "even with the largest computers it is not possible to represent the detailed three-dimensional motions in the atmosphere while including the detailed chemical reactions." Before the "upheavals," scientists seemed to "know" a good deal; afterward, they knew that they knew less.

Our ignorance pertains to the possibility of altogether unknown major effects of nuclear explosions as well as to the magnitude of the known ones and their infinite interactions. Like so much else in science, the discovery of what is known so far about the effects of nuclear explosions is a story of surprises, starting with the surprise that the nucleus could be fissioned at all. Perhaps the second big surprise was the extent of harmful fallout; this came to light in the fifteen-megaton test at Bikini in 1954, when, to the amazement of the designers of the test, fallout began to descend on Marshall

Islanders and on American servicemen manning weather stations on atolls at supposedly safe distances from the explosion. It was not until this test that the world was alerted to the real magnitude—or, at any rate, to the magnitude as it is understood so far—of the peril from nuclear fallout. The next surprise was the extent of the effects of the electromagnetic pulse. Probably the most recent surprise has been the discovery, in the nineteen-seventies, of the peril to the ozone layer. Around 1970, a number of scientists became worried that the use of supersonic transports, which fly in the stratosphere and emit oxides of nitrogen, would deplete the ozone layer, and it occurred to two Columbia physicists—Henry M. Foley and Malvin A. Ruderman—that since nuclear weapons were known to produce nitric oxide in the stratosphere, the capacity of this compound for depleting the ozone might be tested by trying to find out whether ozone levels had dropped as a result of the atmospheric testing of nuclear weapons. The investigation was inconclusive, but it led the two men to worry about the fate of the ozone in the event of a nuclear holocaust. Their concern awakened the concern of other scientists, and in 1975 the National Academy of Sciences produced its report "Long-Term Worldwide Effects of Multiple Nuclear-Weapons Detonations," which attempted, among other things, to measure this peril. The sequence of events leading to our present awareness of this peril is illuminating, because it shows how a broad new development in scientific thought—in this case, the growing awareness in the nineteen-seventies of the vulnerability of the ecosphere to human intervention—brought to light an immense effect of nuclear weapons which had previously gone unnoticed. It is always difficult to become aware of one's ignorance, but as we try to give due weight to our present ignorance it can help us to recall that little more than a decade ago possibly the gravest global consequence of a holocaust which we now know of was totally unsuspected. Given the incomplete state of our knowledge of the earth, it seems unjustified at this point to assume that further developments in science will not bring forth further surprises.

The embryonic state of the earth sciences is one reason for our uncertainty concerning the outcome of a nuclear holocaust, but

there is a moral and political reason that may be even more fundamental. Epistemologically, the earth is a special object. Scientific
inquiry into the effects of a holocaust, like every other form of inquiry into this subject, is restricted by our lack of experience with
large-scale nuclear destruction. But the lack of experience is not the
result of neglect or accident, or even of our reluctance to face the
horror of our predicament. In scientific work, experience means
experiments, and scientific knowledge is not considered to be knowledge until it has been confirmed by experiment—or, at least, by
observation. Until then, no matter how plausible a theory sounds,
and no matter how dazzling it may appear intellectually, it is relegated to the limbo of hypothesis. But when it comes to judging the
consequences of a nuclear holocaust there can be no experimentation, and thus no empirical verification. We cannot run experiments
with the earth, because we have only one earth, on which we depend for our survival; we are not in possession of any spare earths
that we might blow up in some universal laboratory in order to
discover their tolerance of nuclear holocausts. Hence, our knowledge of the resiliency of the earth in the face of nuclear attack is
limited by our fear of bringing about just the event—human extinction—whose likelihood we are chiefly interested in finding out about.
The famous uncertainty principle, formulated by the German physicist Werner Heisenberg, has shown that our knowledge of atomic
phenomena is limited because the experimental procedures with
which we must carry out our observations inevitably interfere with
the phenomena that we wish to measure. The question of extinction by nuclear arms—or by any other means, for that matter—presents us with an opposite but related uncertainty principle: our
knowledge of extinction is limited because the experiments with
which we would carry out our observations interfere with us, the
observers, and, in fact, might put an end to us. This uncertainty
principle complements the first. Both principles recognize that a
limit to our knowledge is fixed by the fact that we are incarnate
beings, not disembodied spirits, and that observation, like other
human activities, is a physical process and so can interfere both
with what is under observation and with the observer. Therefore,

it is ultimately extinction itself that fixes the boundary to what we can know about extinction. No human being will ever be able to say with confidence, "*Now* I see how many megatons it takes for us to exterminate ourselves." To the extent that this check stands in the way of investigation, our uncertainty is forced on us not so much by the limitations of our intellectual ability as by the irreducible fact that we have no platform for observation except our mortal frames. In these circumstances, which are rudiments of the human condition, toleration of uncertainty is the path of life, and the demand for certainty is the path toward death.

We have had some experience of moral and political restraints on research in the field of medicine, in which, in all civilized countries, there are restrictions on experimenting with human beings; when the results might be injurious, laboratory animals are used instead. However, in investigating the properties of the earth we lack even any recourse that would be analogous to the use of these animals, for if we have no extra, dispensable earths to experiment with, neither are we in possession of any planets bearing life of some different sort. (As far as we now know, among the planets in the solar system the earth stands alone as a bearer of life.) And while it is true that we can run experiments in various corners of the earth and try to extrapolate the results to the earth as a whole, what is always missing from the results is the totality of the ecosphere, with its endless pathways of cause and effect, linking the biochemistry of the humblest alga and global chemical and dynamic balances into an indivisible whole. This whole is a mechanism in itself; indeed, it may be regarded as a single living being. Dr. Thomas, for one, has likened the earth to a cell. The analogy is compelling, but in one noteworthy respect, at least, there is a difference between the earth and a cell: whereas each cell is one among billions struck from the same genetic mold, the earth, as the mother of all life, has no living parent. If the behavior of cells is often predictable, it is because they exist en masse, and what a billion of them, programmed by their genetic material, have done a billion times the billion and first is likely to do again. But the earth is a member of no class as yet open to our observation which would permit the drawing of such inferences by generalization. When it comes to trying to predict its tolerance to perturbances, we are in the position of someone asked to deduce the whole of medicine by observing one human being. With respect to its individuality, then, the earth is not so much like a cell as like an individual person. Like a person, the earth is unique; like a person, it is sacred; and, like a person, it is unpredictable by the generalizing laws of science.

If we had no knowledge at all of the likely consequences of a holocaust for the earth, there would, of course, be no basis whatever for judgment. However, given the extent of what there is to know about the earth, it is no contradiction to say that while our ignorance is vast and, in a certain sense, irremediable (although, at the same time, the amount that we can and certainly will find out is also probably measureless), our knowledge is also vast, and that what we know is extremely alarming. Since in a global holocaust even the so-called local effects of the explosions may cover the whole land mass of the Northern Hemisphere, they may have secondary consequences that are truly global. The destruction of estuarine life throughout the Northern Hemisphere and the radioactive poisoning of the local waters could cause general harm to life in the oceans. Ecological collapse on the land in large parts of the Northern Hemisphere could have large consequences for the climate of the earth as a whole. Loss of vegetation, for example, increases the surface reflectivity of the earth, and this has a cooling effect on the atmosphere. In heavily irradiated zones, the mutation of plant pathogens might create virulent strains that could, in the words of the 1975 N.A.S. report, "produce disease epidemics that would spread globally." The irradiated northern half of the earth would in general become a huge radioecological laboratory, in which many species would be driven to extinction, others would flourish and possibly invade unharmed parts of the earth, and still others would evolve into new and unpredictable forms.

But more important by far, in all probability, than the global aftereffects of the local destruction would be the direct global effects, the most important of which is ozone loss. The concentration of ozone in the earth's atmosphere is very small—not more than ten parts by weight per million parts of air. Yet the ozone layer has a critical importance to life on earth, because it protects the earth's surface from the harmful ultraviolet radiation in sunlight, which would otherwise be "lethal to unprotected organisms as we now know them," to quote Dr. Martyn M. Caldwell, a leading authority on the biological effects of ultraviolet radiation, in a recent article of his in *BioScience* titled "Plant Life and Ultraviolet Radiation: Some Perspective in the History of the Earth's UV Climate." I have already mentioned Glasstone's remark that without the absorption of solar ultraviolet radiation by the ozone "life as currently known could not exist except possibly in the ocean." The 1975 N.A.S. report states, "As biologists, geologists, and other students of evolution recognize, the development of an oxygen-rich atmosphere, with its *ozone layer, was a precondition to the development of multicelled plants and animals, and all life forms on land have evolved under this shield*" (italics in the original). B. W. Boville, of the Canadian Atmospheric Environment Service, has written that the ozone layer is "a crucial element to climate and to the existence of all life on earth." Dr. Fred Iklé, who served as the director of the Arms Control and Disarmament Agency under Presidents Nixon and Ford, and now serves as Under Secretary of Defense for Policy under President Reagan, has stated that severe reduction of the ozone layer through nuclear explosions could "shatter the ecological structure that permits man to remain alive on this planet." And a paper delivered at a United Nations-sponsored scientific conference in March, 1977, states, "The whole biological world, so dependent on micro-organisms, may, if doses [of ultraviolet radiation] increase, be in serious trouble."

As the passage from the N.A.S. report states, the beginnings of multicelled life are associated with the formation of an ozone layer. In the earliest stages of evolution, when there was little or no oxygen in the atmosphere, and no ozone layer—ozone (O_3) is formed when sunlight strikes oxygen (O_2) in the upper atmosphere—ultraviolet radiation, which would then have reached the surface of the earth relatively unimpeded, may have been one of the most important sources of the energy that built up the first biological macromolecules, about three and a half billion years ago. But about two billion years ago, when those molecules had formed into single-celled organisms, the organisms freed themselves from dependence on ultraviolet light as a source of energy by coming to rely instead on photosynthesis—a method of extracting energy from sunlight by making use of carbon dioxide and water, which were available everywhere in the environment, as they are today. Photosynthesis was "probably the largest single step on the evolutionary path leading to the growth of higher life forms" (according to Dr. Michael McElroy, a physicist at Harvard's Center for Earth and Planetary Physics, who has done important new work in the study of the earth's atmosphere), and set the stage for terrestrial life as it exists today. For that life to develop, however, the genetic material, DNA, had also to develop, and ultraviolet light, as it happens, is particularly destructive of DNA, causing it to lose "biological activity," as Dr. Caldwell notes. Furthermore, ultraviolet light inhibits photosynthesis, and thus on the earth of two billion years ago it placed another barrier in the way of what turned out to be the next step in evolution. And there was still another barrier to evolution in the fact that oxygen, a by-product of photosynthesis, was poisonous to existing organisms. At first, it is suggested, organisms solved their oxygen problem by fixing oxygen to ferrous iron—a procedure that would explain the existence of banded iron formations found in sedimentary rock that is some two billion years old. But it was life's second solution to its oxygen problem—the development of enzymes capable of returning oxygen harmlessly to the environment—that proved to be the more successful one. It lifted the barriers to evolution just mentioned: by detoxifying oxygen it liberated life from its dependence on iron, leaving life "free to proliferate in the ocean, with rapid growth in oxygen" (McElroy); and by enriching the atmosphere with oxygen it assured the gradual creation of an ozone layer, which blocked out much of the ultraviolet radiation. Once this was done, the way was cleared, in the opinion of some scientists, for the "eruptive proliferation of species" (Caldwell) that geologists find in the fossil record of the Cambrian period, nearly six hundred million years ago. A hundred and eighty million years later, in the Silurian, life made a second leap ahead when, after more than three billion years in the ocean, it made its "dramatic appearance" (Caldwell) on land, and this leap, too, can be associated with the growth of the ozone shield, which, it is thought, around that time reached a density that would permit organisms to survive on land, without the partial protection from ultraviolet radiation which water affords.

If the formation of the ozone layer was one of the necessary preconditions for the "dramatic appearance" of life on land, then the question naturally arises whether heavy depletion of the ozone, by nuclear explosions or any other cause, might not bring about a dramatic disappearance of life, including human life, from the land. (Spray cans, incongruously, are one possible cause of harm to the ozone, because they put chlorocarbons into the atmosphere, and these are broken down by sunlight, releasing chlorine, which depletes ozone.) But that question, having been raised, is one of those which cannot be answered with confidence, given the present state of our knowledge of the workings of the earth. Even the estimates of ozone loss that would be brought about by holocausts of different sizes are highly uncertain (in calculating some of these figures, the National Academy of Sciences found the largest computers insufficient)—as is made clear in the 1975 N.A.S. report, which found that the explosion of ten thousand megatons of nuclear weapons would increase the amount of nitric oxide in the stratosphere to something between five and fifty times the normal amount (a tenfold uncertainty is characteristic of calculations in this field), that it would (as has been mentioned) reduce the ozone layer in the Northern Hemisphere, where the report assumes that the explosions would occur, by anything from thirty to seventy per cent, and that it would reduce it in the Southern Hemisphere by anything from twenty to forty per cent. I recently asked Dr. McElroy what the current estimation of danger to the ozone layer from man-made oxides of nitrogen in general was. "In the years after the N.A.S. report of 1975, the estimates of harm were lowered, but since about 1977 they

81

have risen again," he told me. He went on to discuss a possible increase in nitrous oxide in the atmosphere brought about by, say, agricultural fertilizers. "At present, it is estimated that a doubling of the nitrous oxide in the troposphere, which becomes nitric oxide —one of the compounds that deplete ozone—after it reaches the stratosphere, would bring about a fifteen-per-cent reduction in the ozone. That is a higher estimate for the nitrous-oxide effect than the one made in 1975. However, a nuclear holocaust would inject nitric oxide directly into the stratosphere, and in amounts much greater than would be produced, indirectly, by the twofold increase in nitrous oxide, and no one has done any study of the consequences for the ozone of these larger amounts in the light of the knowledge acquired since 1975. But my guess is that the figures would not have changed radically, and that the estimates for ozone reduction by a nuclear holocaust given in 1975 would not be far off." In mid-1981, the first measurement of an actual reduction of the ozone layer was made. The National Aeronautics and Space Administration reported "preliminary" findings indicating that ozone in a region of the stratosphere some twenty-five miles up—in the higher part of the ozone layer—had decreased at the rate of approximately half a per cent a year over the past decade. While this chilling discovery does not bear directly on the consequences of a holocaust for the ozone, it does tend to confirm the more general hypothesis that the ozone is vulnerable to human intervention.

The extent of the biological damage that would be done by various increases in ultraviolet radiation is, if anything, even less well known than what the increases caused by nuclear detonations might be, but the available information suggests that the damage to the whole ecosphere would be severe. One reason is that certain wavelengths of ultraviolet that are known to be particularly harmful biologically would be disproportionately increased by ozone reduction. Moreover, the cause of the biological damage—increased ultraviolet radiation—would be similar everywhere, but the effects would be different for each of the earth's species and ecosystems. And the effects of those effects, spreading outward indefinitely through the interconnected web of life, are not within the realm of the calculable. However, it is known with certainty that ultraviolet radiation is harmful or fatal to living things. In fact, precisely because of its abiotic qualities ultraviolet light has long been in use as a sterilizing agent in medical and other scientific work. The most comprehensive study of ultraviolet's effects which has been done so far is the Department of Transportation's Climatic Impact Assessment Program report "Impacts of Climatic Change on the Biosphere." It states that "excessive UV-B radiation"—the part of the ultraviolet spectrum which would be significantly increased by ozone depletion—"is a decidedly detrimental factor for most organisms, including man," and continues, "Even current levels of solar UV-B irradiance can be linked with phenomena such as increased mutation rates, delay of cell division, depression of photosynthesis in phytoplankton, skin cancer in humans, cancer eye in certain cattle, and lethality of many lower organisms, such as aquatic invertebrates and bacteria."

Research concerning the effects of UV-B irradiance on specific organisms—and especially on organisms in their natural habitats—has been slight, and in a recent conversation Dr. Caldwell, who was chairman of the scientific panel that produced the Climatic Impact Assessment Program report, told me that not enough experiments have been done for anyone to generalize with confidence about the ultimate fate of living things subjected to increased ultraviolet radiation. From the experiments that have been done, however, it is known that, among mammals, human beings are especially vulnerable, because of their lack of body hair. Since some ultraviolet light reaches the earth in normal circumstances, human beings (and other creatures) have developed adaptations to deal with it. The main adaptation in man is tanning, which helps to prevent sunburn. The susceptibility of fair-skinned people to these ailments and also to skin cancer is traceable to their relative inability to tan, and one consequence of reduced ozone could be higher rates of skin cancer among human beings. Of much greater seriousness, though, would be the temporary loss of sight through photophthalmia, or snow blindness, which can be contracted by exposure to heightened ultraviolet radiation and may last for several days after each exposure.

Photophthalmia is, in the words of the 1975 N.A.S. report, "disabling and painful"; also, "there are no immune groups," and "there is no adaptation." One can avoid photophthalmia by wearing goggles whenever one goes outside, but so far the world has made no provision for each person on earth to have a pair of goggles in case the ozone is depleted. However, if the higher estimates of depletion turn out to be correct, people will not be able to stay outdoors very long anyway. At these levels, "incapacitating" sunburn would occur in several minutes; if the reduction of the ozone reached the seventy per cent maximum that the report assigns to the Northern Hemisphere, the time could be ten minutes. Moreover, the report states that in the months immediately following the attack ozone depletion could be even higher than seventy per cent. "We have no simple way," the report observes, "to estimate the magnitude of short-term depletion." The ten-minute rule is not one that the strategists of "recovery" after a nuclear attack usually figure into their calculations. If high levels of ultraviolet radiation occur, then anyone who crawls out of his shelter after radiation from fallout has declined to tolerable levels will have to crawl back in immediately. In the meantime, though, people would not have been able to go out to produce food, and they would starve. A further possible harmful consequence—in itself a potential human and ecological catastrophe of global proportions—is that increased ultraviolet light would raise the amounts of Vitamin D in the skin of mammals and birds to toxic levels. But the experimentation necessary to determine whether or not this sweeping catastrophe would occur has not been done. The 1975 N.A.S. report observes, alarmingly but inconclusively, "We do not know whether man and other vertebrate animals could tolerate an increased Vitamin D synthesis that might result from a large and rapid increase in [ultraviolet] exposure." The report "urgently" recommends further study of the question.

The skin of many mammals would be protected by fur or other covering, but their eyes would remain exposed. In a recent lecture, Dr. Tsipis said that ozone reduction might bring about the blinding of the world's animals, and that this effect alone would have the makings of a global ecological catastrophe. I discussed the subject with Dr. Frederick Urbach, who teaches medicine at Temple University and is the editor of a volume titled "The Biologic Effects of Ultraviolet Radiation with Emphasis on the Skin," and who has conducted extensive research on the effect of ultraviolet radiation on animals. He confirmed that the peril to the eyes of animals is vast and real. "If you go much above fifty per cent reduction of the ozone, the increase in ultraviolet radiation begins to do injury to the cornea," he told me. "You get a bad sunburn of the eye. People don't usually get it, because at normal levels the anatomy of the face gives protection. But when there is snow on the ground the ultraviolet radiation is reflected back up into the eye. The problem is easily remedied by wearing glasses, but animals will hardly be able to do that. There is a story—probably apocryphal—that when Hannibal crossed the Alps, where ultraviolet is more intense, some of his elephants went blind. When animals can't see, they can't protect themselves. A blind animal does not survive well in nature. Repeated injury causes scarring of the cornea, and this would eventually make the animals permanently blind. We see this happening to the mice that we irradiate with ultraviolet wavelengths in the laboratory; after a while, they develop opaque corneas. In the event of ozone depletion, the same thing would happen not only to mammals but to insects and birds."

Sight and smell permit animals to find their way in the environment and to fulfill the roles mapped out for them by nature, and the loss of sight would throw the environment into disarray as billions of blinded beasts, insects, and birds began to stumble through the world. The disorientation of insects would be fateful not only for them but for plant life, much of which depends on insects for pollination and other processes essential to survival. Ultraviolet light is, in fact, known to play a role in many activities of insects, including phototaxis, celestial navigation, and sex identification, and an increase in ultraviolet light would no doubt impair these capacities. But plant life would in any case be under direct assault from increased ultraviolet radiation. While confident generalization about the fate of plants has to be ruled out, experiments that have been performed with crops show that while some are quite resistant, others, including tomatoes, beans, peas, and onions, would be killed or "severely scalded," according to the N.A.S. report. Because ultraviolet radiation breaks down DNA, which regulates reproduction, and because it also represses photosynthesis, which is the chief metabolic process of plants, the direct effect of increased ultraviolet radiation on plant life is likely to be widespread and serious. And because many species, the N.A.S. report states, "survive at an upper limit of tolerance," any increase in ultraviolet radiation is "a threat to the survival of certain species and accordingly to entire ecosystems." The global damage to plants and the global damage to the insects are synergistic: the damage to the insects damages the plants, which in turn, damage the insects again, in a chain of effects whose outcome is unforeseeable. On the question of the harm to the insects that would be caused by the harm to the rest of the ecosphere, Ting H. Hsiao, a professor of entomology at Utah State University, has written in the Climatic Impact Assessment Program report, "Since insects are important in the world's ecosystems, any changes in other components of the ecosystem could have an impact on insect populations. Ultraviolet radiation is a physical factor that directly influences all biotic components of the ecosystem. . . . A change in abiotic factors, such as temperature, rainfall, or wind, associated with elevated ultraviolet radiation could profoundly affect behavior, biology, population structure, dispersal, and migration of insects." Dr. Hsiao's observations about insects and the ecosphere can, in fact, be generalized to include all global effects of a holocaust, for there are few that do not have potentially large consequences for the character and severity of all the others.

The web of life in the oceans, perhaps more than any other part of the environment, is vulnerable to damage from increased ultraviolet radiation. John Calkins, of the Department of Radiation Medicine of the University of Kentucky, and D. Stuart Nachtwey, a professor of radiation biology at Oregon State University, remark in the Climatic Impact Assessment Program report that the experimentation that has been done so far, though it is inadequate, suggests that "many aquatic micro-organisms and invertebrates have little reserve capacity to cope with surface levels of solar UV-B." The organisms at greatest risk are the unicellular organisms that lie at the base of the marine food chain, and thus ultimately sustain the higher creatures in the oceans. Since the removal of an organism from the food chain can eliminate all the organisms above it in the chain, the loss of even part of the chain's base could have huge consequences. Once again, quantitative judgments are not possible, but such experiments as have been carried out make the danger clear. In the early nineteen-seventies, researchers discovered that even normal levels of UV-B radiation are harmful or fatal to many aquatic organisms if they are not permitted to descend deeper into the water or otherwise shield themselves from exposure. The finding is important, because it means that the question to be asked about increased UV-B radiation is not whether it would be biologically harmful but whether the intensity would be great enough to overpower the mechanisms of defense that organisms have built up over billions of years of evolution to deal with normal levels of ultraviolet radiation. The defense mechanisms include the screening of the DNA molecules with less critical molecules; enzymatic mechanisms by which damage done in the daytime is repaired at night; and delay of cell divisions (when cells can be most sensitive to ultraviolet radiation) until the nighttime. But fleeing, which can save some organisms from the ultraviolet peril, may get them into other kinds of trouble. In general, organisms find the niche in the environment that is best suited to them, and if they are suddenly forced to leave it they may die. Or, if they survive, they may destroy the ecological niche that permits some other species to survive. If a change in the environment occurs slowly, an organism may prove able to adapt, but a holocaust would bring a sudden change, and the usefulness of adaptation would be greatly reduced. A glimpse of a few of the complexities involved in ultraviolet stress is offered by some experiments that were done by Dr. Nachtwey and several colleagues on the unicellular alga called *Chlamydomonas reinhardi*. If the alga is resting near the surface of the ocean on a cloudy day, and the sun suddenly appears, it will dive for safety, and if ultraviolet radiation is at normal levels it will get deep enough fast enough to survive. But if the ozone has been decreased by as little as sixteen per cent, the alga will be killed in mid-dive by the more intense ultraviolet rays. The crucial factor for *C. reinhardi* turns out to be its swimming speed.

Because experimentation has been so slight, and because the complexities are so immense, both the Climatic Impact Assessment Program report and the N.A.S. report hold back from sweeping judgments about the fate of oceanic life as a whole in the event of severe ozone reduction, but at one point the N.A.S. report does state that "under extreme circumstances, certain habitats could become devoid of living organisms," and at another point, speaking of the global effects in their entirety, it states, "Large-scale detonations will create conditions sufficient to modify the oceanic environment, on a global basis, with a resultant modification of the marine biota. In areas of major perturbations this influence will be in the form of local or extensive extinctions or reduction in susceptible species, with a subsequent disruption of the normal food web."

A second global consequence of ozone reduction would be climatic change. The earth's climate, like the ecosphere as a whole, the 1975 N.A.S. report reminds us, is "holocoenotic"; in other words, it is a whole in which "any action influencing a single part of the system can be expected to have an effect on all other parts of the system." As is hardly surprising, the totality of those effects is unknown even for a single major climatic disturbance, and the N.A.S. report notes that "no adequate climatic models exist that would permit prediction of the nature and degree of climatic changes that might result from a large-scale nuclear event." Of the three large components of the earth's surface—land, sea, and air—the air is probably the most changeable. The parts of this delicately balanced whole include, among many others, the chemical composition of both the troposphere and the stratosphere; the temperature levels of the atmosphere and the degree of moisture at all altitudes; the temperature and reflectivity of the earth's surface; the circulatory patterns of the air; the circulatory patterns of the ocean currents; and the degree of retention of the earth's reflected warmth by the atmosphere, in the so-called greenhouse effect. Each of these parts could be disturbed by a holocaust, and the disturbance of any one could disturb many or all of the others. According to present thinking, a depletion of the ozone layer would simultaneously act to warm the surface of the earth, by permitting more solar radiation to reach it, and act to cool it, by reducing the layer's capacity to radiate back to earth the heat reflected from the earth's surface. But, according to the N.A.S. report, the cooling at the surface of the earth, which might last for several years, is expected to exceed the warming by, at most, an amount estimated (very tentatively, considering that "no adequate climatic models exist") at approximately one degree Fahrenheit. Temperature change at the surface, however, may be less important than temperature change elsewhere in the atmosphere. For example, cooling of the upper troposphere and of the lower stratosphere "is likely to be much larger" than cooling at the surface, and may cause alterations in the cloud cover, which would, in turn, influence the climate. This whole subject, however, is one of the many subjects that remain relatively unexplored. It is estimated that dust and smoke lofted by the explosions would add to the cooling by another degree Fahrenheit. Temperatures on earth can fluctuate tens of degrees in a single day, yet the net reduction of a couple of degrees in the temperature of the entire surface of the earth after a holocaust would be of great consequence. For example, it could cut the biological productivity of deciduous forests by as much as twenty per cent, shift the monsoons in Asia in a way that could be ruinous for both agriculture and ecosystems, and eliminate all wheat-growing in Canada. The N.A.S. report also mentions that climatic change identified as "dramatic" and "major," but not otherwise specified, "cannot be ruled out," and adds that although the change is likely to last only a few years, the possibility exists that it "may not be reversible." Greater reductions would, of course, have larger consequences. Another global consequence of the injection of oxides of nitrogen into the stratosphere by nuclear explosions would be pollution of the environment as these gases fell back into the troposphere. Nitrogen dioxide, for example, is one of the most harmful components of the smog that afflicts many modern cities, such as Los Angeles. It reacts with hydrocarbons present in the air above these cities, actually causing in the process some ozone formation. While ozone in the stratosphere is beneficial to human beings, ozone near ground level is not. It has been found not only to increase respiratory problems among human beings but to be harmful to some plant life. The formation of nitrogen dioxide, accordingly, is still another global effect of a holocaust whose consequences are not calculable. In addition, nitrogen dioxide is responsible in polluted cities for turning the sky brown, and after a holocaust it might happen that the sky of the whole earth would turn from blue to brown for as long as the pollution lasted (perhaps several years).

The known consequences of global contamination by stratospheric fallout (as distinct from the tropospheric fallout on the targeted countries) would seem great in comparison with anything except other nuclear effects, but against this backdrop they seem moderate—although, as usual, the state of knowledge precludes confident prediction. The stratospheric portion of the fallout is much less intense than the tropospheric portion, because it can remain in the atmosphere for several years, and by the time it descends to earth its radioactivity has declined to very low levels. The N.A.S. report estimates that a ten-thousand-megaton holocaust would deliver over the following twenty to thirty years a dose of four rems to every person in the Northern Hemisphere and a third of that to every person in the Southern Hemisphere, and would cause a two-per-cent rise in the death rate from cancer. The same doses would cause serious genetic disease to increase around the world by up to about two per cent, with a noticeable but decreasing number of mutations appearing in the next thirty generations. There would, however, be "hot spots" in some parts of the world, where, because of certain patterns of weather, the doses of radiation would be many times as great. Also, the world would be contaminated with particles of plutonium, which would cause an as yet unestimated rise in the incidence of lung cancer. (All these effects, which were

90

calculated by the N.A.S. in 1975 for a ten-thousand-megaton holocaust, would presumably be greater in a twenty-thousand-megaton
holocaust.)

In recent years, scientists in many fields have accumulated enough
knowledge to begin to look on the earth as a single, concrete mechanism, and to at least begin to ask how it works. One of their discoveries has been that life and life's inanimate terrestrial surroundings
have a strong reciprocal influence on each other. For life, the land,
oceans, and air have been the environment, but, equally, for the
land, oceans, and air life has been the environment—the condition-
ing force. The injection of oxygen into the atmosphere by living
things, which led to the formation of an ozone layer, which, in turn,
shut out lethal ultraviolet rays from the sun and permitted the rise
of multicellular organisms, was only one of life's large-scale interventions. The more closely scientists look at life and its evolution,
the less they find it possible to draw a sharp distinction between
"life," on the one hand, and an inanimate "environment" in which it
exists, on the other. Rather, "the environment" of the present day
appears to be a house of unimaginable intricacy which life has to a
very great extent built and furnished for its own use. It seems that
life even regulates and maintains the chemical environment of the
earth in a way that turns out to suit its own needs. In a far-reaching
speculative article entitled "Chemical Processes in the Solar System: A Kinetic Perspective," Dr. McElroy has described the terrestrial cycles by which the most important elements of the atmosphere—oxygen, carbon, and nitrogen—are kept in proportions that
are favorable to life. He finds that in each case life itself—its birth,
metabolism, and decay—is chiefly responsible for maintaining the
balance. For example, he calculates that if for some reason respira-
tion and decay were suddenly cut off, photosynthesis would devour
all the inorganic carbon on the surface of the ocean and in the atmosphere within forty years. Thereafter, carbon welling up from
the deep ocean would fuel photosynthesis in the oceans for another

thousand years, but then "life as we know it would terminate." Dr. McElroy also observes that the amount of ozone in the stratosphere is influenced by the amount of organic decay, and thus by the amount of life, on earth. Nitrous oxide is a product of organic decay, and because it produces nitric oxide—one of the compounds responsible for ozone depletion—it plays the role of regulator. In the absence of human intervention, living things are largely responsible for introducing nitrous oxide into the atmosphere. When life is exceptionally abundant, it releases more nitrous oxide into the atmosphere, and may thus act to cut back on the ozone, and that cutback lets in more ultraviolet rays. On the other hand, when life is sparse and depleted, nitrous-oxide production is reduced, the ozone layer builds up, and ultraviolet rays are cut back. These speculative glimpses of what might be called the metabolism of the earth give substance to the growing conviction among scientists that the earth, like a single cell or a single organism, is a systemic whole, and in a general way they tend to confirm the fear that any large man-made perturbation of terrestrial nature could lead to a catastrophic systemic breakdown. Nuclear explosions are far from being the only perturbations in question; a heating of the global atmosphere through an increased greenhouse effect, which could be caused by the injection of vast amounts of carbon dioxide into the air (for instance, from the increased burning of coal), is another notable peril of this kind. But a nuclear holocaust would be unique in its suddenness, which would permit no observation of slowly building environmental damage before the full—and, for man, perhaps the final—catastrophe occurred. The geological record does not sustain the fear that sudden perturbations can extinguish all life on earth (if it did, we would not be here to reflect on the subject), but it does suggest that sudden, drastic ecological collapse is possible. It suggests that life as a whole, if it is given hundreds of millions of years in which to recuperate and send out new evolutionary lines, has an astounding resilience, and an ability to bring forth new and ever more impressive life forms, but it also suggests that abrupt interventions can radically disrupt any particular evolutionary configuration and dispatch hundreds of thousands of species into extinction.

The view of the earth as a single system, or organism, has only recently proceeded from poetic metaphor to actual scientific investigation, and on the whole Dr. Thomas's observation that "we do not really understand nature, at all" still holds. It is as much on the basis of this ignorance, whose scope we are only now in a position to grasp, as on the basis of the particular items of knowledge in our possession that I believe that the following judgment can be made: Bearing in mind that the possible consequences of the detonations of thousands of megatons of nuclear explosives include the blinding of insects, birds, and beasts all over the world; the extinction of many ocean species, among them some at the base of the food chain; the temporary or permanent alteration of the climate of the globe, with the outside chance of "dramatic" and "major" alterations in the structure of the atmosphere; the pollution of the whole ecosphere with oxides of nitrogen; the incapacitation in ten minutes of unprotected people who go out into the sunlight; the blinding of people who go out into the sunlight; a significant decrease in photosynthesis in plants around the world; the scalding and killing of many crops; the increase in rates of cancer and mutation around the world, but especially in the targeted zones, and the attendant risk of global epidemics; the possible poisoning of all vertebrates by sharply increased levels of Vitamin D in their skin as a result of increased ultraviolet light; and the outright slaughter on all targeted continents of most human beings and other living things by the initial nuclear radiation, the fireballs, the thermal pulses, the blast waves, the mass fires, and the fallout from the explosions; and, considering that these consequences will all interact with one another in unguessable ways and, furthermore, are in all likelihood an incomplete list, which will be added to as our knowledge of the earth increases, one must conclude that a full-scale nuclear holocaust could lead to the extinction of mankind.

To say that human extinction is a certainty would, of course, be a misrepresentation—just as it would be a misrepresentation to say that extinction can be ruled out. To begin with, we know that a holocaust may not occur at all. If one does occur, the adversaries may not use all their weapons. If they do use all their weapons, the global effects, in the ozone and elsewhere, may be moderate. And if the effects are not moderate but extreme, the ecosphere may prove resilient enough to withstand them without breaking down catastrophically. These are all substantial reasons for supposing that mankind will not be extinguished in a nuclear holocaust, or even that extinction in a holocaust is unlikely, and they tend to calm our fear and to reduce our sense of urgency. Yet at the same time we are compelled to admit that there *may* be a holocaust, that the adversaries *may* use all their weapons, that the global effects, including effects of which we are as yet unaware, *may* be severe, that the ecosphere *may* suffer catastrophic breakdown, and that our species *may* be extinguished. We are left with uncertainty, and are forced to make our decisions in a state of uncertainty. If we wish to act to save our species, we have to muster our resolve in spite of our awareness that the life of the species may not now in fact be jeopardized. On the other hand, if we wish to ignore the peril, we have to admit that we do so in the knowledge that the species may be in danger of imminent self-destruction. When the existence of nuclear weapons was made known, thoughtful people everywhere in the world realized that if the great powers entered into a nuclear-arms race the human species would sooner or later face the possibility of extinction. They also realized that in the absence of international agreements preventing it an arms race would probably occur. They knew that the path of nuclear armament was a dead end for mankind. The discovery of the energy in mass—of "the basic power of the universe"—and of a means by which man could release that energy altered the relationship between man and the source of his life, the earth. In the shadow of this power, the earth became small and the life of the human species doubtful. In that sense, the question of human extinction has been on the political agenda of the world ever since the first nuclear weapon was detonated, and there was no need for the world to build up its present tremendous arsenals before starting to worry about it. At just what point the species crossed, or will have crossed, the boundary between merely having the technical knowledge to destroy itself and actually having the arsenals at hand, ready to be used at any second, is not precisely knowable. But it is clear that at present, with some twenty thousand megatons of nuclear explosive power in existence, and with more being added every day, we have entered into the zone of uncertainty, which is to say the zone of risk of extinction. But the mere risk of extinction has a significance that is categorically different from, and immeasurably greater than, that of any other risk, and as we make our decisions we have to take that significance into account. Up to now, every risk has been contained within the frame of life; extinction would shatter the frame. It represents not the defeat of some purpose but an abyss in which all human purposes would be drowned for all time. We have no right to place the possibility of this limitless, eternal defeat on the same footing as risks that we run in the ordinary conduct of our affairs in our particular transient moment of human history. To employ a mathematical analogy, we can say that although the risk of extinction may be fractional, the stake is, humanly speaking, infinite, and a fraction of infinity is still infinity. In other words, once we learn that a holocaust *might* lead to extinction we have no right to gamble, because if we lose, the game will be over, and neither we nor anyone else will ever get another chance. Therefore, although, scientifically speaking, there is all the difference in the world between the mere possibility that a holocaust will bring about extinction and the certainty of it, morally they are the same, and we have no choice but to address the issue of nuclear weapons as though we knew for a certainty that their use would put an end to our species. In weighing the fate of the earth and, with it, our own fate, we stand before a mystery, and in tampering with the earth we tamper with a mystery. We are in deep ignorance. Our ignorance should dispose us to wonder, our wonder should make us humble, our humility should inspire us to reverence and caution, and our reverence and caution should lead us to act without delay to withdraw the threat we now pose to the earth and to ourselves.

In trying to describe possible consequences of a nuclear holocaust, I have mentioned the limitless complexity of its effects on human society and on the ecosphere—a complexity that sometimes seems to be as great as that of life itself. But if these effects should lead to human extinction, then all the complexity will give way to the utmost simplicity—the simplicity of nothingness. We—the human race—shall cease to be.

II.
THE SECOND DEATH

I F A COUNCIL WERE TO BE EMPOWERED by the people of the earth to do whatever was necessary to save humanity from extinction by nuclear arms, it might well decide that a good first step would be to order the destruction of all the nuclear weapons in the world. When the order had been carried out, however, warlike or warring nations might still rebuild their nuclear arsenals—perhaps in a matter of months. A logical second step, accordingly, would be to order the destruction of the factories that make the weapons. But, just as the weapons might be rebuilt, so might the factories, and the world's margin of safety would not have been increased by very much. A third step, then, would be to order the destruction of the factories that make the factories that make the weapons—a measure that might require the destruction of a considerable part of the world's economy. But even then lasting safety would not have been reached, because in some number of years—at most, a few decades—everything could be rebuilt, including the nuclear arsenals, and mankind would again be ready to extinguish itself. A determined council might next decide to try to arrest the world economy in a pre-nuclear state by throwing the blueprints and technical manuals for reconstruction on the bonfires that had by then consumed every-thing else, but that recourse, too, would ultimately fail, because the blueprints and manuals could easily be redrawn and rewritten. As long as the world remained acquainted with the basic physical laws that underlie the construction of nuclear weapons—and these laws include the better part of physics as physics is understood in our century—mankind would have failed to put many years between itself and its doom. For the fundamental origin of the peril of human extinction by nuclear arms lies not in any particular social or politi-cal circumstances of our time but in the attainment by mankind as a whole, after millennia of scientific progress, of a certain level of knowledge of the physical universe. As long as that knowledge is in our possession, the atoms themselves, each one stocked with its prodigious supply of energy, are, in a manner of speaking, in a perilously advanced state of mobilization for nuclear hostilities, and any conflict anywhere in the world can become a nuclear one. To return to safety through technical measures alone, we would have to disarm matter itself, converting it back into its relatively safe, inert, nonexplosive nineteenth-century Newtonian state—something that not even the physics of our time can teach us how to do. (I mention these farfetched, wholly imaginary programs of demolition and suppression in part because the final destruction of all mankind is so much more farfetched, and therefore seems to give us license to at least consider extreme alternatives, but mainly because their obvious inadequacy serves to demonstrate how deeply the nuclear peril is ingrained in our world.)

It is fundamental to the shape and character of the nuclear predicament that its origins lie in scientific knowledge rather than in social circumstances. Revolutions born in the laboratory are to be sharply distinguished from revolutions born in society. Social revolutions are usually born in the minds of millions, and are led up to by what the Declaration of Independence calls "a long train of abuses," visible to all; indeed, they usually cannot occur unless they are widely understood by and supported by the public. By contrast, scientific revolutions usually take shape quietly in the minds of a few men, under cover of the impenetrability to most laymen of scientific theory, and thus catch the world by surprise. In the case of nuclear weapons, of course, the surprise was greatly increased by the governmental secrecy that surrounded the construction of the first bombs. When the world learned of their existence, Mr. Fukai had already run back into the flames of Hiroshima, and tens of thousands of people in that city had already been killed. Even long after scientific discoveries have been made and their applications have transformed our world, most people are likely to remain ignorant of the underlying principles at work, and this has been particularly true of nuclear weapons, which, decades after their invention, are still surrounded by an aura of mystery, as though they had descended from another planet. (To most people, Einstein's famous formula $E=mc^2$, which defines the energy released in nuclear explosions, stands as a kind of symbol of everything that is esoteric and incomprehensible.)

But more important by far than the world's unpreparedness for scientific revolutions are their universality and their permanence once they have occurred. Social revolutions are restricted to a particular time and place; they arise out of particular circumstances, last for a while, and then pass into history. Scientific revolutions, on the other hand, belong to all places and all times. In the words of Alfred North Whitehead, "Modern science was born in Europe, but its home is the whole world." In fact, of all the products of human hands and minds, scientific knowledge has proved to be the most durable. The physical structures of human life—furniture, buildings, paintings, cities, and so on—are subject to inevitable natural decay, and human institutions have likewise proved to be transient. Hegel, whose philosophy of history was framed in large measure in an attempt to redeem the apparent futility of the efforts of men to found something enduring in their midst, once wrote, "When we see the evil, the vice, the ruin that has befallen the most flourishing kingdoms which the mind of man ever created, we can scarce avoid being filled with sorrow at this universal taint of corruption; and, since this decay is not the work of mere Nature, but of Human Will —a moral embitterment—a revolt of the Good Spirit (if it have a place within us) may well be the result of our reflections." Works of thought and many works of art have a better chance of surviving, since new copies of a book or a symphony can be transcribed from old ones, and so can be preserved indefinitely; yet these works, too, can and do go out of existence, for if every copy is lost, then the work is also lost. The subject matter of these works is man, and they seem to be touched with his mortality. The results of scientific work, on the other hand, are largely immune to decay and disappearance. Even when they are lost, they are likely to be rediscovered, as is shown by the fact that several scientists often make the same discovery independently. (There is no record of several poets' having independently written the same poem, or of several composers' having independently written the same symphony.) For both the subject matter and the method of science are available to all capable minds in a way that the subject matter and the method of the arts are not. The human experiences that art deals with are, once over, lost forever, like the people who undergo them, whereas matter, energy, space, and time, alike everywhere and in all ages, are always available for fresh inspection. The subject matter of science is the physical world, and its findings seem to share in the immortality of the physical world. And artistic vision grows out of the unrepeatable individuality of each artist, whereas the reasoning power of the mind—its ability to add two and two and get four—is the same in all competent persons. The rigorous exactitude of scientific methods does not mean that creativity is any less individual, intuitive, or mysterious in great scientists than in great artists, but it does mean that scientific findings, once arrived at, can be tested and confirmed by shared canons of logic and experimentation. The agreement among scientists thus achieved permits science to be a collective enterprise, in which each generation, building on the accepted findings of the generations before, makes amendments and additions, which in their turn become the starting point for the next generation. (Philosophers, by contrast, are constantly tearing down the work of their predecessors, and circling back to re-ask questions that have been asked and answered countless times before. Kant once wrote in despair, "It seems ridiculous that while every science moves forward ceaselessly, this [metaphysics], claiming to be wisdom itself, whose oracular pronouncements everyone consults, is continually revolving in one spot, without advancing one step.") Scientists, as they erect the steadily growing structure of scientific knowledge, resemble nothing so much as a swarm of bees working harmoniously together to construct a single, many-chambered hive, which grows more elaborate and splendid with every year that passes. Looking at what they have made over the centuries, scientists need feel no "sorrow" or "moral embitterment" at any "taint of corruption" that supposedly undoes all human achievements. When God, alarmed that the builders of the Tower of Babel would reach Heaven with their construction, and so become as God, put an end to their undertaking by making them all speak different languages, He apparently overlooked the scientists, for they, speaking what is often called the "universal language" of their disciplines from country to country and generation to generation, went on to build a new tower—the edifice of scientific knowledge. Their phenomenal success, beginning not with Einstein but with Euclid and Archimedes, has provided the unshakable structure that supports the world's nuclear peril. So durable is the scientific edifice that if we did not know that human beings had constructed it we might suppose that the findings on which our whole technological civilization rests were the pillars and crossbeams of an invulnerable, inhuman order obtruding into our changeable and perishable human realm. It is the crowning irony of this lopsided development of human abilities that the only means in sight for getting rid of the knowledge of how to destroy ourselves would be to do just that—in effect, to remove the knowledge by removing the knower.

Although it is unquestionably the scientists who have led us to the edge of the nuclear abyss, we would be mistaken if we either held them chiefly responsible for our plight or looked to them, particularly, for a solution. Here, again, the difference between scientific revolutions and social revolutions shows itself, for the notion that scientists bear primary responsibility springs from a tendency to confuse scientists with political actors. Political actors, who, of course, include ordinary citizens as well as government officials, act with definite social ends in view, such as the preservation of peace, the establishment of a just society, or, if they are corrupt, their own aggrandizement; and they are accordingly held responsible for the consequences of their actions, even when these are unintended ones, as they so often are. Scientists, on the other hand (and here I refer to the so-called pure scientists, who search for the laws of nature for the sake of knowledge itself, and not to the applied scientists, who make use of already discovered natural laws to solve practical problems), do not aim at social ends, and, in fact, usually do not know what the social results of their findings will be; for that matter, they cannot know what the findings themselves will be, because science is a process of discovery, and it is in the nature of discovery that one cannot know beforehand what one will find. This element of the unexpected is present when a researcher sets out to unravel some small, carefully defined mystery—say, the chemistry of a certain enzyme—but it is most conspicuous in the synthesis of the great laws of science and in the development of science as a whole, which, over decades and centuries, moves toward destinations that no one can predict. Thus, only a few decades ago it might have seemed that physics, which had just placed nuclear energy at man's disposal, was the dangerous branch of science, while biology, which underlay improvements in medicine and also helped us to understand our dependence on the natural environment, was the beneficial branch; but now that biologists have begun to fathom the secrets of genetics, and to tamper with the genetic substance of life directly, we cannot be so sure. The most striking illustration of the utter disparity that may occur between the wishes of the scientist as a social being and the social results of his scientific findings is certainly the career of Einstein. By nature, he was, according to all accounts, the gentlest of men, and by conviction he was a pacifist, yet he made intellectual discoveries that led the way to the invention of weapons with which the species could exterminate itself. Inspired wholly by a love of knowledge for its own sake, and by an awe at the creation which bordered on the religious, he made possible an instrument of destruction with which the terrestrial creation could be disfigured.

A disturbing corollary of the scientists' inability even to foresee the path of science, to say nothing of determining it, is that while science is without doubt the most powerful revolutionary force in our world, no one directs that force. For science is a process of submission, in which the mind does not dictate to nature but seeks out and then bows to nature's laws, letting its conclusions be guided by that which *is*, independent of our will. From the political point of view, therefore, scientific findings, some lending themselves to evil, some to good, and some to both, simply pour forth from the laboratory in senseless profusion, offering the world now a neutron bomb, now bacteria that devour oil, now a vaccine to prevent polio, now a cloned frog. It is not until the pure scientists, seekers of knowledge for its own sake, turn their findings over to the applied scientists that social intentions begin to guide the results. The applied scientists do indeed set out to make a better vaccine or a bigger bomb, but even they, perhaps, deserve less credit or blame than we are sometimes inclined to give them. For as soon as our intentions enter the picture we are in the realm of politics in the broadest sense, and in politics it is ultimately not technicians but governments and citizens who are in charge. The scientists in the Manhattan Project could not decide to make the first atomic bomb; only President Roosevelt, elected to office by the American people, could do that.

If scientists are unable to predict their discoveries, neither can they cancel them once they have been made. In this respect, they are like the rest of us, who are asked not whether we would like to live in a world in which we can convert matter into energy but only what we want to do about it once we have been told that we do live in such a world. Science is a tide that can only rise. The individual human mind is capable of forgetting things, and mankind has collectively forgotten many things, but we do not know how, as a species, to *deliberately* set out to forget something. A basic scientific finding, therefore, has the character of destiny for the world. Scientific discovery is in this regard like any other form of discovery; once Columbus had discovered America, and had told the world about it, America could not be hidden again.

Scientific progress (which can and certainly will occur) offers little more hope than scientific regression (which probably cannot occur) of giving us relief from the nuclear peril. It does not seem likely that science will bring forth some new invention—some anti-ballistic missile or laser beam—that will render nuclear weapons harmless (although the unpredictability of science prevents any categorical judgment on this point). In the centuries of the modern scientific revolution, scientific knowledge has steadily increased the destructiveness of warfare, for it is in the very nature of knowledge, apparently, to increase our might rather than to diminish it. One of the most common forms of the hope for deliverance from the nuclear peril by technical advances is the notion that the species will be spared extinction by fleeing in spaceships. The thought seems to be that while the people on earth are destroying themselves communities in space will be able to survive and carry on. This thought does an injustice to our birthplace and habitat, the earth. It assumes that if only we could escape the earth we would find safety—as though it were the earth and its plants and animals that threatened us, rather than the other way around. But the fact is that wherever human beings went there also would go the knowledge of how to build nuclear weapons, and, with it, the peril of extinction. Scientific progress may yet deliver us from many evils, but there are at least two evils that it cannot deliver us from: its own findings and our own destructive and self-destructive bent. This is a combination that we will have to learn to deal with by some other means.

We live, then, in a universe whose fundamental substance contains a supply of energy with which we can extinguish ourselves. We shall never live in any other. We now know that we live in such a universe, and we shall never stop knowing it. Over the millennia, this truth lay in waiting for us, and now we have found it out, irrevocably. If we suppose that it is an integral part of human existence to be curious about the physical world we are born into, then, to speak in the broadest terms, the origin of the nuclear peril lies, on the one hand, in our nature as rational and inquisitive beings and, on the other, in the nature of matter. Because the energy that nuclear weapons release is so great, the whole species is threatened by them, and because the spread of scientific knowledge is unstoppable, the whole species poses the threat: in the last analysis, it is all of mankind that threatens all of mankind. (I do not mean to overlook the fact that at present it is only two nations—the United States and the Soviet Union—that possess nuclear weapons in numbers great enough to possibly destroy the species, and that they thus now bear the chief responsibility for the peril. I only wish to point out that, regarded in its full dimensions, the nuclear peril transcends the rivalry between the present superpowers.)

The fact that the roots of the nuclear peril lie in basic scientific knowledge has broad political implications that cannot be ignored if the world's solution to the predicament is to be built on a solid foundation, and if futile efforts are to be avoided. One such effort would be to rely on secrecy to contain the peril—that is, to "classify" the "secret" of the bomb. The first person to try to suppress knowledge of how nuclear weapons can be made was the physicist Leo Szilard, who in 1939, when he first heard that a nuclear chain reaction was possible, and realized that a nuclear bomb might be possible, called on a number of his colleagues to keep the discovery secret from the Germans. Many of the key scientists refused. His failure foreshadowed a succession of failures, by whole governments, to restrict the knowledge of how the weapons are made. The first, and most notable, such failure was the United States' inability to monopolize nuclear weapons, and prevent the Soviet Union from building them. And we have subsequently witnessed the failure of the entire world to prevent nuclear weapons from spreading. Given the nature of scientific thought and the very poor record of past attempts to suppress it, these failures should not have surprised anyone. (The Catholic Church succeeded in making Galileo recant his view that the earth revolves around the sun, but we do not now believe that the sun revolves around the earth.) Another, closely related futile effort—the one made by our hypothetical council—

would be to try to resolve the nuclear predicament through disarmament alone, without accompanying political measures. Like the hope that the knowledge can be classified, this hope loses sight of the fact that the nuclear predicament consists not in the possession of nuclear weapons at a particular moment by certain nations but in the circumstance that mankind as a whole has now gained possession once and for all of the knowledge of how to make them, and that all nations—and even some groups of people which are not nations, including terrorist groups—can potentially build them. Because the nuclear peril, like the scientific knowledge that gave rise to it, is probably global and everlasting, our solution must at least aim at being global and everlasting. And the only kind of solution that holds out this promise is a global political one. In defining the task so broadly, however, I do not mean to argue against short-term palliatives, such as the Strategic Arms Limitation Talks between the United States and the Soviet Union, or nuclear-nonproliferation agreements, on the ground that they are short-term. If a patient's life is in danger, as mankind's now is, no good cause is served by an argument between the nurse who wants to give him an aspirin to bring down his fever and the doctor who wants to perform the surgery that can save his life; there is need for an argument only if the nurse is claiming that the aspirin is all that is necessary. If, given the world's discouraging record of political achievement, a lasting political solution seems almost beyond human powers, it may give us confidence to remember that what challenges us is simply our extraordinary success in another field of activity—the scientific. We have only to learn to live politically in the world in which we already live scientifically.

Since 1947, the *Bulletin of the Atomic Scientists* has included a "doomsday clock" in each issue. The editors place the hands farther away from or closer to midnight as they judge the world to be farther away from or closer to a nuclear holocaust. A companion clock can be imagined whose hands, instead of metaphorically representing a judgment about the likelihood of a holocaust, would represent an estimate of the amount of time that, given the world's technical and political arrangements, the people of the earth can be sure they have left before they are destroyed in a holocaust. At present, the hands would stand at, or a fraction of a second before, midnight, because none of us can be sure that at any second we will not be killed in a nuclear attack. If, by treaty, all nuclear warheads were removed from their launchers and stored somewhere else, and therefore could no longer descend on us at any moment without warning, the clock would show the amount of time that it would take to put them back on. If all the nuclear weapons in the world were destroyed, the clock would show the time that it would take to manufacture them again. If in addition confidence-inspiring political arrangements to prevent rearmament were put in place, the clock would show some estimate of the time that it might take for the arrangements to break down. And if these arrangements were to last for hundreds or thousands of years (as they must if mankind is to survive this long), then some generation far in the future might feel justified in setting the clock at decades, or even centuries, before midnight. But no generation would ever be justified in retiring the clock from use altogether, because, as far as we can tell, there will never again be a time when self-extinction is beyond the reach of our species. An observation that Plutarch made about politics holds true also for the task of survival, which has now become the principal obligation of politics: "They are wrong who think that politics is like an ocean voyage or a military campaign, something to be done with some end in view, something which levels off as soon as that end is reached. It is not a public chore, to be got over with; it is a way of life."

The scientific principles and techniques that make possible the construction of nuclear weapons are, of course, only one small portion of mankind's huge reservoir of scientific knowledge, and, as I have mentioned, it has always been known that scientific findings can be made use of for evil as well as for good, according to the intentions of the user. What is new to our time is the realization that, acting quite independently of any good or evil intentions of ours, the human enterprise as a whole has begun to strain and

109

erode the natural terrestrial world on which human and other life depends. Taken in its entirety, the increase in mankind's strength has brought about a decisive, many-sided shift in the balance of strength between man and the earth. Nature, once a harsh and feared master, now lies in subjection, and needs protection against man's powers. Yet because man, no matter what intellectual and technical heights he may scale, remains embedded in nature, the balance has shifted against him, too, and the threat that he poses to the earth is a threat to him as well. The peril to nature was difficult to see at first, in part because its symptoms made their appearance as unintended "side effects" of our intended goals, on which we had fixed most of our attention. In economic production, the side effects are the peril of gradual pollution of the natural environment—by, for example, global heating through an increased "greenhouse effect." In the military field, the side effects, or prospective side effects —sometimes referred to by the strategists as the "collateral effects" —include the possible extinction of the species through sudden, severe harm to the ecosphere, caused by global radioactive contamination, ozone depletion, climatic change, and the other known and unknown possible consequences of a nuclear holocaust. Though from the point of view of the human actor there might be a clear difference between the "constructive" economic applications of technology and the "destructive" military ones, nature makes no such distinction: both are beachheads of human mastery in a defenseless natural world. (For example, the ozone doesn't care whether oxides of nitrogen are injected into it by the use of supersonic transports or by nuclear weapons; it simply reacts according to the appropriate chemical laws.) It was not until recently that it became clear that often the side effects of both the destructive and the constructive applications were really the main effects. And now the task ahead of us can be defined as one of giving the "side effects," including, above all, the peril of self-extinction, the weight they deserve in our judgments and decisions. To use a homely metaphor, if a man discovers that improvements he is making to his house threaten to destroy its foundation he is well advised to rethink them.

A nuclear holocaust, because of its unique combination of immensity and suddenness, is a threat without parallel; yet at the same time it is only one of countless threats that the human enterprise, grown mighty through knowledge, poses to the natural world. Our species is caught in the same tightening net of technical success that has already strangled so many other species. (At present, it has been estimated, the earth loses species at the rate of about three per day.) The peril of human extinction, which exists not because every single person in the world would be killed by the immediate explosive and radioactive effects of a holocaust—something that is exceedingly unlikely, even at present levels of armament—but because a holocaust might render the biosphere unfit for human survival, is, in a word, an *ecological* peril. The nuclear peril is usually seen in isolation from the threats to other forms of life and their ecosystems, but in fact it should be seen as the very center of the ecological crisis—as the cloud-covered Everest of which the more immediate, visible kinds of harm to the environment are the mere foothills. Both the effort to preserve the environment and the effort to save the species from extinction by nuclear arms would be enriched and strengthened by this recognition. The nuclear question, which now stands in eerie seclusion from the rest of life, would gain a context, and the ecological movement, which, in its concern for plants and animals, at times assumes an almost misanthropic posture, as though man were an unwanted intruder in an otherwise unblemished natural world, would gain the humanistic intent that should stand at the heart of its concern.

Seen as a planetary event, the rising tide of human mastery over nature has brought about a categorical increase in the power of death on earth. An organism's ability to renew itself during its lifetime and to reproduce itself depends on the integrity of what biologists call "information" stored in its genes. What endures—what lives—in an organism is not any particular group of cells but a configuration of cells which is dictated by the genetic information. What survives in a species, correspondingly, is a larger configuration, which takes in all the individuals in the species. An ecosystem is a still larger configuration, in which a whole constellation of spe-

111

cies forms a balanced, self-reproducing, slowly changing whole. The ecosphere of the earth—Dr. Lewis Thomas's "cell"—is, finally, the largest of the living configurations, and is a carefully regulated and balanced, self-perpetuating system in its own right. At each of these levels, life is coherence, and the loss of coherence—the sudden slide toward disorder—is death. Seen in this light, life is information, and death is the loss of information, returning the substance of the creature to randomness. However, the death of a species or an ecosystem has a role in the natural order that is very different from that of the death of an organism. Whereas an individual organism, once born, begins to proceed inevitably toward death, a species is a source of new life that has no fixed term. An organism is a configuration whose demise is built into its plan, and within the life of a species the death of individual members normally has a fixed, limited, and necessary place, so that as death moves through the ranks of the living its pace is roughly matched by the pace of birth, and populations are kept in a rough balance that enables them to coexist and endure in their particular ecosystem. A species, on the other hand, can survive as long as environmental circumstances happen to permit. An ecosystem, likewise, is indefinitely self-renewing. But when the pace of death is too much increased, either by human intervention in the environment or by some other event, death becomes an extinguishing power, and species and ecosystems are lost. Then not only are individual creatures destroyed but the sources of all future creatures of those kinds are closed down, and a portion of the diversity and strength of terrestrial life in its entirety vanishes forever. And when man gained the ability to intervene directly in the workings of the global "cell" as a whole, and thus to extinguish species wholesale, his power to encroach on life increased by still another order of magnitude, and came to threaten the balance of the entire planetary system of life.

Hence, there are two competing forces at work in the terrestrial environment—one natural, which acts over periods of millions of years to strengthen and multiply the forms of life, and the other man-made and man-operated, which, if it is left unregulated and unguided, tends in general to deplete life's array of forms. Indeed, it is a striking fact that both of these great engines of change on earth depend on stores of information that are passed down from generation to generation. There is, in truth, no closer analogy to scientific progress, in which a steadily growing pool of information makes possible the creation of an ever more impressive array of artifacts, than evolution, in which another steadily growing pool of information makes possible the development of ever more complex and astonishing creatures—culminating in human beings, who now threaten to raze both the human and the natural structures to their inanimate foundations. One is tempted to say that only the organic site of the evolutionary information has changed— from genes to brains. However, because of the extreme rapidity of technological change relative to natural evolution, evolution is unable to refill the vacated niches of the environment with new species, and, as a result, the genetic pool of life as a whole is imperilled. Death, having been augmented by human strength, has lost its appointed place in the natural order and become a counter-evolutionary force, capable of destroying in a few years, or even in a few hours, what evolution has built up over billions of years. In doing so, death threatens even itself, since death, after all, is a part of life: stones may be lifeless but they do not die. The question now before the human species, therefore, is whether life or death will prevail on the earth. This is not metaphorical language but a literal description of the present state of affairs.

One might say that after billions of years nature, by creating a species equipped with reason and will, turned its fate, which had previously been decided by the slow, unconscious movements of natural evolution, over to the conscious decisions of just one of its species. When this occurred, human activity, which until then had been confined to the historical realm—which, in turn, had been supported by the broader biological current—spilled out of its old boundaries and came to menace both history and biology. Thought and will became mightier than the earth that had given birth to them. Now human beings became actors in the geological time span, and the laws that had governed the development and the survival of life began to be superseded by processes in the mind of man. Here, however, there were no laws; there was only choice, and the thinking and feeling that guide choice. The reassuring, stable, self-sustaining prehistoric world of nature dropped away, and in its place mankind's own judgments, moods, and decisions loomed up with an unlooked-for, terrifying importance.

Regarded objectively, as an episode in the development of life on earth, a nuclear holocaust that brought about the extinction of mankind and other species by mutilating the ecosphere would constitute an evolutionary setback of possibly limited extent—the first to result from a deliberate action taken by the creature extinguished but perhaps no greater than any of several evolutionary setbacks, such as the extinction of the dinosaurs, of which the geological record offers evidence. (It is, of course, impossible to judge what course evolution would take after human extinction, but the past record strongly suggests that the reappearance of man is not one of the possibilities. Evolution has brought forth an amazing variety of creatures, but there is no evidence that any species, once extinguished, has ever evolved again. Whether or not nature, obeying some law of evolutionary progress, would bring forth another creature equipped with reason and will, and capable of building, and perhaps then destroying, a world, is one more unanswerable question, but it is barely conceivable that some gifted new animal will pore over the traces of our self-destruction, trying to figure out what went wrong and to learn from our mistakes. If this should be possible, then it might justify the remark once made by Kafka: "There is infinite hope, but not for us." If, on the other hand, as the record of life so far suggests, terrestrial evolution is able to produce only once the miracle of the qualities that we now associate with human beings, then all hope rides with human beings.) However, regarded subjectively, from within human life, where we are all actually situated, and as something that would happen to us, human extinction assumes awesome, inapprehensible proportions. It is of the essence of the human condition

114

that we are born, live for a while, and then die. Through mishaps of all kinds, we may also suffer untimely death, and in extinction by nuclear arms the number of untimely deaths would reach the limit for any one catastrophe: everyone in the world would die. But although the untimely death of everyone in the world would in itself constitute an unimaginably huge loss, it would bring with it a separate, distinct loss that would be in a sense even huger—the cancellation of all future generations of human beings. According to the Bible, when Adam and Eve ate the fruit of the tree of knowledge God punished them by withdrawing from them the privilege of immortality and dooming them and their kind to die. Now our species has eaten more deeply of the fruit of the tree of knowledge, and has brought itself face to face with a second death —the death of mankind. In doing so, we have caused a basic change in the circumstances in which life was given to us, which is to say that we have altered the human condition. The distinctness of this second death from the deaths of all the people on earth can be illustrated by picturing two different global catastrophes. In the first, let us suppose that most of the people on earth were killed in a nuclear holocaust but that a few million survived and the earth happened to remain habitable by human beings. In this catastrophe, billions of people would perish, but the species would survive, and perhaps one day would even repopulate the earth in its former numbers. But now let us suppose that a substance was released into the environment which had the effect of sterilizing all the people in the world but otherwise leaving them unharmed. Then, as the existing population died off, the world would empty of people, until no one was left. Not one life would have been shortened by a single day, but the species would die. In extinction by nuclear arms, the death of the species and the death of all the people in the world would happen together, but it is important to make a clear distinction between the two losses; otherwise, the mind, overwhelmed by the thought of the deaths of the billions of living people, might stagger back without realizing that behind this already ungraspable loss there lies the separate loss of the future generations.

The possibility that the living can stop the future generations from entering into life compels us to ask basic new questions about our existence, the most sweeping of which is what these unborn ones, most of whom we will never meet even if they are born, mean to us. No one has ever thought to ask this question before our time, because no generation before ours has ever held the life and death of the species in its hands. But if we hardly know how to comprehend the possible deaths in a holocaust of the billions of people who are already in life how are we to comprehend the life or death of the infinite number of possible people who do not yet exist at all? How are we, who are a part of human life, to step back from life and see it whole, in order to assess the meaning of its disappearance? To kill a human being is murder, and there are those who believe that to abort a fetus is also murder, but what crime is it to cancel the numberless multitude of unconceived people? In what court is such a crime to be judged? Against whom is it committed? And what law does it violate? If we find the nuclear peril to be somehow abstract, and tend to consign this whole elemental issue to "defense experts" and other dubiously qualified people, part of the reason, certainly, is that the future generations really are abstract—that is to say, without the tangible existence and the unique particularities that help to make the living real to us. And if we find the subject strangely "impersonal" it may be in part because the unborn, who are the ones directly imperilled by extinction, are not yet persons. What are they, then? They lack the individuality that we often associate with the sacredness of life, and may at first thought seem to have only a shadowy, mass existence. *Where* are they? Are they to be pictured lined up in a sort of fore-life, waiting to get into life? Or should we regard them as nothing more than a pinch of chemicals in our reproductive organs, toward which we need feel no special obligations? What standing should they have among us? How much should their needs count in competition with ours? How far should the living go in trying to secure their advantage, their happiness, their existence?

The individual person, faced with the metaphysical-seeming

perplexities involved in pondering the possible cancellation of people who do not yet exist—an apparently extreme effort of the imagination, which seems to require one first to summon before the mind's eye the countless possible people of the future generations and then to consign these incorporeal multitudes to a more profound nothingness—might well wonder why, when he already has his own death to worry about, he should occupy himself with this other death. Since our own individual death promises to inflict a loss that is total and final, we may find the idea of a second death merely redundant. After all, can everything be taken away from us twice? Moreover, a person might reason that even if mankind did perish he wouldn't have to know anything about it, since in that event he himself would perish. There might actually be something consoling in the idea of having so much company in death. In the midst of universal death, it somehow seems out of order to want to go on living oneself. As Randall Jarrell wrote in his poem "Losses," thinking back to his experience in the Second World War, "it was not dying: everybody died."

However, the individual would misconceive the nuclear peril if he tried to understand it primarily in terms of personal danger, or even in terms of danger to the people immediately known to him, for the nuclear peril threatens life, above all, not at the level of individuals, who already live under the sway of death, but at the level of everything that individuals hold in common. Death cuts off life; extinction cuts off birth. Death dispatches into the nothingness after life each person who has been born; extinction in one stroke locks up in the nothingness before life all the people who have not yet been born. For we are finite beings at both ends of our existence—natal as well as mortal—and it is the natality of our kind that extinction threatens. We have always been able to send people to their death, but only now has it become possible to prevent all birth and so doom all future human beings to uncreation. The threat of the loss of birth—a beginning that is over and done with for every living person—cannot be a source of immediate, selfish concern; rather, this threat assails everything that people hold in common, for it is the ability of our species to produce

117

new generations which assures the continuation of the world in which all our common enterprises occur and have their meaning. Each death belongs inalienably to the individual who must suffer it, but birth is our common possession. And the meaning of extinction is therefore to be sought first not in what each person's own life means to him but in what the world and the people in it mean to him.

In its nature, the human world is, in Hannah Arendt's words, a "common world," which she distinguishes from the "private realm" that belongs to each person individually. (Somewhat surprisingly, Arendt, who devoted so much of her attention to the unprecedented evils that have appeared in our century, never addressed the issue of nuclear arms; yet I have discovered her thinking to be an indispensable foundation for reflection on this question.) The private realm, she writes in "The Human Condition," a book published in 1958, is made up of "the passions of the heart, the thoughts of the mind, the delights of the senses," and terminates with each person's death, which is the most solitary of all human experiences. The common world, on the other hand, is made up of all institutions, all cities, nations, and other communities, and all works of fabrication, art, thought, and science, and it survives the death of every individual. It is basic to the common world that it encompasses not only the present but all past and future generations. "The common world is what we enter when we are born and what we leave behind when we die," Arendt writes. "It transcends our life-span into past and future alike; it was there before we came and will outlast our brief sojourn in it. It is what we have in common not only with those who live with us, but also with those who were here before and with those who will come after us." And she adds, "Without this transcendence into a potential earthly immortality, no politics, strictly speaking, no common world, and no public realm is possible." The creation of a common world is the use that we human beings, and we alone among the earth's creatures, have made of the biological circumstance that while each of us is mortal, our species is biologically immortal. If mankind had not established a common world, the species would still outlast its individual members and be immortal, but this immortality would be unknown to us and would go for nothing, as it does in the animal kingdom, and the generations, unaware of one another's existence, would come and go like waves on the beach, leaving everything just as it was before. In fact, it is only because humanity has built up a common world that we can fear our destruction as a species. It may even be that man, who has been described as the sole creature that knows that it must die, can know this only because he lives in a common world, which permits him to imagine a future beyond his own life. This common world, which is unharmed by individual death but depends on the survival of the species, has now been placed in jeopardy by nuclear arms. Death and extinction are thus complementary, dividing between them the work of undoing, or threatening to undo, everything that human beings are or can ever become, with death terminating the life of each individual and extinction imperilling the common world shared by all. In one sense, extinction is less terrible than death, since extinction can be avoided, while death is inevitable; but in another sense extinction is more terrible—is the more radical nothingness—because extinction ends death just as surely as it ends birth and life. Death is only death; extinction is the death of death.

The world is made a common one by what Arendt calls "publicity," which insures that "everything that appears in public can be seen and heard by everybody." She writes, "A common world can survive the coming and going of the generations only to the extent that it appears in public. It is the publicity of the public realm which can absorb and make shine through the centuries whatever men may want to save from the natural ruin of time." But this publicity does not only shine on human works; it also brings to light the natural foundations of life, enabling us to perceive what our origins are. It thereby permits us not only to endow things of our own making with a degree of immortality but to see and appreciate the preëxisting, biological immortality of our species and of life on the planet, which forms the basis for any earthly immortality whatever. The chief medium of the publicity of the common world is, of course, language, whose possession by man is believed by many to be what separates him from the other animals; but there are also the other "languages" of the arts and sciences. And standing behind language is that of which language is expressive—our reason, our psyche, our will, and our spirit. Through these, we are capable of entering into the lives of others, and of becoming aware that we belong to a community of others that is as wide as our species. The foundation of a common world is an exclusively human achievement, and to live in a common world— to speak and listen to one another, to read, to write, to know about the past and look ahead to the future, to receive the achievements of past generations, and to pass them on, together with achievements of our own, to future generations, and otherwise to participate in human enterprises that outlast any individual life—is part of what it means to be human, and by threatening all this nuclear weapons threaten a part of our humanity. The common world is not something that can be separated from the life we now live; it is intrinsic to our existence—something as close to us as the words we speak and the thoughts we think using those words. Descartes's famous axiom "I think, therefore I am" has perhaps been more extensively rebutted than any other single philosophical proposition. The rebuttal by Lewis Mumford happens to amount to a description of each person's indebtedness to the common world and to the common biological inheritance that the common world has brought to light. "Descartes forgot that before he uttered these words 'I think' . . . he needed the coöperation of countless fellow-beings, extending back to his own knowledge as far as the thousands of years that Biblical history recorded," Mumford writes in "The Pentagon of Power," a book published in 1970. "Beyond that, we know now he needed the aid of an even remoter past that mankind too long remained ignorant of: the millions of years required to transform his dumb animal ancestors into conscious human beings." In our long and arduous ascent out of biological darkness, it seems, we forgot our indebtedness to the natural world of our origins, and now, in consequence, threaten to plunge ourselves into an even deeper darkness. The nuclear predicament is thus in every sense a crisis of life in the common world. Only because there is a common world, in which knowledge of the physical world accumulates over the generations, can there be a threat to the common world and to its natural foundations. Only because there is a common world, which permits us knowledge of other generations and of the terrestrial nature of which human life is a part, can we worry about, or even know of, that threat. And only because there is a common world can we hope, by concerting our actions, to save ourselves and the earth.

The common world has been the work of every generation that has lived in it, back to the remotest ages. Much as poets begin by using language as they find it but, usually as an unself-conscious consequence of their work, leave usage slightly altered behind them, people in general pursue their various ends in the yielding medium of the world and shape its character by their actions. But although the world receives the imprint of the lives of those who pass through it, it has never been given to any single generation to dictate the character of the world. Not even the most thoroughgoing totalitarian regimes have succeeded in wholly shaping the lives of their peoples. One has only to think of Alexander Solzhenitsyn growing up in the Soviet Union but drawing so much of his spiritual sustenance from earlier centuries of Russian life, or to think of China, where so many of the customs and qualities of the people have outlasted what was probably the longest and most concentrated assault in history by a government on the national tradition of its own country, to realize how deeply a people's past is woven into its present.

The links binding the living, the dead, and the unborn were described by Edmund Burke, the great eighteenth-century English conservative, as a "partnership" of the generations. He wrote, "Society is indeed a contract. . . . It is a partnership in all science; a partnership in all art; a partnership in every virtue, and in all perfection. As the ends of such a partnership cannot be obtained except in many generations, it becomes a partnership not only between those who are living, but between those who are living, those who are dead, and those who are to be born." Pericles offered a similar, though not identical, vision of the common life of the generations in his funeral oration, in which he said that all Athens was a "sepul-chre" for the remembrance of the soldiers who had died fighting for their city. Thus, whereas Burke spoke of common tasks that needed many generations for their achievement, Pericles spoke of the immortality that the living confer on the dead by remembering their sacrifices. In the United States, Abraham Lincoln seemed to combine these two thoughts when he said in his Gettysburg address that the sacrifices of the soldiers who had died at Gettysburg laid an obligation on the living to devote themselves to the cause for which the battle had been fought. And, indeed, every political observer or political actor of vision has recognized that if life is to be fully human it must take cognizance of the dead and the unborn.

But now our responsibilities as citizens in the common world have been immeasurably enlarged. In the pre-nuclear common world, we were partners in the protection of the arts, the institutions, the customs, and all "perfection" of life; now we are also partners in the protection of life itself. Burke described as a common inheritance the achievements that one generation passed along to the next. "By a constitutional policy, working after the pattern of nature, we receive, we hold, we transmit our government and our privileges, in the same manner in which we enjoy and transmit our property and our lives," he wrote. "The institutions of policy, the goods of fortune, the gifts of Providence, are handed down, to us and from us, in the same course and order." These words appear in Burke's "Reflections on the Revolution in France"—the revolution being an event that filled him with horror, for in it he believed he saw a single generation violently destroying in a few years the national legacy of hundreds of years. But, whether or not he was right in thinking that the inheritance of France was being squandered by its recipients, the inheriting generations and their successors were at least biologically intact. In our time, however, among the items in the endangered inheritance the inheritors find themselves. Each generation of mankind still receives, holds, and transmits the inheritance from the past, but, being now a part of that inheritance, each generation *is received, is held, and is transmitted*, so that receiver and received, holder and held, transmitter and transmitted are one. Yet our jeopardy is only a part of the jeopardy of all life, and the largest item in the inheritance that we receive, hold, and must transmit is the entire ecosphere. So deep is the change in the structure of human life brought about by this new peril that in retrospect the Burkean concern about the "perfection" of life, indispensable as this concern is to the quality of our existence, seems like only the barest hint or suggestion of the incomparably more commanding obligation that is laid on us by the nuclear predicament. It strikes modern ears as prophetic that when Burke sought to describe the permanence in human affairs which he so valued he often resorted to metaphors drawn from the natural world—speaking, for example, of a "pattern of nature" that human society should imitate—as though he had had a premonition that an almost habitually revolutionary mankind would one day proceed from tearing society apart to tearing the natural world apart. Speaking of the society into which each of us is born, Burke angrily asked whether it could be right to "hack that aged parent in pieces." His words have acquired a deeper meaning than he could ever have foretold for them now that the parent in question is not merely human society but the earth itself.

Since all human aims, personal or political, presuppose human existence, it might seem that the task of protecting that existence should command all the energy at our disposal. However, the claims that the conduct of life lays upon us, including our desire for individual survival, have not suspended themselves in deference to the peril to life as a whole. As long as we keep from extinguishing ourselves, history continues at full flood, and the needs, desires, fears, interests, and ideals that have always moved people assert themselves with their usual vigor, even though extinction threatens them all with termination forever. For example, although people may want the species to survive, they may also want to be free, to be prosperous, to be treated justly, and so on. We are thus required to weigh the value of these goals of human life against the value of human life in its entirety. But while we are used to weighing the various goals of human life against one another, this new task finds us unprepared. For with what measuring rods should we gauge our worth as a species, and how should we rate ourselves against things whose own worth derives from our existence? These questions are by no means academic. Every government and every citizen in the world—but especially the governments and the citizens of the United States and the Soviet Union—face the decision of how much weight to give to the survival of the world compared with the exigencies of business in the world. Ordinarily, when we look out upon each other and upon the world we measure the worth of what we find by making use of standards. For measuring the products of our labor, we may employ a standard of usefulness; for political activity, a standard of justice; for artistic and intellectual work, standards of beauty and truth; for human behavior in general, a standard of goodness. And when the things we value in life are in conflict we weigh them against one another by the perhaps indefinable but nevertheless comprehensible and useful standard of the common good. But none of these standards, including that of the common good, are suitable for gauging the worth of mankind as a whole, for none of them have any meaning or application unless one first assumes the existence of the very thing whose loss they are supposed to measure; namely, mankind. Anyone who prizes the usefulness of things assumes the existence of human beings to whom things can be useful; anyone who loves justice assumes the existence of a society whose parts can be brought into relationships that are just; anyone who loves beauty and truth assumes the existence of minds to which the beautiful and the true can manifest themselves; anyone who loves goodness assumes the existence of creatures who are capable of exhibiting it and being nourished by it; and anyone who wishes to promote the common good assumes the existence of a community whose divergent aims it can harmonize. These standards of worth, and any others that one might think of, are useful only in relating things that are in life to one another, and are inadequate as measures of life itself. We cannot, for example, say in any simple or unqualified sense that the end of the world is bad and its continuation good, because mankind is not in itself good or evil but is the source of both, providing the theatre in which good and evil actions appear as well as the actors by whom they are all enacted. (No stone, tree, or lion ever did anything either good or evil.) Neither can we say that mankind is useful. For to whom are we of any use? Human life is not needed by someone somewhere; rather, it is the seat of need, and need is one of the modes of our being.

The question of the worth of each individual human life, like the question of the worth of mankind, also poses the question of what life might be "for"—if, indeed, it is right to say that life is "for" anything—but with the crucial difference that while the individual can sacrifice his own life "for" others, mankind cannot do the same, since it includes all possible others within itself. Some philosophers, faced with the perplexing fact that although we can try to judge the worth of everything in creation by asking how well it serves as a means to some end of mankind's, mankind itself does not seem to be a means to anything, and therefore, by this estimation, is, strictly speaking, worthless, have attempted to solve the problem (as Kant, for example, did) by saying that man is "an end in himself" or a "final end," by which they meant that service to human beings was the highest good, and that human life was not to be treated as a means for achieving some other, supposedly higher good. However, this description is open to the criticism that by placing mankind at the final stage of a series of means and ends it seems to suggest that man creates himself—since the process of reaching ends through means is a purely human one—whereas in fact he was created by powers over which he had no influence whatever. It would be more appropriate, perhaps, to say that man is a beginning, for all chains of means and ends, no matter what their ultimate goals may be, start up out of man, whose existence they presuppose, and only then circle back into him, and so are wholly enclosed within human life. In that sense, man does not serve as a "final end" so much as stand prior to all means and ends, shaping and defining them according to his nature and his will. But this "beginning," whose existence is a fait accompli as far as we are concerned, is hard for us to see, because as soon as we start

125

thinking something, intending something, enjoying something, or doing something, we have already taken it—"it" being our very selves and our fellow human beings—for granted. The forms that the life of the species can assume appear in innumerable clearly defined, often visible shapes, but mankind itself—the bare structure of human life, which underlies all these permutations—never appears as such, and remains, in a way, invisible.

One reason that standards fail us in our attempt to grasp the worth of our species is that they are meant to provide a common frame of reference against which the individuals in a given class of things can be measured, whereas mankind is a member of no class that we have as yet discovered. It is theoretically possible, of course, that other creatures endowed with the mental, psychological, and spiritual faculties that now distinguish human beings from all other forms of life will be discovered in outer space, and that we will then be able to rate ourselves in relation to them according to some suitable standard that will suggest itself once the creatures are in view. Even now, we are free to imagine that some extraterrestrial creature or god might take the measure of our loss by regarding it as a gap of a certain character and size in the order of a universal living creation of whose existence we are as yet unaware. But these lofty proceedings, in which we exchange our human perspective for a purely speculative superhuman one, are an evasion, for they lift us clean out of the human predicament that it is our obligation to face. By setting up an intelligence that itself escapes extinction and looks down upon the event, and by endowing that intelligence with suspiciously human characteristics, we in effect deny or evade the reality of extinction, for we have covertly manufactured a survivor. (Could it be that the vogue for science fiction and other types of pure fantasy stems in part from the reassurance we get from believing that there are other forms of life in the universe besides ours? The extra worlds offered by science fiction may provide us with an escape in imagination from the tight trap that our species is caught in in reality.) Seen in religious terms, such an assumption of a godlike perspective would be an attempted usurpation by man of God's omniscience, and, as such, a form of blasphemy. A second reason that standards fail us, then, is that employment of the only ones we actually have in our possession or have any real title to apply—the human ones—is terminated by our extinction, and we are left with the impossibility of a judgment without a judge to pass it.

A closely related, and more serious, perversion of religion is the suggestion, made by some Christian fundamentalists, that the nuclear holocaust we threaten to unleash is the Armageddon threatened by God in the Bible. This identification arrogates to ourselves not only God's knowledge but also His will. However, it is not God, picking and choosing among the things of His creation, who threatens us but we ourselves. And extinction by nuclear arms would not be the Day of Judgment, in which God destroys the world but raises the dead and then metes out perfect justice to everyone who has ever lived; it would be the utterly meaningless and completely unjust destruction of mankind by men. To imagine that God is guiding our hand in this action would quite literally be the ultimate evasion of our responsibility as human beings—a responsibility that is ours because (to stay with religious interpretation for a moment) we possess a free will that was implanted in us by God.

Human beings have a worth—a worth that is sacred. But it is *for* human beings that they have that sacred worth, and for them that the other things in the creation have their worth (although it is a reminder of our indissoluble connection with the rest of life that many of our needs and desires are also felt by animals). Hence, while our standards of worth have reference to the various possible worthy things in life, they all also point back to the life of the needy, or suffering, or rejoicing, or despairing, or admiring, or spiritually thirsting person in whose existence the things are found to be worthy or lacking in worth. To borrow elementary philosophical language, as objects the members of the species are among many things in existence that have worth in human eyes, but as the sum of all possible human subjects the species comprises all those "eyes," and in that sense is the sole originator of all worth as it is given to us to be aware of it. The death of an individual person is a loss of one subject, and of all its needs, longings, sufferings, and enthusiasms—of its being. But the extinction of the species goes farther, and removes from the known universe the human *kind* of being, which is different from any other kind that we as yet know of. It is, above all, the death of mankind as this immortal source of all human subjects, not the death of mankind as an object, that makes extinction radically unique and "unthinkable." In extinction, a darkness falls over the world not because the lights have gone out but because the eyes that behold the light have been closed. To assert this, however, is not to assert that only that which the human eye beholds is real. There is nothing in a holocaust that calls into doubt the existence of the physical world, which we can be confident will go on existing whether we destroy ourselves or not. We are even free to suppose that in a certain sense the worth of things will still reside in them in our absence, waiting for creatures who can appreciate it to reappear. But, without entering into the debate over whether beauty is in the eye of the beholder or in "the thing itself," we can at least say that without the beholder the beauty goes to waste. The universe would still exist, but the universe as it is imprinted on the human soul would be gone. Of many of the qualities of worth in things, we can say that they give us a private audience, and that insofar as they act upon the physical world they do so only by virtue of the response that they stir in us. For example, any works of art that survived our extinction would stare off into a void without finding a responding eye, and thus become shut up in a kind of isolation. (The physical qualities of things, on the other hand, will go on interacting among themselves without us.) Or, to put it differently, the qualities of worth find in us their sole home in an otherwise neutral and inhospitable universe. I believe that Rilke was saying something of this kind when, in the "Duino Elegies," he wrote the lines:

> Earth, isn't this what you want: an invisible
> re-arising in us? Is it not your dream
> to be one day invisible? Earth! invisible!
> What is your urgent command, if not transformation?

> Earth, you darling, I will! Oh, believe me, you need
> your Springs no longer to win me: a single one,
> just one, is already more than my blood can endure.

Because we are the ones who hold everything that is of worth to be so, the attempt to assign a worth to our species leads us in an intellectual circle. We find ourselves trying to gauge the usefulness of usefulness, the goodness of goodness, the worth of worth, and these are questions that have no resolution. Mankind is to be thought of not as something that possesses a certain worth (although in the eyes of one another we have that, too)—as something with a certain measurable degree of usefulness, beauty, or goodness (for just as often as we are useful, beautiful, or good we are destructive, ugly, or evil)—but as the inexhaustible source of all the possible forms of worth, which has no existence or meaning without human life. Mankind is not, in the ancient phrase, the measure of all things; he is the measurer, and is himself measureless.

For the generations that now have to decide whether or not to risk the future of the species, the implication of our species' unique place in the order of things is that while things in the life of mankind have worth, we must never raise that worth above the life of mankind and above our respect for that life's existence. To do this would be to make of our highest ideals so many swords with which to destroy ourselves. To sum up the worth of our species by reference to some particular standard, goal, or ideology, no matter how elevated or noble it might be, would be to prepare the way for extinction by closing down in thought and feeling the open-ended possibilities for human development which extinction would close down in fact. There is only one circumstance in which it might be possible to sum up the life and achievement of the species, and that circumstance would be that it had already died; but then, of course, there would be no one left to do the summing up. Only a generation that believed itself to be in possession of final, absolute truth could ever conclude that it had reason to put an end to human life, and only generations that recognized the limits to their own wisdom and virtue would be likely to subordinate their interests and dreams to the as yet unformed interests and undreamed dreams of the future generations, and let human life go on.

From the foregoing, it follows that there can be no justification for extinguishing mankind, and therefore no justification for any nation ever to push the world into nuclear hostilities, which, once inaugurated, may lead uncontrollably to a full-scale holocaust and to extinction. But from this conclusion it does not follow that any action is permitted as long as it serves the end of preventing extinction. The grounds for these two propositions become clearer if we consider the nature of ethical obligation. It seems especially important to consider the ethical side of the question, because the other common justification for military action—self-interest—obviously can never justify extinction, inasmuch as extinction would constitute suicide for the perpetrator; and suicide, whatever else it may be, is scarcely in the interest of the one who commits it.

I shall let the behavior of Socrates at his trial in Athens, in the fourth century B.C., on charges of corrupting youth and denigrating the gods, stand as a model of ethical behavior. His example has a special, direct relevance to the nuclear question, because every attempt to justify the use of nuclear weapons has been based on some variation of the conviction, first given full expression by him, in words that still sound with their full force, that the highest good is not life itself—mere survival—but the moral life. The possible application of the Socratic principle to the question of extinction is obvious: if under certain circumstances it is the duty of the individual to sacrifice his life for something higher than his life, might it not be the obligation of mankind under certain circumstances to do the same? The philosopher Karl Jaspers, for one, thought so, and was one of the few who have had the courage to state such a belief outright. In his book "The Future of Mankind," published in 1958, he writes, concerning the nuclear question, "Man is born to be free, and the free life that he tries to save by all possible means is more than mere life. Hence, life in the sense of existence—individual life as well as all life—can be staked and sacrificed for the sake of the life that is worth living." He asks, "And if no such way [to the life worth living] is found, does the substance of humanity then lie where failure is no longer an objection—where indeed man's ultimately real, truly serious purpose is his doom?" To which he answers, "It could be necessary only as a sacrifice made for the sake of eternity." I have suggested, though, that doom can never be a human purpose at all, truly serious or otherwise, but, rather, is the end of all human purposes, none of which can be fulfilled outside of human life.

Jaspers's opposite conclusion, I believe, depends on an application to the species as a whole of a canon of morality that properly applies only to each individual person. Ethical commandments have often been regarded as "absolute" for the individual (and thus as justifying any sacrifice made in their name), and, in a certain sense, Socrates regarded them in that light, too. He even claimed that a "voice," or "God," sometimes commanded him not to do certain things. The commands were absolute in two ways. First, once the voice, which we may take to be the voice of conscience, had spoken, he could not be released from it by appeal to any outside authority, such as the majority voice of the community. Second, the commands were absolutely binding on him, and had to be followed even unto death. Therefore, when the city of Athens put him on trial he was not at liberty to abandon the dictates of his conscience and to save his life. Instead, he chided the jury for "trying to put an innocent man to death," and added, for good measure, that since to commit such an injustice would be in his opinion a worse fate than to suffer it, then "so far from pleading on my own behalf, as might be supposed, I am really pleading on yours." In these bold words and actions, which cost him his life, Socrates asserted the absolute sovereignty of his conscience over his actions. But, having asserted that sovereignty, he did not go on to suppose that he had thereby won the right to exercise a similar sovereignty over others. On the contrary, it was of the essence of his conduct at the trial and at the execution that he placed himself wholly at the service of his community, and that his belief in the worth of his actions in fact consisted in this. His radical assertion of the independence of his conscience was thus inseparable from a no less radical subordination of his interests to the good of his city. This subordination was evident in his decision to stand trial, in his decision after the trial to stay in Athens and suffer the death penalty rather than flee (as friends advised him to do), and in the words that he spoke throughout the proceedings. He persisted in dedicating himself to the service of his community even though the community might kill him for his pains. In this devotion, he resembled Christ, of course, who appeared on earth to be "a servant of all," and gave up His life for the sake of the people who put Him to death.

In the present context, the point is that if Socrates is taken as the example, there are no ethics apart from service to the human community, and therefore no ethical commandments that can justify the extinction of humanity. Ethical obligation begins with the assumption that we are naturally inclined to look out for our own interests, and asks that we pay regard to the interests of others—that we do unto them as we would have them do unto us. But since extinction annihilates the community of others it can never be an ethical act, and to say that it could be is like saying that to kill the children in a school would be an educational experience for them, or to starve a country to death would be a beneficial economic measure for it. And even if all the people in the world somehow managed to persuade themselves that their death was justified (thus overlooking the question of for what or for whom it was justified), this suicidal action would still be wrong, because it would also cancel the unconsulted and completely innocent future generations. (Can anybody be more innocent than they are?) In actuality, of course, no one is proposing the voluntary suicide of everyone on earth; on the contrary, what is being claimed is that one or two countries have the right to jeopardize all countries and their descendants in the name of certain beliefs. Hence, those who, to defend risking extinction, start with the moral obligation of "individual life" to sacrifice itself and generalize from that to an obligation of "all life" to sacrifice itself (in Jaspers's phrases) in fact pass from a principle of individual self-sacrifice to a principle of aggression by a few against all—"all" in this case including the unborn generations.

The question remains whether there might be some superethical, ultramundane principle, perhaps of religious inspiration, that could justify the destruction of the world. Is it possible, for example, that one day it might be our obligation to set both human interests and human morality aside and destroy the species for the sake of God? There is a long history of wars waged in the name of one god or another, but in the possible justifications for a nuclear holocaust theological principles could play a role of special importance, because they might seem to offer something to "fight" for that would not itself be destroyed in a holocaust. For example, the extinction of an "evil" mankind might be regarded as acceptable or pleasing to a wrathful God—or, at least, as representing the fulfillment of some plan of His (as in the identification by some Christian fundamentalists of a holocaust with Armageddon). When armies take up the banner of God, the "absolute" sovereignty of each person's individual conscience over his own actions is transmuted into a claim of absolute sovereignty over other people; and the absolute submission owed by each person to the voice of conscience is transmuted into a claim of submission owed by other people to those who, as representatives of religious orthodoxy, have taken it on themselves to speak for God. Then the Christian commandment to sacrifice oneself for one's neighbor at God's command is transformed into permission to sacrifice one's neighbor for God's sake. In the pre-nuclear world, the assumption of these claims led to considerable slaughter; in the nuclear world, it could lead to the end of the species. But all this is infinitely remote from the teaching of Christ, at least, who taught people not to kill their enemies but to love them, and who died rather than lift His hand in violence against His tormentors. It speaks powerfully against any Christian justification for destroying the world that when the Christian God appeared on earth in human form not only did He not sacrifice a single human being for His sake but He suffered a lonely, anguishing, degrading human death so that the world might be saved.

In no saying of His did Christ ever suggest that the two great commandments—to love God and to love one's neighbor—could in any way be separated, or that the former could be used as a justification for violating the latter. In fact, He explicitly stated that religious faith that is divorced from love of human beings is empty and dangerous. For example, He said, "If thou bring thy gift to the altar, and there rememberest that thy brother hath aught against thee; Leave there thy gift before the altar, and go thy way; first be reconciled to thy brother, and then come and offer thy gift." We who have planned out the deaths of hundreds of millions of our brothers plainly have a great deal of work to do before we return to the altar. Clearly, the corpse of mankind would be the least acceptable of all conceivable offerings on the altar of this God.

If there is nothing in the teachings of either Socrates or Christ that could justify the extinction of mankind—nothing, in fact, that could teach us to do anything in regard to this act but hold back from performing it—neither is there anything that would justify the commission of crimes in order to prevent extinction. In the teachings of both men, a person's obligation is to answer even the utmost evil not with more evil but with good. This refusal to be goaded by evil into evil may be the closest thing to an "absolute" that there is in their teachings. (I wonder whether it might not have been this absolute refusal to participate in evil which was in the back of Jaspers's mind when he said that in order to avoid certain evils it was permissible to perpetrate extinction.) Rather, the altogether un-Socratic and un-Christian teaching that the end justifies the means is the basis on which governments, in all times, have licensed themselves to commit crimes of every sort; the *raison d'état* of governments, in fact, enshrines the opposite of the Socratic principle, for it holds that states may do virtually anything whatever in the name of survival. Extinction nullifies the ends-means justification by destroying every end that might justify the means (the *raison d'état* is not well served if the nation is biologically exterminated), but the goal of *preventing* extinction, if it ever became operative as

134

an end, could lend to this expedient line of thinking an immensely enlarged scope, since if the end justifies the means, and the end is human survival, then any means short of human extinction can be countenanced. Herein lies another peril of the nuclear predicament—albeit a lesser one by far than extinction itself, since any political system, no matter how entrenched, is subject to change and decline, whereas extinction is eternal. In most countries, "national security" is found to be justification enough for abusing every human right, and we can only imagine what governments might feel entitled to do once they had begun to claim that they were defending not just national but human survival.

It has not been the mistake of governments of our time to lay too much emphasis on the imperative of human survival, yet in the period of détente between the United States and the Soviet Union the world was given a glimpse of policies in which the aim of avoiding extinction was offered as a justification for repression. Both superpowers, while hardly abandoning the defense of their national interests, made a disturbingly smooth transition between using national interests to rationalize repression and using human survival to rationalize it. In the Soviet Union, a totalitarian country, it was not long before the authorities were supplementing their usual list of charges against critics of the regime by calling them "wreckers of détente," and the like. And in the United States, a democracy, but one that was presided over at the time by an Administration with a criminal and authoritarian bent, President Nixon was quick to invite the public to accept his usurpations and violations of the Constitution as a small price for the country to pay for the grandiose "structure of peace" that he believed he was building together with the Soviets. This incipient alliance of the champions of peace in repression went a step further when the Soviet leaders emerged as vocal defenders of Nixon's constitutional abuses in the Watergate crisis. It is noteworthy also that the Nixon Administration was conspicuously silent about abuses of human rights in the Soviet Union. Regrettably, it may be that the cause of peace can be used no less readily than war as a justification for repression. There is even a superficial resemblance between peace and repression—both tend to be quiet—which should put us on our guard. In the period of détente, the first, tentative steps were taken toward nuclear-arms control (only to stall subsequently), but the totalitarian murk around the world thickened noticeably.

Having said that each generation has an obligation to survive, so that the future generations may be born, I would like to guard against a possible misinterpretation. It has become fashionable recently to suggest that in circumstances of extreme evil—including, especially, imprisonment in concentration camps—personal survival becomes a moral principle, and one that, indeed, takes precedence over the obligation to treat others decently. If this notion were accepted, then the Socratic message that mere survival is empty, and only an honorable life is worth living, would be overruled, and each person would be invited to treat other people however he liked as long as he survived. It might be thought that the obligation of the species to survive adds weight to this point of view. However, each generation's obligation to survive does not in fact lead to a similar obligation on the part of the individual, any more than the individual's obligation to sacrifice himself implies an obligation of self-sacrifice on the part of the species. On the contrary, the species' obligation to survive lays on each individual a new obligation to set aside his personal interest in favor of the general interest. (After all, his personal survival, which cannot last beyond the natural span of his life in any case, in no way aids the survival of the species, since the world's peril does not stem from any shortage of people.) For whereas there is no principle, whether practical, ethical, or divine, that overarches mankind and would offer a justification for its self-destruction, mankind still overarches each person, as it always has done, and summons him, at times, to act in favor of something larger than he is.

Implicit in everything that I have said so far about the nuclear predicament there has been a perplexity that I would now like to take up explicitly, for it leads, I believe, into the very heart of our response—or, rather, our lack of response—to the predicament. I have pointed out that our species is the most important of all the things that, as inhabitants of a common world, we inherit from the past generations, but it does not go far enough to point out this superior importance, as though in making our decision about extinction we were being asked to choose between, say, liberty, on the one hand, and the survival of the species, on the other. For the species not only overarches but contains all the benefits of life in the common world, and to speak of sacrificing the species for the sake of one of these benefits involves one in the absurdity of wanting to destroy something in order to preserve one of its parts, as if one were to burn down a house in an attempt to redecorate the living room, or to kill someone to improve his character. But even to point out this absurdity fails to take the full measure of the peril of extinction, for mankind is not some invaluable object that lies outside us and that we must protect so that we can go on benefitting from it; rather, it is we ourselves, without whom everything there is loses its value. To say this is another way of saying that extinction is unique not because it destroys mankind as an object but because it destroys mankind as the source of all possible human subjects, and this, in turn, is another way of saying that extinction is a second death, for one's own individual death is the end not of any object in life but of the subject that experiences all objects. Death, however, places the mind in a quandary. One of the confounding characteristics of death—"tomorrow's zero," in Dostoevski's phrase—is that, precisely because it removes the person himself rather than something in his life, it seems to offer the mind nothing to take hold of. One even feels it inappropriate, in a way, to try to speak "about" death at all, as though death were a thing situated somewhere outside us and available for objective inspection, when the fact is that it is within us—is, indeed, an essential part of what we are. It would be more appropriate, perhaps, to say that death, as a fundamental element of our being, "thinks" in us and through us about whatever we think about, coloring our thoughts and moods with its presence throughout our lives.

Extinction is another such intangible, incomprehensible, yet all-important presence, surrounding and pervading life without ever showing its face directly. Extinction is, in truth, even less tangibly present than death, because while death continually strikes down those around us, thereby at least reminding us of what death is, and reminding us that we, too, must die, extinction can, by definition, strike only once, and is, therefore, entirely hidden from our direct view; no one has ever seen extinction and no one ever will. Extinction is thus *a human future that can never become a human present.* For who will suffer this loss, which we somehow regard as supreme? We, the living, will not suffer it; we will be dead. Nor will the unborn shed any tears over their lost chance to exist; to do so they would have to exist already. The perplexity underlying the whole question of extinction, then, is that although extinction might appear to be the largest misfortune that mankind could ever suffer, it doesn't seem to happen *to* anybody, and one is left wondering where its impact is to be registered, and by whom.

Lucretius wrote, "Do you not know that when death comes, there will be no other you to mourn your memory, and stand above you prostrate?" And Freud wrote, "It is indeed impossible to imagine our own death: and whenever we attempt to do so, we can perceive that we are in fact still present as spectators." Thought and feeling try to peer ahead and catch a glimpse of death, but they encounter their own demise along the way, for their death is what death is. In the same way, when we try to picture extinction we come up against the fact that the human faculties with which someone might see, hear, feel, or understand this event are obliterated in it, and we are left facing a blankness, or emptiness. But even the words "blankness" and "emptiness" are too expressive—too laden with human response—because, inevitably, they connote the *experience* of blankness and emptiness, whereas extinction is the end of human experience. It thus seems to be in the nature of extinction to repel emotion and starve thought, and if the mind, brought face to face with extinction, descends into a kind of exhaustion and dejection it is surely in large part because we know that mankind cannot be a "spectator" at its own funeral any more than any individual person can.

It might be well to consider for a moment the novel shape of the mental and emotional predicament that the nuclear peril places us in—a predicament that exists not because of a psychological failing or the inadequacy of the human mind but because of the actual nature of the thing that we are trying to think about. Strange as it may seem, we may have to teach ourselves to think about extinction in a meaningful way. (This seems less strange when we recall that whereas people may have a natural aversion to death no similar instinct moves them to ward off extinction—although most people's spontaneous reaction to the idea is hardly favorable, either. Like the peril of extinction itself, recognition of the peril and understanding of it can come only as a product of our life together in the common world—as a product, that is, not of instinct but of civilization. Other species not only do not resist extinction but are completely unaware that it is happening; the last passenger pigeon had no way of knowing that it *was* the last passenger pigeon, much less of doing anything about it.) On first looking into the consequences of a nuclear holocaust, one is struck by the odd fact that, beyond a certain point, the larger the imagined attack is, the less there is to say about it. At "low" levels of attack—the tens or hundreds of megatons—there is the complexity of the countless varieties of suffering and social and ecological breakdown to reflect on. But at higher levels—the thousands of megatons—the complexity steadily gives way to the simplicity and nothingness of death. Step by step, the "spectators" at the "funeral"—the sufferers of the calamity, in whose eyes it retains a human reality, and in whose lives it remains a human experience—dwindle away, until at last, when extinction is reached, all the "spectators" have themselves gone to the grave, and only the stones and stars, and whatever algae and mosses may have made it through, are present to witness the end.

Yet no matter how poor and thin a thing for imagination to grasp extinction may be, it seems to be in imagination alone that it can be grasped at all. Lacking the possibility of experience, all we have left is thought, since for us extinction is locked away forever in a future that can never arrive. Like the thought "I do not exist," the thought "Humanity is now extinct" is an impossible one for a rational person, because as soon as *it* is, *we* are not. In imagining any other event, we look ahead to a moment that is still within the stream of human time, which is to say within a time in which other human beings will exist, and will be responding to whatever they see, looking back to our present time and looking forward to future times that will themselves be within the sequence of human time. But in imagining extinction we gaze past everything human to a dead time that falls outside the human tenses of past, present, and future. By adopting a coldly scientific frame of mind, we can imagine that inert scene, but the exercise is oddly fruitless, and seems to hold no clue to the meaning of extinction. Instead, we find that almost everything that might engage our attention or stir our interest—even if only to repel us—has passed away. Struggling in this way to grasp the meaning of extinction, we may be led to wonder whether it can be grasped at all, and begin to suspect that nature provided an instinctual drive for the perpetuation of the species because it knew that our consciousness and will were so poorly equipped to deal with this task.

Given the special role of our mental faculties in any attempt to come to terms with extinction, it is not very surprising that a great deal of the writing that has been done about nuclear strategy is characterized by a highly abstract tone. The atmosphere in which this work goes forward is perfectly suggested by the nickname for the sort of institution in which much of it takes place: "the think tank." This term, evoking a hermetic world of thought, exactly reflects the intellectual circumstances of those thinkers whose job it is to deduce from pure theory, without the lessons of experience, what might happen if nuclear hostilities broke out. But, as Herman Kahn, the director of one of these think tanks (the Hudson Institute), and the author of "Thinking About the Unthinkable," among other works on nuclear strategy, has rightly said, "it will do no good to inveigh against theorists; in this field, everyone is a theorist." Hence, while in one sense Kahn is right to call a nuclear holocaust "unthinkable," it is also true, as his remark suggests, that when it comes to grasping the nature of this peril thinking about it is all that we *can* do.

The intellectual and affective difficulties involved in trying to understand the nuclear predicament have no precedent (unless one is to count individual death as a precedent), but they were foreshadowed in at least some respects by certain barriers that have impeded understanding of other sudden revolutionary developments of the modern age. In "Democracy in America," Tocqueville, speaking of the democratic revolution of his times, wrote, "Although the revolution that is taking place in the social condition, the laws, the opinions, and the feelings of men is still very far from being terminated, yet its results already admit of no comparison with anything that the world has ever before witnessed. I go back from age to age up to the remotest antiquity, but I find no parallel to what is occurring before my eyes; as the past has ceased to cast its light upon the future, the mind of man wanders in obscurity." But if in Tocqueville's day the past had ceased to cast its light upon the future, the present—what was occurring before his eyes—could still do so. Although the democratic revolution had not "terminated," it was nevertheless in full swing, and democratic America provided Tocqueville with enough factual material to fill the two thick volumes of his book. Drawing on this material, he was able to cast so much light on the future that we still see by it today.

The radical novelty of events became an even more troubling impediment to the understanding of totalitarian revolutions of our century. Arendt, who, more than anyone else, performed the offices of a Tocqueville in casting light on totalitarianism, wrote, "The gap between past and future ceased to be a condition peculiar only to the activity of thought and restricted as an experience to those few who made thinking their primary business. It became a tangible reality and perplexity for all; that is, it became a fact of political relevance." The totalitarian regimes, of course, made active attempts to revise or erase the factual record of both the past and the present. Yet these attempts have not been successful, and, in spite of the sense of unreality we feel when we confront the acts of the totalitarian regimes, totalitarianism is for us today something that has left its bloody marks on history, and these events, when we are told of them by credible witnesses, fill us with active revulsion. In Hitler's Germany and Stalin's Russia, horrifying events of dreamlike incredibility occurred, and pure, everyday common sense might reject their very possibility if the historical record were not there. In Arendt's "Eichmann in Jerusalem," we read the following description of the gassing to death by the Nazis of Jews in Poland:

> This is what Eichmann saw: The Jews were in a large room; they were told to strip; then a truck arrived, stopping directly before the entrance to the room, and the naked Jews were told to enter it. The doors were closed and the truck started off. "I cannot tell [how many Jews entered, Eichmann said later], I hardly looked. I could not; I could not; I had had enough. The shrieking, and . . . I was much too upset, and so on, as I later told Müller when I reported to him; he did not get much profit out of my report. I then drove along after the van, and then I saw the most horrible sight I had thus far seen in my life. The truck was making for an open ditch, the doors were opened, and the corpses were thrown out, as though they were still alive, so smooth were their limbs. They were hurled into the ditch, and I can still see a civilian extracting the teeth with tooth plyers."

We don't want to believe this; we find it all but impossible to believe this. But our wishful disbelief is stopped cold by the brute historical fact that it *happened:* we are therefore forced to believe. But extinction *has not happened,* and hides behind the veil of a future time which human eyes can never pierce. It is true that the testimony of those who survived the bombings of Hiroshima and Nagasaki offers us a vivid record of devastation by nuclear arms, but this record, which already seems to exhaust our powers of emotional response, illumines only a tiny corner of a nuclear holocaust, and, in any case, does not reach the question of extinction, which, instead of presenting us with scenes of horror, puts an end to them, just as it puts an end to all other scenes that are enacted by human beings. After several centuries of bringing a variety of nightmarish futures into existence, we have now invented one so unbelievable and overwhelming that it cannot come to pass at all. ("Come to pass" is a perfect phrase to describe what extinction cannot do. It can "come," but not "to pass," for with its arrival the creature that divides time into past, present, and future—the creature before whose eyes it would "pass"—is annihilated.) Deprived of both past and present experience to guide us as we try to face the nuclear predicament, we are left in the unpromising position of asking the future to shed light on itself.

As we look ahead to the possibility of extinction, our secret thought, which is well founded in the facts of the case, may be that since everyone will then be dead no one will have to worry about it, so why should we worry about it now? Following this unacknowledged but logical line of thinking, we may be led to the shrug of indifference that seems to have characterized most people's conscious reaction to the nuclear peril for the last thirty-six years. If extinction is nothing, we may unconsciously ask ourselves, may not no reaction be the right one? By contrast, our thoughts and feelings experience no such defeat when we consider a privation of future generations which falls short of denying them their existence—when we imagine, for example, that their supply of oil will run out, or that their supply of food will grow short, or that their civilization will go into decline. Then, through the widest possible extension of our respect for individual life, we can picture their plight, sympathize with their suffering, and perhaps take some action to forestall the evil. In effect, we are still following the ethical precept of doing unto others as we would have them do unto us, now expanding our understanding of who the others are to include the unborn, as Burke did. This comes naturally to us, as Burke pointed out, because a moment's reflection reveals to us the debt of gratitude that we owe past generations. However, in extending our sympathetic concern in this way, of course, we make the tacit assumption that there will *be* future generations, taking it for granted that nature, acting in and through us, will bring them forth, as it always has done. And in the pre-nuclear world, before it was in our power to extinguish the species, this confidence was warranted. But now the creation of new human beings is just the thing that is in question; and, in our attempt to grasp not the suffering and death of future generations but their failure to come into existence in the first place, a sympathetic response is inappropriate, for sympathy can extend only to living beings, and extinction is the foreclosure of life. The shuddering anticipation that we may feel on behalf of others when we realize that they are threatened with harm is out of place, because the lack of any others is the defining feature of extinction.

In removing the sufferer and his suffering with one blow, extinction again shows its resemblance to death. Montaigne writes, "Death can put an end, and deny access, to all our other woes," and adds, "What stupidity to torment ourselves about passing into exemption from all torment!" Extinction likewise brings not suffering but the end of suffering. Among feelings, suffering and joy are opposites, but both, like all feelings, are manifestations of life, and, as such, are together opposites of either death or extinction. Never having faced the end of human life before, we are led by mental habit to try to respond to it as though it were a disaster of one kind or another, in which people were going to be harmed or bereaved. But in doing so we strain for a reaction that, to our puzzlement, perhaps, does not come, for the excellent reason that in extinction there is no disaster: no falling buildings, no killed or injured people, no shattered lives, no mourning survivors. All of that is dissolved in extinction, along with everything else that goes on in life. We are left only with the ghostlike cancelled future generations, who, metaphorically speaking, have been waiting through all past time to enter into life but have now been turned back by us.

The distinction between harm to people in the world and the end of the world—or even the end of *a* world, such as occurred to European Jewry under Hitler—may give us some clue to the nature of what Arendt, borrowing a phrase of Kant's in order to describe the unparalleled crimes of Hitler's Germany and Stalin's Soviet Union, has called "radical evil." The "true hallmark" of radical evil, "about whose nature so little is known," she says, is that we do not know either how to punish these offenses or how to forgive them, and they therefore "transcend the realm of human affairs and the potentialities of human power, both of which they radically destroy wherever they make their appearance." By crimes that "transcend the realm of human affairs and the potentialities of human power," she means, I believe, crimes so great that they overwhelm the capacity of every existing system of jurisprudence, or other organized human response, to deal with them adequately. She goes on to say, "Here, where the deed itself dispossesses us of all power, we can indeed only repeat with Jesus: 'It were better for him that a millstone were hanged about his neck, and he cast into the sea.'" I would like to suggest that evil becomes radical whenever it goes beyond destroying individual victims (in whatever numbers) and, in addition, mutilates or destroys the *world* that can in some way respond to—and thus in some measure redeem—the deaths suffered. This capacity of evil was demonstrated on a large scale in modern times by the totalitarian regimes, which, in a manner of speaking, attempted to tear gaping, unmendable holes in the fabric of the world—holes into which entire peoples or classes would sink without a trace—but now it has fully emerged in the capacity of the species for self-extinction, which, by ending the world altogether, would "dispossess us of all power" forever. When crimes are of a certain magnitude and character, they nullify our power to respond to them adequately because they smash the human context in which human losses normally acquire their meaning for us. When an entire community or an entire people is destroyed, most of those who would mourn the victims, or bring the perpetrators to justice, or forgive them, or simply remember what occurred, are themselves destroyed. When that community is all mankind, the loss of the human context is total, and no one is left to respond. In facing this deed, we will either respond to it before it is done, and thus avoid doing it, or lose any chance to respond, and pass into oblivion.

If this interpretation is correct, every episode of radical evil is already a small extinction, and should be seen in that light. Between individual death and biological extinction, then, there are other possible levels of obliteration, which have some of the characteristics of extinction. The "end of civilization"—the total disorganization and disruption of human life, breaking the links between mankind's past and its future—is one. Genocide—the destruction of a people—which can be seen as an extinction *within* mankind, since it eliminates an element in the interior diversity of the species is another; in fact, genocide, including, above all, Hitler's attempt to extinguish the Jewish people, is the closest thing to a precursor of the extinction of the species that history contains. What the end of civilization, genocide, and extinction all have in common is that they are attacks not merely on existing people and things but on either the biological or the cultural heritage that human beings transmit from one generation to the next; that is, they are crimes against the future. The connection between genocide and extinction is further suggested by the fact that what the superpowers *intend* to do if a holocaust breaks out (leaving aside the unintended "collateral effects" for the moment) is to commit genocide against one another—to erase the other side as a culture and as a people from the face of the earth. In its nature, human extinction is and always will be without precedent, but the episodes of radical evil that the world has already witnessed are warnings to us that gigantic, insane crimes are not prevented from occurring merely because they are "unthinkable." On the contrary, they may be all the more likely to occur for that reason. Heinrich Himmler, a leading figure in the carrying out of the destruction of the Jews, assured his subordinates from time to time that their efforts were especially noble because by assuming the painful burden of making Europe "Jew-free" they were fighting "battles which future generations will not have to fight again." His remark applies equally well to a nuclear holocaust, which might render the earth "human-free." This is another "battle" (and the word is as inappropriate for a nuclear holocaust as it was for the murder of millions of Jews) that "future generations will not have to fight again."

If our usual responses to disasters and misfortunes are mismatched to the peril of extinction, then we have to look in some other quarter of our being to find its significance. Individual death once more offers a point of departure. We draw closer to death throughout our lives, but we never arrive there, for just as we are about to arrive we are gone. Yet although death thus always stands outside life, it nevertheless powerfully conditions life. Montaigne writes, "You are in death while you are in life; for you are after death when you are no longer in life. Or, if you prefer it this way, you are dead after life; but during life you are dying; and death affects the dying much more roughly than the dead, and more keenly and essentially." We are similarly "in extinction" while we are in life, and are after extinction when we are extinct. Extinction, too, thus affects the living "more roughly" and "more keenly and essentially" than it does the nonliving, who in its case are not the dead but the unborn. Like death, extinction is felt not when it has arrived but beforehand, as a deep shadow cast back across the whole of life. The answer to the question of who experiences extinction and when, therefore, is that we the living experience it, now and in all the moments of our lives. Hence, while it is in one sense true that extinction lies outside human life and never happens to anybody, in another sense extinction saturates our existence and never stops happening. If we want to find the meaning of extinction, accordingly, we should start by looking with new eyes at ourselves and the world we live in, and at the lives we live. The question to be asked then is no longer what the features and characteristics of extinction are but what it says about us and what it does to us that we are preparing our own extermination.

Because the peril is rooted in basic scientific knowledge, which is likely to last as long as mankind does, it is apparently a permanent one. But in the presence of that peril opposite poles of re-

147

sponse, both in feeling and, above all, in action, are possible, and the quality of the lives we live together is conditioned in opposite ways according to which response we choose. The choice is really between two entire ways of life. One response is to decline to face the peril, and thus to go on piling up the instruments of doom year after year until, by accident or design, they go off. The other response is to recognize the peril, dismantle the weapons, and arrange the political affairs of the earth so that the weapons will not be built again. I remarked that we do not have two earths at our disposal—one for experimental holocausts and the other to live on. Neither do any of us have two souls—one for responding to the nuclear predicament and the other for living the rest of our lives. In the long run, if we are dull and cold toward life in its entirety we will become dull and cold toward life in its particulars—toward the events of our own daily lives—but if we are alert and passionate about life in its entirety we will also be alert and passionate about it in its dailiness.

It is a matter of record that in our thirty-six years of life in a nuclear-armed world we have been largely dead to the nuclear peril, and I would like to consider more closely what this failure of response seems to have been doing to our world. Pascal, taking note of the cerebral character of the condition of mortality, once observed that "it is easier to endure death without thinking about it than to endure the thought of death without dying." His observation perfectly describes our response so far to the peril of extinction: we have found it much easier to dig our own grave than to think about the fact that we are doing so. Almost everyone has acknowledged on some level that the peril exists, but the knowledge has been without consequences in our feelings and our actions, and the superpowers have proceeded with their nuclear buildups, in the recent words of George Kennan, "like the victims of some sort of hypnotism, like men in a dream, like lemmings heading for the sea."

For a very short while before and after the first bomb was produced, a few men at and near the top of the American government seemed prepared to deal with the nuclear predicament at its proper depth. One of them was Secretary of War Henry Stimson, who knew of the Manhattan Project and, in March of 1945—four months before the Trinity test, at Alamogordo—confided to his diary an account of a discussion he had had about the new weapon with Harvey Bundy, his closest personal assistant. "Our thoughts," he wrote, "went right down to the bottom facts of human nature, morals, and governments, and it is by far the most searching and important thing that I have had to do since I have been here in the Office of the Secretary of War because it touches matters which are deeper even than the principles of present government." Yet those deep thoughts somehow did not take root firmly enough in the hearts of the American leaders or of the world at large, and the old ways of thinking returned, in the teeth of the new facts. The true dimensions of the the nuclear peril, and of its significance for mankind, had been glimpsed, but then the awareness faded and the usual exigencies of international political life—including, shortly, the Cold War between the United States and the Soviet Union—laid claim to people's passions and energies. The nuclear buildup that has continued to this day began, and the nuclear question, having emerged abruptly from the twofold obscurity of scientific theory and governmental secrecy, was almost immediately thrust into the new obscurity of the arcane, abstract, denatured world of the theorists in the think tanks, who were, in effect, deputized to think the "unthinkable" thoughts that the rest of us lacked the will to think.

Thus began the strange double life of the world which has continued up to the present. On the one hand, we returned to business as usual, as though everything remained as it always had been. On the other hand, we began to assemble the stockpiles that could blow this supposedly unaltered existence sky-high at any second. When the scientists working on the Manhattan Project wanted to send word to President Truman, who was at the Potsdam Conference, that the detonation near Alamogordo had been successful, they chose the horrible but apt code phrase "Babies satisfactorily born." Since then, these "babies"—which are indeed like the off-spring of a new species, except that it is a species not of life but of anti-life, threatening to end life—have "proliferated" steadily under our faithful care, bringing forth "generation" after "generation" of weapons, each more numerous and more robust than the last, until they now threaten to do away with their creators altogether. Yet while we did all this we somehow kept the left hand from knowing —or from dwelling on—what the right hand was doing; and the separation of our lives from awareness of the doom that was being prepared under us and around us was largely preserved.

It is probably crucial psychologically in maintaining this divorce that, once Hiroshima and Nagasaki had been pushed out of mind, the nuclear peril grew in such a way that while it relentlessly came to threaten the existence of everything, it physically touched nothing, and thus left people free not to think about it if they so chose. Like a kindhearted executioner, the bomb permitted its prospective victims to go on living seemingly ordinary lives up to the day that the execution should suddenly and without warning be carried out. (If one nuclear bomb had gone off each year in one of the world's cities, we can well imagine that public attitudes toward the nuclear peril would now be quite different.) The continuity, however illusory, between the pre-nuclear world and the nuclear world which was made possible by these years of not using nuclear weapons was important in preserving the world's denial of the peril because it permitted a spurious normality to be maintained—although "normality" was at times embraced with a fervor that betrayed an edge of hysterical insecurity. The spectacle of life going on as usual carried with it a strong presumption that nothing much was wrong. When we observed that no one seemed to be worried, that no one was showing any signs of alarm or doing anything to save himself, it was hard to resist the conclusion that everything was all right. After all, if we were reasonable people and we were doing nothing how could there be anything the matter? The totality of the peril, in particular, helped to disguise it, for, with everyone and everything in the world similarly imperilled, there was no flight from imperilled things to safe things—no flow of capital from country to country, or migration of people from one place to another. Thoughts of the nuclear peril were largely banned from waking life, and relegated to dreams or to certain fringes of society, and open, active concern about it was restricted to certain "far-out" people, whose ideas were on the whole not so much rejected by the supposedly sober, "realistic" people in the mainstream as simply ignored. In this atmosphere, discussion of the nuclear peril even took on a faintly embarrassing aura, as though dwelling on it were somehow melodramatic, or were a sophomoric excess that serious people outgrew with maturity.

It was not unless one lifted one's gaze from all the allegedly normal events occurring before one's eyes and looked at the executioner's sword hanging over everyone's head that the normality was revealed as a sort of mass insanity. This was an insanity that consisted not in screaming and making a commotion but precisely in *not* doing these things in the face of overwhelming danger, as though everyone had been sedated. Passengers on a ship who are eating, sunning themselves, playing shuffleboard, and engaging in all the usual shipboard activities appear perfectly normal as long as their ship is sailing safely in quiet seas, but these same passengers doing these same things appear deranged if in full view of them all their ship is caught in a vortex that may shortly drag it and them to destruction. Then their placidity has the appearance of an unnatural loss of normal human responses—of a pathetic and sickening acquiescence in their own slaughter. T. S. Eliot's well-known lines "This is the way the world ends/Not with a bang but a whimper" may not be literally correct—there will decidedly be a very big bang—but in a deeper sense it is certainly right; if we do end the world, the sequence is likely to be not a burst of strong-willed activity leading to a final explosion but enervation, dulled senses, enfeebled will, stupor, and paralysis. Then death.

Since we have not made a positive decision to exterminate ourselves but instead have chosen to live on the edge of extinction, periodically lunging toward the abyss only to draw back at the last second, our situation is one of uncertainty and nervous insecurity rather than of absolute hopelessness. We know that we may fall into the abyss at any moment, but we also know that we may not. So life proceeds—what else should it do?—but with a faltering and hesitant step, like one who gropes in darkness at the top of a tall precipice. Intellectually, we recognize that we have prepared ourselves for self-extermination and are improving the preparations every day, but emotionally and politically we have failed to respond. Accordingly, we have begun to live *as if* life were safe, but living *as if* is very different from just living. A split opens up between what we know and what we feel. We place our daily doings in one compartment of our lives and the threat to all life in another compartment. However, this split concerns too fundamental a matter to remain restricted to that matter alone, and it begins to influence the rest of life. Before long, denial of reality becomes a habit—a dominant mode in the life of society—and unresponsiveness becomes a way of life. The society that has accepted the threat of its utter destruction soon finds it hard to react to lesser ills, for a society cannot be at the same time asleep and awake, insane and sane, against life and for life.

To say that we and all future generations are threatened with extinction by the nuclear peril, however, is to describe only half of our situation. The other half is that we are the authors of that extinction. (For the populations of the superpowers, this is true in a positive sense, since we pay for extinction and support the governments that pose the threat of it, while for the peoples of the non-nuclear-armed world it is true only in the negative sense that they fail to try to do anything about the danger.) Like all those who are inclined to suicide, we approach the action in two capacities: the capacity of the one who would kill and that of the one who would be killed. As when we dream, we are both the authors and the sufferers of our fate. Therefore, when we hide from ourselves the immense preparations that we have made for our self-extermination we do so for two compelling reasons. First, we don't want to recognize that at any moment our lives may be taken away from us and our world blasted to dust, and, second, we don't want to face the fact that we are potential mass killers. The moral cost of nuclear armament is that it makes of all of us underwriters of the slaughter of hundreds of millions of people and of the cancellation of the future generations—an action whose utter indefensibility is not altered in the slightest degree by the fact that each side contemplates performing it only in "retaliation." In fact, as we shall see, this retaliation is one of the least justified actions ever contemplated, being wholly pointless. It is another nonsensical feature of the nuclear predicament that while each side regards the population of the other side as the innocent victims of unjust government, each proposes to punish the other government by annihilating that already suffering and oppressed population. Nor is there any exoneration from complicity in this slaughter in the theoretical justification that we possess nuclear arms not in order to use them but in order to prevent their use, for the fact is that even in theory prevention works only to the degree that it is backed up by the plausible threat of use in certain circumstances. Strategy thus commits us all to actions that we cannot justify by any moral standard. It introduces into our lives a vast, morally incomprehensible—or simply immoral —realm, in which every scruple or standard that we otherwise claim to observe or uphold is suspended. To be targeted from the cradle to the grave as a victim of indiscriminate mass murder is degrading in one way, but to target others for similar mass murder is degrading in another and, in a sense, a worse way. We endeavor to hold life sacred, but in accepting our roles as the victims and the perpetrators of nuclear mass slaughter we convey the steady message— and it is engraved more and more deeply on our souls as the years roll by—that life not only is not sacred but is worthless; that, somehow, according to a "strategic" logic that we cannot understand, it has been judged acceptable for everybody to be killed.

As it happens, our two roles in the nuclear predicament have been given visual representation in the photographs of the earth that we have taken with the aid of another technical device of our time, the spaceship. These pictures illustrate, on the one hand, our mastery over nature, which has enabled us to take up a position in the heavens and look back on the earth as though it were just one more celestial body, and, on the other, our weakness and frailty in the face of that mastery, which we cannot help feeling when we see the smallness, solitude, and delicate beauty of our planetary home. Looking at the earth as it is caught in the lens of the camera, reduced to the size of a golf ball, we gain a new sense of scale, and are made aware of a new relation between ourselves and the earth: we can almost imagine that we might hold this earth between the giant thumb and forefinger of one hand. Similarly, as the possessors of nuclear arms we stand outside nature, holding instruments of cosmic power with which we can blot life out, while at the same time we remain embedded in nature and depend on it for our survival.

Yet although the view from space is invaluable, in the last analysis the view that counts is the one from earth, from within life—the view, let us say, from a bedroom window in some city, in the evening, overlooking a river, perhaps, and with the whole colored by some regret or some hope or some other human sentiment. Whatever particular scene might come to mind, and whatever view and mood might be immediately present, from this earthly vantage point another view—one even longer than the one from space— opens up. It is the view of our children and grandchildren, and of all the future generations of mankind, stretching ahead of us in time—a view not just of one earth but of innumerable earths in succession, standing out brightly against the endless darkness of space, of oblivion. The thought of cutting off life's flow, of amputating this future, is so shocking, so alien to nature, and so contradictory to life's impulse that we can scarcely entertain it before turning away in revulsion and disbelief. The very incredibility of the action protects it from our gaze; our very love of life seems to rush forward to deny that we could do this. But although we block out the awareness of this self-posed threat as best we can, engrossing ourselves in life's richness to blind ourselves to the jeopardy to life, ultimately there is no way that we can remain unaffected by it. For finally we know and deeply feel that the ever-shifting, ever-dissolving moments of our mortal lives are sustained and given meaning by the broad stream of life, which bears us along like a force at our backs. Being human, we have, through the establishment of a common world, taken up residence in the enlarged space of past, present, and future, and if we threaten to destroy the future generations we harm ourselves, for the threat we pose to them is carried back to us through the channels of the common world that we all inhabit together. Indeed, "they" are we ourselves, and if their existence is in doubt our present becomes a sadly incomplete affair, like only one word of a poem, or one note of a song. Ultimately, it is subhuman.

Because the weight of extinction, like the weight of mortality, bears down on life through the mind and spirit but otherwise, until the event occurs, leaves us physically undisturbed, no one can prove that it alters the way we live. We can only say that it hardly stands to reason that the largest peril that history has ever produced —a peril in which, indeed, history would swallow itself up—should leave the activities of life, every one of which is threatened with dissolution, unaffected; and that we actually do seem to find life changing in ways that might be expected. Since the future generations are specifically what is at stake, all human activities that assume the future are undermined directly. To begin with, desire, love, childbirth, and everything else that has to do with the biological renewal of the species have been administered a powerful shock by the nuclear peril. The timeless, largely unspoken confidence of the species that although each person had to die, life itself would go on—the faith that on earth life was somehow favored, which found one of its most beautiful expressions in Christ's admonition "Consider the lilies of the field, how they grow; they toil not, neither do they spin: And yet I say unto you, That even Solomon in all his glory was not arrayed like one of these"—has been shaken, and with it the also largely unspoken confidence that people had in their own instinctual natures has been upset. It seems significant that Freud, who pioneered our century's self-consciousness in sexual matters, should have been one of the first observers to warn that humanity was headed down a path of self-destruction. In the last paragraph of "Civilization and Its Discontents," published in 1930, he wrote: ·

The fateful question for the human species seems to me to be whether and to what extent their cultural development will succeed in mastering the disturbance of their communal life by the human instinct of aggression and self-destruction. It may be that in this respect precisely the present time deserves a special interest. Men have gained

control over the forces of nature to such an extent that
with their help they would have no difficulty in exterminating one another to the last man. They know this, and
hence comes a large part of their current unrest, their un-
happiness and their mood of anxiety. And now it is to be
expected that the other of the two "Heavenly Powers,"
eternal Eros, will make an effort to assert himself in the
struggle with his equally immortal adversary [death].
But who can foresee with what success and with what
result?

It is as though Freud perceived that the balance between man's
"lower," animal, and instinctual nature, which had historically been
so much feared and despised by religious men and philosophers as
a disruptive force in man's spiritual development, and his "higher,"
rational nature had tipped in favor of the latter—so that now the
greater danger to man came not from rampant, uncontrolled instinct breaking down the restraining bonds of reason and self-
control but from rampant reason oppressing and destroying instinct
and nature. And rampant reason, man found, was, if anything, more
to be feared than rampant instinct. Bestiality had been the cause
of many horrors, but it had never threatened the species with extinction; some instinct for self-preservation was still at work. Only
"selfless" reason could ever entertain the thought of self-extinction.
Freud's merciful, solicitous attitude toward the animal in our nature
foreshadowed the solicitude that we now need to show toward the
animals and plants in our earthly environment. Now reason must sit
at the knee of instinct and learn reverence for the miraculous instinctual capacity for creation.

It may be a symptom of our disordered instinctual life that,
increasingly, sexuality has lost its hiding place in the privacy of the
bedroom and been drawn into the spotlight of public attention,
where it becomes the subject of debate, advice, and technical instruction, just like any other fully public matter. In Freud's day,
open discussion of sexual questions helped to free people from a
harshly restrictive Victorian morality, but in our day it appears that

sex, which no longer suffers from that traditional suppression, is drawn into the open because something has gone wrong with it and people want to repair it. By making it a public issue, they seem to acknowledge indirectly that our instincts have run up against an obstacle, as indeed they have, and are in need of public assistance, as indeed they are. Odd as it may seem, the disorder of our private, or once private, lives may require a political solution, for it may not be until the human future has been restored to us that desire can again find a natural place in human life.

The biological continuity of the species is made into a fully human, worldly continuity by, above all, the institution of marriage. Marriage lends permanence and a public shape to love. Marriage vows are made by a man and a woman to one another, but they are also made before the world, which is formally present at the ceremony in the role of witness. Marriage *solemnizes* love, giving this most inward of feelings an outward form that is acknowledged by everyone and commands everyone's respect. In swearing their love in public, the lovers also let it be known that their union will be a fit one for bringing children into the world—for receiving what the Bible calls "the grace of life." And the world, by insisting on a ceremony, and by attending in the role of witness, announces its stake in its own continuity. Thus, while in one sense marriage is the most personal of actions, in another sense it belongs to everybody. In a world that is perpetually being overturned and plowed under by birth and death, marriage—which for this reason is rightly called an "institution"—lays the foundation for the stability of a human world that is built to house all the generations. In this sense as well as in the strictly biological sense and the emotional sense, love creates the world.

The peril of extinction surrounds such love with doubt. A trembling world, poised on the edge of self-destruction, offers poor soil for enduring love to grow in. Everything that this love would build up, extinction would tear down. "Eros, builder of cities" (in Auden's phrase, in his poem eulogizing Freud on the occasion of his death) is thwarted. Or, to put it brutally but truthfully, every generation that holds the earth hostage to nuclear destruction holds a gun to the head of its own children. In laying this trap for the species, we show our children no regard, and treat them with indifference and neglect. As for love itself, love lives in the moment, but the moment is dying, as we are, and love also reaches beyond its moment to dwell in a kind of permanence. For

> Love's not Time's fool, though rosy lips and cheeks
> Within his bending sickle's compass come;
> Love alters not with his brief hours and weeks,
> But bears it out even to the edge of doom.

But if doom's edge draws close, love's vast scope is narrowed and its resolve may be shaken. The approach of extinction drives love back into its perishable moment, and, in doing so, tends to break up love's longer attachments, which now, on top of all the usual vicissitudes, have the weight of the whole world's jeopardy to bear.

There is, in fact, an odd resemblance between the plight of love and the plight of war in the nuclear world. Military hostilities, having been stopped by dread of extinction from occurring on the field of battle, are relegated to a mental plane—to the world of strategic theory and war games, where the generals of our day sit at their computer terminals waging shadow wars with the ostensible aim of making sure that no real hostilities ever happen. Love, too, although it has not been prevented altogether, has in a way lost its full field of action—the world that included the future generations—and so has tended to withdraw to a mental plane peculiarly its own, where it becomes an ever more solitary affair: impersonal, detached, pornographic. It means something that we call both pornography and nuclear destruction "obscene." In the first, we find desire stripped of any further human sentiment or attachment—of any "redeeming social value," in the legal phrase. In the second, we find violence detached from any human goals, all of which would be engulfed in a holocaust—detached, that is, from all redeeming social value.

The Japanese used to call the pleasure quarters of their cities "floating worlds." Now our entire world, cut adrift from its future and its past, has become a floating world. The cohesion of the social realm—the dense and elaborate fabric of life that is portrayed for us in the novels of the nineteenth century, among other places, inspiring "nostalgic" longing in us—is disintegrating, and people seem to be drifting apart and into a weird isolation. The compensation that is offered is the license to enjoy life in the moment with fewer restrictions; but the present moment and its pleasures provide only a poor refuge from the emptiness and loneliness of our shaky, dreamlike, twilit world. The moment itself, unable to withstand the abnormal pressure of expectation, becomes distorted and corrupted. People turn to it for rewards that it cannot offer—certainly not when it is ordered to do so. Plucked out of life's stream, the moment—whether a moment of love or of spiritual peace, or even of simple pleasure in a meal—is no longer permitted to quietly unfold and be itself but is strenuously tracked down, manipulated, harried by instruction and advice, bought and sold, and, in general, so roughly manhandled that the freshness and joy that it can yield up when it is left alone are corrupted or destroyed.

It is fully understandable that in the face of the distortion and disintegration of human relationships in a doom-ridden world a "conservative" longing for a richer, more stable, and more satisfying social existence should spring up. Unfortunately, however, this longing, instead of inspiring us to take political measures that would remove the world from jeopardy, and thus put life on a solid footing again, all too often takes the form of a simple *wish* that the world would stop being the way it is now and return to its former state, with what are often called "the old values" intact. Rather than take cognizance of the radical causes of the world's decline, with a view to doing something about them, these would-be upholders of the past tend to deny the existence of our new situation. It is only one more part of this denial—the most dangerous part—to imagine that war, too, still exists in its traditional form, in which one's enemies can be defeated on the field of battle without bringing an end to everything. Conservatism in personal and social questions has often gone together with militarism in the past, but now the combination is far more perilous than ever before. It represents a denial of what the world has now become which could lead to the end of the world. If a nation indulges itself in the illusion that, even with nuclear arms, war is possible, and that "victory" can be won with them, it risks bringing about its own and the world's extinction by mistake. Alert and realistic conservatives, by contrast, would see that everything that anyone might wish to conserve is threatened by nuclear weapons, and would recognize in them a threat not only to "the old values" but to any values whatever. And instead of dreaming of the vanished wars of past times they would place themselves in the forefront of a movement for disarmament.

Politics, as it now exists, is even more thoroughly compromised than personal and social life by the peril of extinction. Marriage lays down its map of hereditary lines across the unmarked territory of generational succession, shaping the rudiments of a common world out of biological reproduction, which without marriage would continue anyway, as it did before civilization was born, and does still among animals. Marriage is thus half submerged in the unconscious, instinctual, biological life of the species, and only half emergent into the "daylight" (in Hegel's term) of history and the common world. Politics, on the other hand, is wholly the creature of the common world, and could have no existence without it. (If people did not have reason and language, they could still reproduce but they could not set up a government among themselves.) There is no political "moment," as there is a sensual moment, to fall back on in an attempted retreat from the futility of a jeopardized common world. Politics, accordingly, is fully stuck with the glaring absurdity that with one hand it builds for a future that with the other hand it prepares to destroy. Each time a politician raises his voice to speak of making a better world for our children and grandchildren (and this is an intrinsic part of what politics is about, whether or not it happens to be explicitly stated), the peril of extinction is there to gainsay him with the crushing rebuttal: But there may *be* no children or grandchildren. And when, far more ridiculously, politicians let us know of their desire for a "place in history," it is not only their swollen vanity that invites anger but their presumption in trying to reserve a place in a history whose continued existence their own actions place in doubt.

Since Aristotle, it has often been said that the two basic aims of political association are, first, to assure the survival of members of society (that is, to protect life) and, second, to give them a chance to fulfill themselves as social beings (that is, to enable them to lead a noble or a good life). The threat of self-extermination annuls both of these objectives, and leaves the politics of our day in the ludicrous position of failing even to aim at the basic goals that have traditionally justified its existence. If our economy were to produce a wonderful abundance of silverware, glasses, and table napkins but no food, people would quickly rebel and insist on a different system. The world's political arrangements, which now aim at providing some accoutrements of life but fail to lift a finger to save life itself, are in no less drastic need of replacement. People cannot for long place confidence in institutions that fail even to recognize the most urgent requirement of the whole species, and it is therefore not surprising that, more and more, people do actually look on politicians with contempt, though perhaps without having quite figured out why.

As long as politics fails to take up the nuclear issue in a determined way, it lives closer than any other activity to the lie that we have all come to live—the pretense that life lived on top of a nuclear stockpile can last. Meanwhile, we are encouraged not to tackle our predicament but to inure ourselves to it: to develop a special, enfeebled vision, which is capable of overlooking the hugely obvious; a special, sluggish nervous system, which is conditioned not to react even to the most extreme and urgent peril; and a special, constricted mode of political thinking, which is permitted to creep around the edges of the mortal crisis in the life of our species but never to meet it head on. In this timid, crippled thinking, "realism" is the title given to beliefs whose most notable characteristic is their failure to recognize the chief reality of the age, the pit into which our species threatens to jump; "utopian" is the term of scorn for any plan that shows serious promise of enabling the species to keep from killing itself (if it is "utopian" to want to survive, then it must be "realistic" to be dead); and the political arrangements that keep us on the edge of annihilation are deemed "moderate," and are found to be "respectable," whereas new arrangements, which might enable us to draw a few steps back from the brink, are called "extreme" or "radical." With such fear-filied, thought-stopping epithets as these, the upholders of the status quo defend the anachronistic structure of their thinking, and seek to block the revolution in thought and in action which is necessary if mankind is to go on living.

Works of art, history, and thought, which provide what Arendt calls the "publicity" that makes an intergenerational common world possible, are undermined at their foundations by the threat of self-extermination. Each such work is a vessel that bears the distillation of some thought, feeling, or experience from one generation to another. In his 1970 Nobel Prize acceptance speech, Solzhenitsyn said, "Woe to that nation whose literature is disturbed by the intervention of power. Because that is not just a violation against 'freedom of print,' it is the closing down of the heart of the nation, a slashing to pieces of its memory." In reminding us that totalitarian governments seek to break the connections between generations, which are so inconvenient to all monomaniacal campaigns, Solzhenitsyn might well have been demonstrating that totalitarianism is indeed one of the precursors of the peril of extinction, which puts an end to all the generations. (The difference is that whereas totalitarianism destroys the memories, extinction destroys all the rememberers.) A work of art will often celebrate the most evanescent thing—a glance, a vague longing, the look of a certain shadow—but as soon as the artist picks up his brush or his pen he takes up residence in the immortal common world inhabited by all generations together. As the poets have always told us, art rescues love and other mortal things from time's destruction. And it is not only the artists who reach beyond their own lifetimes with art; it is also the readers, listeners, and viewers, who while they are in the presence of a work of art are made contemporary with it and, in a way, with all other readers, listeners, and viewers, in all ages. Through art, we "are able to break bread with the dead, and without communion with the dead a fully human life is impossible" (Auden). The timeless appeal of the greatest works of art, in fact, testifies to our common humanity as few other things do, and is one of the strongest grounds we have for supposing that a political community that would embrace the whole earth and all generations is also possible.

The other side of art's communion with the dead (which is the basis for Camus's lovely remark "As an artist . . . I began by admiring others, which in a way is heaven on earth") is its communion with the unborn. In nothing that we do are the unborn more strongly present than in artistic creation. It is the very business of artists to speak to future audiences, and therefore it is perhaps not surprising that they—probably more than any other observers, at least in the modern age—have been gifted with prophetic powers. (In our century, the name of Kafka, who seemed to foresee in so many particulars the history of our time, inevitably comes to mind.) Indeed, great works of art are often so closely attuned to the future that it takes the world a few decades to understand them. There is no doubt that art, which breaks into the crusted and hardened patterns of thought and feeling in the present as though it were the very prow of the future, is in radically altered circumstances if the future is placed in doubt. The ground on which the artist stands when he turns to his work has grown unsteady beneath his feet. In the pre-nuclear world, an artist who hoped to enable future generations to commune with his time might be worried that his work would be found wanting by posterity and so would pass into oblivion, but in the nuclear world the artist, whose work is still subject to this danger, must also fear that even if he produces nothing but timeless masterpieces they will fall into oblivion anyway, because there will be no posterity. The masterpieces cannot be timeless if time itself stops. The new uncertainty is not that one's work will be buried and forgotten in the tumult of history but that history, which alone offers the hope of saving anything from time's destruction, will itself be buried in the indifference of the nonhuman universe, dragging all human achievements down with it. The two fates, which now constitute a double jeopardy for artistic creation, are utterly different. In the first, it is life—the "onslaught of the generations," in Arendt's phrase—that undoes the work while itself surviving. In the second, it is death that swallows up both life and the work. The first peril makes us feel our individual mortality more keenly, but, for that very reason, makes us feel the common life of the species more strongly, and both feelings may inspire us to increase our efforts to accomplish whatever it is that we hope to offer the world before we die. The second peril threatens not each individual work but the world to which all works are offered, and makes us feel that even if we did accomplish our individual aims it would be pointless, thus undercutting our will to accomplish anything at all.

It would be futile to try to prescribe to art what it "can" and "cannot" do, as though we in the present had a visionary capacity to foresee art's future forms and, like an omniscient critic, accept some while ruling out others; but it is possible to reflect on what has already occurred, and to wonder what role political and other events in the world may have played in this or that development. Bearing in mind the irreducible mysteriousness of artistic creativity, we may note that some of the developments in art in recent decades have the look of logical, if unconscious, adjustments to the newly imperilled condition of the species. The art critic and social and political observer Harold Rosenberg has spoken of a "de-definition" of art, by which he meant a blurring of the boundary lines that have traditionally separated artistic creation from other human activities. Among the distinctions that have been lost—or deliberately breached —are the ones between the artist and his work of art and between the work of art and its audience. Rosenberg found the first breach in Action painting, in which the meaning of the work came to reside in the act of painting rather than in the finished canvas, and he found the second in all those artistic events that are called "happenings," in which the audience is more or less dispensed with and the "aesthetic effects are given by the event itself, without intervention on the part of the spectator-participant." In trying to do away with the enduring, independently existing art product and its audience, and concentrating on the act of creation, these artists, who "left art behind," seemed to be working toward an art that would fulfill itself—like the sexual act that is isolated from the past and the future—in the moment, thus giving up on communion with the dead and with the unborn: doing away, in fact, with art's whole

164

dependence on the common world, which assumes the existence of the human future. If art could manage this, of course, it would escape the futility of trying to communicate with generations that now may never arrive. Politics is simply powerless to cut itself off from the future and compress itself into a highly charged present (although some of the radical students of the nineteen-sixties seemed at times to be making the attempt), but art may have more leeway for experimentation, perhaps because, as the traditional rescuer of fleeting things from oblivion, it starts off being closer to life in the moment. Whether these experiments can produce much that is worthwhile is another question. Rosenberg spoke of "all those ruses of scrutinizing itself and defiantly denying its own existence" by which art has survived in recent decades, but he held out little hope that these devices could sustain art much longer. Looked at in terms of the predicament of the species as a whole, art appears to be in a quandary. Art attempts both to reflect the period in which it was produced and to be timeless. But today, if it wishes to truthfully reflect the reality of its period, whose leading feature is the jeopardy of the human future, art will have to go out of existence, while if it insists on trying to be timeless it has to ignore this reality —which is nothing other than the jeopardy of human time—and so, in a sense, tell a lie. Art by itself is powerless to solve its predicament, and artists, like lovers, are in need of assistance from statesmen and ordinary citizens.

By threatening to cancel the future generations, the nuclear peril not only throws all our activities that count on their existence into disorder but also disturbs our relationship with the past generations. We need the assurance that there will be a future if we are to take on the burden of mastering the past—a past that really does become the proverbial "dead past," an unbearable weight of millennia of corpses and dust, if there is no promise of a future. Without confidence that we will be followed by future generations, to whom we can hand on what we have received from the past, it becomes intolerably depressing to enter the tombs of the dead to gather what they have left behind; yet without that treasure our life is impoverished. The present is a fulcrum on which the future and the past lie balanced, and if the future is lost to us, then the past must fall away, too.

Death lies at the core of each person's private existence, but part of death's meaning is to be found in the fact that it occurs in a biological and social world that survives. No one can be a spectator at his own funeral, but others can be there, and the anticipation of their presence, which betokens the continuity of life and all that that means for a mortal creature, is consolation to each person as he faces his death. Death suffered in the shadow of doom lacks this consolation. It is a gap that threatens soon to be lost in a larger gap —a death within a greater death. When human life itself is overhung with death, we cannot go peacefully to our individual deaths. The deaths of others, too, become more terrible: with the air so full of death, every death becomes harder to face. When a person dies, we often turn our thoughts to the good he did while he was alive—to that which he gave to the world, and which therefore outlasts him in the world's affection. (When someone who did great harm to the world dies, we feel that death has had a more thorough victory, since there is so little of his that the world wishes to preserve. Rather, it may wish to bury him even more thoroughly than any grave can.) But when the whole world, in which the dead in a sense live on, is imperilled, this effort at remembrance and preservation seems to lose its point, and all lives and deaths are threatened with a common meaninglessness.

There have been many deaths in our century that in certain respects resembled those that would be suffered in a nuclear holocaust: the deaths of the millions of people who died in the concentration camps of the totalitarian regimes, which sought not only to kill their victims but to extirpate their memory from the historical record. Because the camps threatened people not only with death but with oblivion, remembrance has become for some survivors a passion and a sacred obligation. When Solzhenitsyn accepted the Nobel Prize, he was at pains to remind the world that he spoke on behalf of millions who had not survived, and his whole historical reconstruction of the Soviet camp system is pitted against totalitarian forgetfulness. Likewise, the command "Never forget," so often heard in connection with the Nazis' genocidal attack on the Jews, is important not only because it may help the world to prevent any repetition but because remembering is in itself an act that helps to defeat the Nazis' attempt to send a whole people into oblivion. Just because genocide, by trying to prevent the future generations of people from being born, commits a crime against the future, it lays a special obligation on the people of the future to deal with the crime, even long after its perpetrators are themselves dead. The need to bear witness and then to remember was felt first by the inmates of the camps and only later by the world at large. The French journalist David Rousset, a survivor of several camps, including Buchenwald, has written of his experiences in those camps:

> How many people here still believe that a protest has even historic importance? This skepticism is the real masterpiece of the S.S. Their great accomplishment. They have corrupted all human solidarity. Here the night has fallen on the future. When no witnesses are left, there can be no testimony. To demonstrate when death can no longer be postponed is an attempt to give death a meaning, to act beyond one's own death. In order to be successful, a gesture must have social meaning. There are hundreds of thousands of us here, all living in absolute solitude.

Thanks to a few heroic witnesses, and to the existence outside the totalitarian world of a nontotalitarian world, which could find out about what happened and then remember it, the connections between the camp victims and the rest of humanity were never altogether severed. There *was* testimony, the "historic importance" of the events in the camps *was* preserved, "human solidarity" *was* partly maintained, however tragically late, and the "masterpiece" of the S.S. was spoiled. Indeed, if we read the testimony of those in the camps deeply enough it may help us in our effort to avoid our extinction. Arendt, writing in her classic study "The Origins of Totalitarianism," made the connection:

Here [in the camps], there are neither political nor historical nor simply moral standards but, at the most, the realization that something seems to be involved in modern politics that actually should never be involved in politics as we used to understand it, namely all or nothing—all, and that is an undetermined infinity of forms of human living-together, or nothing, for a victory of the concentration-camp system would mean the same inexorable doom for human beings as the use of the hydrogen bomb would mean the doom of the human race.

Yet we must insist, I think, that in fact extinction by nuclear arms would be the more profound oblivion, since then the very possibility of remembrance or renewal—of the existence of a Solzhenitsyn or Rousset to bear witness, or of an Arendt to reflect on their testimony, or of readers to ponder what happened and take it to heart—would be gone. In extinction, and only in extinction, the connections between the victims and the rest of humanity would really be severed forever, and the "masterpiece" of the mass murderers would be perfected, for the night would have "fallen on the future" once and for all. Of all the crimes against the future, extinction is the greatest. It is the murder of the future. And because this murder cancels all those who might recollect it even as it destroys its immediate victims the obligation to "never forget" is displaced back onto us, the living. It is we—the ones who will either commit this crime or prevent it—who must bear witness, must remember, and must arrive at the judgment.

A nuclear holocaust would destroy the living and cancel the unborn in the same blow, but it is possible, as I mentioned earlier, at least to imagine that, through sterilization of the species, the future generations could be cancelled while the living were left unharmed. Although the condition of being extinct is by definition beyond experience this remnant—the living cells of the dead body of mankind—would, like a prisoner who knows that he is condemned to die on a certain day, be forced to look extinction in the face in a way that we, who can always tell ourselves that we may yet

168

escape extinction, are not. To them, the futility of all the activities
of the common world—of marriage, of politics, of the arts, of learn-
ing, and, for that matter, of war—would be driven home inexorably.
They would experience in their own lives the breakdown of the ties
that bind individual human beings together into a community and a
species, and they would feel the current of our common life grow
cold within them. And as their number was steadily reduced by
death they would witness the final victory of death over life. One
wonders whether in these circumstances people would want to go
on living at all—or whether they might not choose to end their own
lives. By killing off the living quickly, extinction by nuclear arms
would spare us those barren, bitter decades of watching and feeling
the end close in. As things are, we will never experience the approach of extinction in that pure form, and are left in an irremediable uncertainty. Nevertheless, the spectre of extinction hovers
over our world and shapes our lives with its invisible but terrible
pressure. It now accompanies us through life, from birth to death.
Wherever we go, it goes, too; in whatever we do, it is present. It
gets up with us in the morning, it stays at our side throughout the
day, and it gets into bed with us at night. It is with us in the
delivery room, at the marriage ceremony, and on our deathbeds.
It is the truth about the way we now live. But such a life cannot go
on for long.

Because the unborn generations will never experience their cancellation by us, we have to look for the consequences of extinction
before it occurs, in our own lives, where it takes the form of a spiritual sickness that corrupts life at the invisible, innermost starting
points of our thoughts, moods, and actions. This emphasis on us,
however, does not mean that our only reason for restraining ourselves from elimination of the future generations is to preserve
them as auxiliaries to *our* needs—as the audience for our works of
art, as the outstretched hands to receive our benefactions (and so to
bring our otherwise frustrated charitable impulses to fulfillment),
as the minds that will provide us with immortality by remembering

our words and deeds, and as the successors who will justify us by carrying on with the tasks that we have started or advanced. To adopt such an expedient view of the future generations would be to repeat on a monumental scale the error of the philanthropist who looks on the needy only as a convenient prop with which he can develop and demonstrate his moral superiority, or the more familiar and more dangerous figure of the politician who looks on the public only as a ladder on which he can climb to power. It would also put us in the company of those who, in pursuit, very often, of visionary social goals, make the opposite but closely related error of regarding the *present* generations only as auxiliaries—as the expendable bricks and mortar to be used in the construction of a glorious palace in which the future generations will take up residence. (We have merely to remember how many people have been murdered so that "history" might "go forward" to be reminded how great the costs of this mistake have been.) Whether we were subordinating the living or the unborn generations, this reduction of human beings to a supporting role in the completion of cross-generational tasks would suggest that we had come to place a higher value on the achievements of life than we did on life itself, as though we were so dazzled by the house man lives in that we had forgotten who lives there. But no human being, living or unborn, should be regarded as an auxiliary. Although human beings have their obligations to fulfill, they are not to be seen as beasts of burden whose purpose in existing is to carry on with enterprises that are supposedly grander and more splendid than they are. For in the last analysis these enterprises, which together make up the common world, are meant to serve life, not to be served by it. Life does not exist for the sake of the governments, the buildings, the books, and the paintings; all these exist for the sake of life. The works of man are great, but man himself is greater.

The reason that so much emphasis must be laid on the living generations is not that they are more important than the unborn but only that at any given moment they, by virtue of happening to be the ones who exist, are the ones who pose the peril, who can feel the consequences of the peril in their lives, and who can respond to the peril on behalf of all other generations. To cherish life—whether one's own or someone else's, a present life or an unborn life—one must already be in life, and only the living have this privilege. The question that the peril of extinction puts before the living, however, is: Who would miss human life if they extinguished it? To which the only honest answer is: Nobody. That being so, we have to admit that extinction is no loss, since there cannot be loss when there is no loser: and we are thus driven to seek the meaning of extinction in the mere anticipation of it by the living, whose lives this anticipation corrupts and degrades. However, there is another side to the entire question. For while it is true that extinction cannot be felt by those whose fate it is—the unborn, who would stay unborn—the same cannot be said, of course, for extinction's alternative, survival. If we shut the unborn out of life, they will never have a chance to lament their fate, but if we let them into life they will have abundant opportunity to be glad that they were born instead of having been prenatally severed from existence by us. The idea of escaping extinction before one was born is a strange one for us, since it is so new, but to generations that live deep in nuclear time, and who know that their existence has depended on the wisdom and restraint of a long succession of generations before them, we can be sure that the idea will be familiar.

Of every other bequest that the present makes to the future it can be said that that which would be gratefully received if it was given would also be sorely missed if it was withheld. Of life alone is it the case that while its receipt can be welcomed, its denial cannot be mourned. The peril of extinction, by bringing us up against this reality, concentrates our attention in a new way on the simple and basic fact that before there can be good or evil, service or harm, lamenting or rejoicing there *must be life.* (Even those who wish to exploit and harm other human beings must first want human beings to exist.) In coming to terms with the peril of extinction, therefore, what we must desire first of all is that people be born, for their own sakes, and not for any other reason. Everything else—our wish to serve the future generations by preparing a decent world for them to live in, and our wish to lead a decent life ourselves in a common world made secure by the safety of the future generations—flows from this commitment. Life comes first. The rest is secondary.

To recapitulate: In a nuclear holocaust great enough to extinguish the species, every person on earth would die; but in addition to that, and distinct from it, is the fact that the unborn generations would be prevented from ever existing. However, precisely because the unborn are not born, they cannot experience their plight, and its meaning has to be sought among the living, who share a common world with the unborn as well as with the dead, and who find that if they turn their backs on the unborn, and deny them life, then their own lives become progressively more twisted, empty, and despairing. On the other hand, if instead of asking what the act of extinction means we ask what the act of survival means—and in the nuclear world survival has, for the first time, become an act—we find that the relationship between the generations is reconstituted, and we can once again ask what the meaning of our actions will be for the people directly affected by them, who now, because they are presumed to exist, can be presumed to have a response. By acting to save the species, and repopulating the future, we break out of the cramped, claustrophobic isolation of a doomed present, and open a path to the greater space—the only space fit for human habitation—of past, present, and future. Suddenly, we can think and feel again. Even by merely imagining for a moment that the nuclear peril has been lifted and human life has a sure foothold on the earth again, we can feel the beginnings of a boundless relief and calm—a boundless peace. But we can open this path only if it is our desire that the unborn exist for their own sake. We trace the effects of extinction in our own world because that is the only place where they can ever appear, yet those sad effects, important as they are, are only the side effects of our shameful failure to fulfill our main obligation of valuing the future human beings themselves. And if at first we find these future people to be somewhat abstract we have only to remind ourselves that we, too, were once "the future generation," and that every unborn person will be as vivid and important to himself as each of us is to himself. We gain the right perspective on extinction not by trying to peer into the inhuman emptiness of a

post-human universe but by putting ourselves in the shoes of someone in the future, who, precisely because he has been allowed to be
born, can rejoice in the fact of being alive.

With the generation that has never known a world unmenaced by
nuclear weapons, a new order of the generations begins. In it, each
person alive is called on to assume his share of the responsibility for
guaranteeing the existence of all future generations. And out of the
new sense of responsibility must come a worldwide program of
action for preserving the species. This program would be the guarantee of existence for the unborn and the measure of the honor and
the humanity of the living. Its inauguration would mark the foundation of a new common world, which would greatly transcend the old,
pre-nuclear common world in importance and in the strength of its
ties. Without such a program in place, nothing else that we under-
take together can make any practical or moral sense. Thus, the
nuclear peril, while for the first time in history placing the whole
common world in jeopardy, at the same time draws into that common world much that was formerly left out, including, above all,
the terrestrial biological inheritance. Through the jeopardy of our
biological substance, even the things that belong to what Arendt
called the "private realm" are affected, so that ultimately it is not
only the institutions, arts, and sciences—the enduring, heavy structure of the world—whose meaning is changed but also the fleeting
things: sensation, desire, "the summer lightning of individual happiness" (Alexander Herzen). Against the background of the new
double mortality of life, the fleeting things seem even more flicker-
ing, and more to be protected and cherished.

By threatening life in its totality, the nuclear peril creates new
connections between the elements of human existence—a new min-
gling of the public and the private, the political and the emotional,
the spiritual and the biological. In a strikingly pertinent remark,
Arendt, speaking of the individual's capacity for action, writes,
"With word and deed we insert ourselves into the human world,
and this insertion is like a second birth, in which we confirm and

take upon ourselves the naked fact of our original physical appearance." Now the whole species is called on literally to take on itself the naked fact of its original physical appearance—to protect our being through an act of our will. Formerly, the future was simply given to us; now it must be achieved. We must become the agriculturalists of time. If we do not plant and cultivate the future years of human life, we will never reap them. This effort would constitute a counterpart in our conscious life of reason and will of our instinctual urge to procreate. And in so doing it would round out and complete the half-finished common world of pre-nuclear times, which, by the time nuclear weapons were invented, had enabled mankind to learn and to suffer but not to act as one.

In asking us to cherish the lives of the unborn, the peril of extinction takes us back to the ancient principle of the sacredness of human life, but it conducts us there by a new path. Instead of being asked not to kill our neighbors, we are asked to let them be born. If it is possible to speak of a benefit of the nuclear peril, it would be that it invites us to become more deeply aware of the miracle of birth, and of the world's renewal. "For unto us a child is born." This is indeed "good news." Yet when we turn from extinction, which silences us with its nothingness, to the abundance of life, we find ourselves tongue-tied again, this time by the fullness of what lies before our eyes. If death is one mystery, life is another, greater one. We find ourselves confronted with the essential openness, unfathomability, and indefinability of our species. (Auden has observed that human nature is indefinable because definition is a historical act that can upset the human reality it seeks to define.) We can only feel awe before a mystery that both is what we are and surpasses our understanding.

Without violating that mystery, we can perhaps best comprehend the obligation to save the species simply as a new relationship among human beings. Because the will to save the species would be a will to let other people into existence rather than a will to save oneself, it is a form of respect for others, or, one might say, a form of love. (By contrast, the will to avoid the holocaust, which would kill off every living person, involves self-interest, and would grow, in part, out of fear. Thus, as we face the nuclear predicament in its entirety, both love and fear are present, but they are inspired by threats to different things.) This love, I believe, would bear a resemblance to the generative love of parents, who in wanting to bring children into the world have some experience of what it is to hope for the renewal of life. They know that when a child is born the whole world is reborn with it, as in a sunrise, since it is only in the mind, heart, and spirit of each human being that the human world has existence. If the ideal for the relationship among living people is brotherhood, then the ideal for the relationship of the living to the unborn is parenthood. Universal brotherhood, which seeks to safeguard lives that are already in existence, embodies the solicitude and protectiveness of love, and its highest command, therefore, is "Thou shalt not kill." Universal parenthood, which would seek to bring life into existence out of nothing, would embody the creativity and abundant generosity of love, and its highest commandment, therefore, would be "Be fruitful and multiply." But this commandment is not the strictly biological one. The nuclear peril makes all of us, whether we happen to have children of our own or not, the parents of all future generations. Parental love, which begins even before any child exists, is unconditional. It does not attach to any quality of the beloved; it only wants him to be. But then all love, when it is deep, has something in it of this character, and is ready to forgive every particular failing in the beloved. Shakespeare says that "love is not love which alters when it alteration finds," and we know from the Bible that "love keeps no accounts."

The common world itself can be seen as a product of the superabundance of life's fruitfulness. It is like a surplus, beyond what each generation can use for itself, that is passed on in a steadily growing accumulation, enabling all the generations to participate in a *life* of mankind which transcends individual life and is not undone by individual death. Extinction is a second death, and this second life is the life that it destroys.

Since the future generations will surely do and suffer wrong, it is part of the work of this love to come to terms with evil. Love is given Job's task: to accept and affirm the creation even in the full knowledge of the unspeakable injustice and suffering that it contains. Thus, while our capacity for sympathizing with the suffering of others is of no help in understanding extinction, because there is no suffering (or any other human experience) in it, it would not be right to say that the question of suffering does not come up, for *in saving* the future generations we will bring them every kind of suffering that life holds (together with every other human experience). The fact that it is not extinction but life that brings suffering, and even death, is the clearest proof that extinction is misconceived as a disaster in any ordinary sense. On the contrary, survival means disaster—endlessly, as long as life is beset by accident and folly. In the pre-nuclear common world, our aim was to spare all generations every particular evil that it was in our power to resist, but now our determination must be first to give the future generations all the evils, which are as much a part of life as breathing, and only then to set about mitigating them. Fortunately or unfortunately, we cannot pick and choose which experiences of life to give the future generations. Either we keep them out of life completely or we get them in for all of it.

To favor life on these terms is difficult, but it is not inhuman. We find this affirmation in one form in parental love and we find it in another form in religious faith, as the example of Job attests. Augustine wrote that after his introduction to Christianity "no more did I long for better things, because I thought of all things, and with a sounder judgment I held that the higher things are indeed better than the lower, but that all things together are better than the higher things alone." And he wrote, "All things, by the very fact that they *are*, are good." A Japanese Buddhist monk seems to have been saying the same thing even more simply when he said, "Every day is a good day." A similar affirmation runs through the ceremonial words of Christian sacramental occasions. Marriage vows, in which the couple swear to love one another in sickness and in health and "for better for worse," seem to signify an affirmation not only of the married condition but of the whole human condition. And in the words sometimes spoken in burial services the affirmation is made outright: "Ashes to ashes, dust to dust. The Lord gave, and the Lord hath taken away; blessed be the name of the Lord."

The first principle of life in the new common world would be respect for human beings, born and unborn, based on our common love of life and our common jeopardy in the face of our own destructive powers and inclinations. This respect would grow out of each generation's gratitude to past generations for having permitted it to exist. Each generation would look on itself as though it were a delegation that had been chosen by an assembly of all the dead and all the unborn to represent them in life. The living would thus look on the gift of life the way any political representative should look on election to office—as a temporary trust to be used for the common good. For if the surface of the globe is the breadth of the world, time, which politics is now called on to guarantee, is its depth, and we cannot expect the world to cohere horizontally if it is not joined together vertically as well. In this new world, the people of the present generations, if they acquit their responsibility, would be the oldest of the grandfathers, and their role would be that of founders.

A second principle of life in the nuclear common world would be respect for the earth. This is nothing but a full realization of the ecological principle, according to which the earth's environment is seen not merely as a surrounding element in which it is more or less pleasant to live but as the foundation of human as of other life. The oneness of the earth as a system of support for life is already visible around us. Today, no matter how strenuously statesmen may assert the "sovereign" power of their nations, the fact is that they are all caught in an increasingly fine mesh of global life, in which the survival of each nation depends on the survival of all. There is no "sovereign" right to destroy the earthly creation on which everyone depends for survival (although such a right is exactly what each superpower now claims for itself). More and more, the earth is coming to resemble a single body, or, to use Dr. Thomas's metaphor, a single cell, which is inhabited by billions of separate intelligences and wills. In these circumstances, the use of violence is like the left hand attacking the right, or like both hands attacking the throat. We want to maintain the independence of each person's mind and will—for our liberty consists in this—but in doing so we must not kill the one terrestrial body in which we are all incarnated together.

A third principle would be respect for God or nature, or whatever one chooses to call the universal dust that made, or became, us. We need to remember that neither as individuals nor as a species have we created ourselves. And we need to remember that our swollen power is not a power to create but only a power to destroy. We can kill all human beings and close down the source of all future human beings, but we cannot create even one human being, much less create those terrestrial conditions which now permit us and other forms of life to live. Even our power of destruction is hardly our own. As a fundamental property of matter, nuclear energy was nature's creation, and was only discovered by us. (What is truly our own is the knowledge that has enabled us to exploit this energy.) With respect to creation, things still stand as they have always stood, with extra-human powers performing the miracle, and human beings receiving the fruits. Our modest role is not to create but only to preserve ourselves. The alternative is to surrender ourselves to absolute and eternal darkness: a darkness in which no nation, no society, no ideology, no civilization will remain; in which never again will a child be born; in which never again will human beings appear on the earth, and there will be no one to remember that they ever did.

III.
THE CHOICE

Four and a half billion years ago, the earth was formed. Perhaps a half billion years after that, life arose on the planet. For the next four billion years, life became steadily more complex, more varied, and more ingenious, until, around a million years ago, it produced mankind—the most complex and ingenious species of them all. Only six or seven thousand years ago—a period that is to the history of the earth as less than a minute is to a year—civilization emerged, enabling us to build up a human world, and to add to the marvels of evolution marvels of our own: marvels of art, of science, of social organization, of spiritual attainment. But, as we built higher and higher, the evolutionary foundation beneath our feet became more and more shaky, and now, in spite of all we have learned and achieved—or, rather, because of it—we hold this entire terrestrial creation hostage to nuclear destruction, threatening to hurl it back into the inanimate darkness from which it came. And this threat of self-destruction and planetary destruction is not something that we will pose one day in the future, if we fail to take certain precautions; it is here now, hanging over the heads of all of us at every moment. The machinery of destruction is complete, poised on a hair trigger, waiting for the "button" to be "pushed" by some misguided or deranged human being or for some faulty computer chip to send out the instruction to fire. That so much should be balanced on so fine a point—that the fruit of four and a half billion years can be undone in a careless moment—is a fact against which belief rebels. And there is another, even vaster measure of the loss, for stretching ahead from our present are more billions of years of life on earth, all of which can be filled not only with human life but with human civilization. The procession of generations that extends onward from our present leads far, far beyond the line of our sight, and, compared with these stretches of human time, which exceed the whole history of the earth up to now, our brief civilized moment is almost infinitesimal. And yet we threaten, in the name of our transient aims and fallible convictions, to foreclose it all. If our species does destroy itself, it will be a death in the cradle—a case of infant mortality. The disparity between the cause and the effect of our peril is so great that our minds seem all but powerless to encompass it. In addition, we are so fully enveloped by that which is menaced, and so deeply and passionately immersed in its events, which are the events of our lives, that we hardly know how to get far enough away from it to see it in its entirety. It is as though life itself were one huge distraction, diverting our attention from the peril to life. In its apparent durability, a world menaced with imminent doom is in a way deceptive. It is almost an illusion. Now we are sitting at the breakfast table drinking our coffee and reading the newspaper, but in a moment we may be inside a fireball whose temperature is tens of thousands of degrees. Now we are on our way to work, walking through the city streets, but in a moment we may be standing on an empty plain under a darkened sky looking for the charred remnants of our children. Now we are alive, but in a moment we may be dead. Now there is human life on earth, but in a moment it may be gone.

Once, there was time to reflect in a more leisurely way on our predicament. In August, 1945, when the invention of the bomb was made known through its first use on a human population, the people of Hiroshima, there lay ahead an interval of decades which might have been used to fashion a world that would be safe from extinction by nuclear arms, and some voices were in fact heard counselling deep reflection on the looming peril and calling for action to head it off. On November 28, 1945, less than four months after the bombing of Hiroshima, the English philosopher Bertrand Russell rose in the House of Lords and said:

> We do not want to look at this thing simply from the point of view of the next few years; we want to look at it from the point of view of the future of mankind. The question is a simple one: Is it possible for a scientific society to continue to exist, or must such a society inevitably bring itself to destruction? It is a simple question but a very vital one. I do not think it is possible to exaggerate the gravity of the possibilities of evil that lie in the utilization of atomic energy. As I go about the streets and see St. Paul's, the British Museum, the Houses of Parliament, and the other monuments of our civilization, in my mind's eye I see a nightmare vision of those buildings as heaps of rubble with corpses all round them. That is a thing we have got to face, not only in our own country and cities, but throughout the civilized world.

Russell and others, including Albert Einstein, urged full, global disarmament, but the advice was disregarded. Instead, the world set about building the arsenals that we possess today. The period of grace we had in which to ward off the nuclear peril before it became a reality—the time between the moment of the invention of the weapons and the construction of the full-scale machinery for extinction—was squandered, and now the peril that Russell foresaw is upon us. Indeed, if we are honest with ourselves we have to admit that unless we rid ourselves of our nuclear arsenals a holocaust not only *might* occur but *will* occur—if not today, then tomorrow; if not this year, then the next. We have come to live on borrowed time: every year of continued human life on earth is a borrowed year, every day a borrowed day.

In the face of this unprecedented global emergency, we have so far had no better idea than to heap up more and more warheads, apparently in the hope of so thoroughly paralyzing ourselves with terror that we will hold back from taking the final, absurd step. Considering the wealth of our achievement as a species, this response is unworthy of us. Only by a process of gradual debasement of our self-esteem can we have lowered our expectations to this point. For, of all the "modest hopes of human beings," the hope that mankind will survive is the most modest, since it only brings us to the threshold of all the other hopes. In entertaining it, we do not yet ask for justice, or for freedom, or for happiness, or for any of the other things that we may want in life. We do not even necessarily ask for our personal survival; we ask only that we *be survived*. We ask for assurance that when we die as individuals, as we know we must, mankind will live on. Yet once the peril of extinction is present, as it is for us now, the hope for human survival becomes the most tremendous hope, just because it is the foundation for all the other hopes, and in its absence every other hope will gradually wither and die. Life without the hope for human survival is a life of despair.

The death of our species resembles the death of an individual in its boundlessness, its blankness, its removal beyond experience, and its tendency to baffle human thought and feeling, yet as soon as one mentions the hope of survival the similarities are clearly at an end. For while individual death is inevitable, extinction can be avoided; while every person must die, mankind can be saved. Therefore, while reflection on death may lead to resignation and acceptance, reflection on extinction must lead to exactly the opposite response: to arousal, rejection, indignation, and action. Extinction is not something to contemplate, it is something to rebel against. To point this out might seem like stating the obvious if it were not that on the whole the world's reaction to the peril of extinction has been one of numbness and inertia, much as though extinction were

184

as inescapable as death is. Even today, the official response to the sickening reality before us is conditioned by a grim fatalism, in which the hope of ridding the world of nuclear weapons, and thus of surviving as a species, is all but ruled out of consideration as "utopian" or "extreme"—as though it were "radical" merely to want to go on living and to want one's descendants to be born. And yet if one gives up these aspirations one has given up on everything. As a species, we have as yet done nothing to save ourselves. The slate of action is blank. We have organizations for the preservation of almost everything in life that we want but no organization for the preservation of mankind. People seem to have decided that our collective will is too weak or flawed to rise to this occasion. They see the violence that has saturated human history, and conclude that to practice violence is innate in our species. They find the perennial hope that peace can be brought to the earth once and for all a delusion of the well-meaning who have refused to face the "harsh realities" of international life—the realities of self-interest, fear, hatred, and aggression. They have concluded that these realities are eternal ones, and this conclusion defeats at the outset any hope of taking the actions necessary for survival. Looking at the historical record, they ask what has changed to give anyone confidence that humanity can break with its violent past and act with greater restraint. The answer, of course, is that everything has changed. To the old "harsh realities" of international life has been added the immeasurably harsher new reality of the peril of extinction. To the old truth that all men are brothers has been added the inescapable new truth that not only on the moral but also on the physical plane the nation that practices aggression will itself die. This is the law of the doctrine of nuclear deterrence—the doctrine of "mutual assured destruction"—which "assures" the destruction of the society of the attacker. And it is also the law of the natural world, which, in its own version of deterrence, supplements the oneness of mankind with a oneness of nature, and guarantees that when the attack rises above a certain level the attacker will be engulfed in the general ruin of the global ecosphere. To the obligation to honor life is now added the sanction that if we fail in our obligation life will actually be taken away from us, individually and collectively. Each of us will die, and as we die we will see the world around us dying. Such imponderables as the sum of human life, the integrity of the terrestrial creation, and the meaning of time, of history, and of the development of life on earth, which were once left to contemplation and spiritual understanding, are now at stake in the political realm and demand a political response from every person. As political actors, we must, like the contemplatives before us, delve to the bottom of the world, and, Atlas-like, we must take the world on our shoulders.

The self-extinction of our species is not an act that anyone describes as sane or sensible; nevertheless, it is an act that, without quite admitting it to ourselves, we plan in certain circumstances to commit. Being impossible as a fully intentional act, unless the perpetrator has lost his mind, it can come about only through a kind of inadvertence—as a "side effect" of some action that we do intend, such as the defense of our nation, or the defense of liberty, or the defense of socialism, or the defense of whatever else we happen to believe in. To that extent, our failure to acknowledge the magnitude and significance of the peril is a necessary condition for doing the deed. We can do it only if we don't quite know what we're doing. If we did acknowledge the full dimensions of the peril, admitting clearly and without reservation that any use of nuclear arms is likely to touch off a holocaust in which the continuance of all human life would be put at risk, extinction would at that moment become not only "unthinkable" but also undoable. What is needed to make extinction possible, therefore, is some way of thinking about it that at least partly deflects our attention from what it is. And this way of thinking is supplied to us, unfortunately, by our political and military traditions, which, with the weight of almost all historical experience behind them, teach us that it is the way of the world for the earth to be divided up into independent, sovereign states, and for these states to employ war as the final arbiter for settling the disputes that arise among them. This arrangement of the political affairs of the world was not intentional. No one wrote a book proposing it; no parliament sat down to debate its merits and then voted it into existence. It was simply there, at the beginning of recorded history; and until the invention of nuclear weapons it remained there, with virtually no fundamental changes. Unplanned though this arrangement was, it had many remarkably durable features, and certain describable advantages and disadvantages; therefore, I shall refer to it as a "system"—the system of sovereignty. Perhaps the leading feature of this system, and certainly the most important one in the context of the nuclear predicament, was the apparently indissoluble connection between sovereignty and war. For without sovereignty, it appeared, peoples were not able to organize and launch wars against other peoples, and without war they were unable to preserve their sovereignty from destruction by armed enemies. (By "war" I here mean only international war, not revolutionary war, which I shall not discuss.) Indeed, the connection between sovereignty and war is almost a definitional one—a sovereign state being a state that enjoys the right and the power to go to war in defense or pursuit of its interests.

It was into the sovereignty system that nuclear bombs were born, as "weapons" for "war." As the years have passed, it has seemed less and less plausible that they have anything to do with war; they seem to break through its bounds. Nevertheless, they have gone on being fitted into military categories of thinking. One might say that they appeared in the world in a military disguise, for it has been traditional military thinking, itself an inseparable part of the traditional political thinking that belonged to the system of sovereignty, that has provided those intentional goals—namely, national interests—in the pursuit of which extinction may now be brought about unintentionally, or semi-intentionally, as a "side effect." The system of sovereignty is now to the earth and mankind what a polluting factory is to its local environment. The machine produces certain things that its users want—in this case, national sovereignty —and as an unhappy side effect extinguishes the species.

The ambivalence resulting from the attempt to force nuclear weapons into the preëxisting military and political system has led to a situation in which, in the words of Einstein—who was farseeing in his political as well as in his scientific thought—"the unleashed power of the atom has changed everything save our modes of thinking, and we thus drift toward unparalleled catastrophes." As Einstein's observation suggests, the nuclear revolution has gone quite far but has not been completed. The question we have to answer is whether the completion will be extinction or a global political revolution—whether the "babies" that the scientists at Alamogordo brought forth will put an end to us or we will put an end to them. For it is not only our thoughts but also our actions and our institutions—our global political arrangements in their entirety—that we have failed to change. We live with one foot in each of two worlds. As scientists and technicians, we live in the nuclear world, in which whether we choose to acknowledge the fact or not, we possess instruments of violence that make it possible for us to extinguish ourselves as a species. But as citizens and statesmen we go on living in the pre-nuclear world, as though extinction were not possible and sovereign nations could still employ the instruments of violence as instruments of policy—as "a continuation of politics by other means," in the famous phrase of Karl von Clausewitz, the great philosopher of war. In effect, we try to make do with a Newtonian politics in an Einsteinian world. The combination is the source of our immediate peril. For governments, still acting within a system of independent nation-states, and formally representing no one but the people of their separate, sovereign nations, are driven to try to defend merely national interests with means of destruction that threaten not only international but intergenerational and planetary doom. In our present-day world, in the councils where the decisions are made there is no one to speak for man and for the earth, although both are threatened with annihilation.

The peril that the scientists have brought into our lives stems from hitherto unknown properties of the physical universe, but it is not an external, self-propelled peril—as though they had discovered that forces in the interior of the earth were one day going to blow it up, or that a huge asteroid was one day going to collide with it. Rather, the peril comes from our own actions—from within us—and if we had never sought to harm one another the energy latent in matter would have remained locked up there, without posing any threat to anybody. Thus, the peril of extinction by nuclear arms is doubly ours: first, because we have it in our power to prevent the catastrophe, and, second, because the catastrophe cannot occur unless, by pursuing our political aims through violence, we bring it about. Since military action is the one activity through which we deliberately threaten to employ our new mastery over nature to destroy ourselves, nothing could be more crucial to an understanding of the practical dimensions of the nuclear predicament than a precise understanding of what nuclear weapons have done to war, and, through war, to the system of sovereignty of which war has traditionally been an indispensable part. All war is violent, but not all violence is war. War is a violent means employed by a nation to achieve an end, and, like all mere means, is subject to Aristotle's rule "The means to the end are not unlimited, for the end itself sets the limit in each case." The possible ends of war are as varied as the desires and hopes of men, having ranged from the recovery of a single beautiful woman from captivity to world conquest, but every one of them would be annihilated in a nuclear holocaust. War is destructive, but it is also a human phenomenon—complex, carefully wrought, and, in its way, fragile and delicate, like its maker—but nuclear weapons, if they were ever used in large numbers, would simply blow war up, just as they would blow up everything else that is human.

One of the respects in which war is unique among the uses to which mankind's steadily increasing technical skills have been put is that in war no benefit is obtained and no aim achieved unless the powers involved exert themselves to the limit, or near-limit, of their strength. In the words of Clausewitz: "War is an act of violence pushed to its utmost bounds; as one side dictates to the other, there arises a sort of reciprocal action which logically must lead to an extreme." For only at the extremes are victory and defeat—the results of war—brought about. Even when victory and defeat are not absolute, the terms of the disengagement are determined by the nearness of one side to defeat. In this case, the antagonists, like chess players near the end of the game, see the inevitable outcome and spare themselves the trouble of actually going through the final moves. As Clausewitz writes, "everything is subject to a supreme law: which is the *decision by arms*." Therefore, "all action . . . takes place on the supposition that if the solution by force of arms which lies at its foundation should be realized, it will be a favorable one." For "the decision by arms is, for all operations, great and small, what cash payment is in bill transactions," and "however remote from each other these relations, however seldom the realization may take place, still it can never entirely fail to occur." Nuclear arms ruin war by making the decision by arms impossible. The decision by arms can occur only when the strength of one side or the other is exhausted, or when its exhaustion is approached. But in nuclear "war" no one's strength fails until *both* sides have been annihilated. There cannot be a victor without a vanquished, the collapse of whose military efforts signals the end of the hostilities, permitting the victor to collect his spoils. But when both adversaries have nuclear arms that moment of collapse never comes, and the military forces—the missiles—of both countries go on "fighting" after the countries themselves have disappeared. From the point of view of a power contemplating war in the pre-nuclear world, war appeared to depend on the possession of great strength, since the side that possessed the greater strength had the better chance of being victorious. But when war is seen from the point of view of the nuclear world it becomes clear that as an institution—as the mechanism with which sovereign states settled their disputes—war depended, above all, on weakness: the weakness of the defeated party, whose collapse made the decision by arms (the whole purpose of war) possible. And this weakness, in turn, depended on the presence of certain technical limitations on the ability of mankind in general to avail itself of natural forces for destructive purposes. When science made the energy in mass available to man, the crucial limits were removed, for everybody, forever, and the exhaustion of the defeated party—and so the triumph of the victor—was rendered impossible. War itself has thus proved to be a casualty of the tremendous means that were put at its disposal by science. We are now in a position to see that helplessness has always been the specific product of war, and weakness its essential ingredient. War has never been anything but unilateral disarmament—the disarmament of one side by the other. But now, before the exhaustion of either party can be reached, everyone will be dead, and all human aims— the aims pursued in the "war" and all others—will have been nullified. In a nuclear conflict between the United States and the Soviet Union—the holocaust—not only the adversaries but also the world's bystanders will vanish. In this "war," instead of one side winning and the other losing, it is as though all human beings lost and all the weapons won. Clausewitz writes, "War can never be separated from political intercourse, and if, in the consideration of the matter, this is done in any way, all the threads of the different relations are, to a certain extent, broken, and we have before us a senseless thing without an object." War can, for example, decline into mere looting or banditry or some other form of aimless violence. But, of all the "senseless things" that can ever occur when war's violence (its means) is severed from its political purposes (its ends), a nuclear holocaust is the most senseless. To call this senseless thing "war" is, in fact, simply a misnomer, and to go on speaking of "nuclear war," and the like, can only mislead and confuse us. Thus, while the Soviet Union and the United States are perfectly free to fire their thousands of nuclear weapons at one another, the result would not be war, for no end could be served by it. It would be comprehensive destruction—a "senseless thing." With the invention of nuclear weapons, it became impossible for violence to be fashioned into war, or to achieve what war used to achieve. Violence can no longer break down the opposition of the adversary; it can no longer produce victory and defeat; it can no longer attain its ends. It can no longer be war.

It must be emphasized that what nuclear weapons have ruined is not only "nuclear war" but all war (that is, all war between nuclear powers). "Conventional war," which in fact encompasses everything that deserves to be called war, is ruined because as long as nuclear weapons are held in reserve by the combatants, in accordance with the supposedly agreed-upon rules of some "limited war," the hostilities have not run to that extreme of violence at which the essential helplessness of one side or the other has been produced. If a decision were to be reached while the "defeated" party held potentially decisive means of violence in its possession, then that decision would be not "by arms" but by something else. We have to imagine that this power would accept its defeat while knowing that the use of its bombs would reverse it. A current example illustrates how little willingness there is among nuclear powers to accept such an outcome. For some time, it has been widely believed that the Soviet Union enjoys a preponderance in conventional forces over the NATO powers in Europe, and the United States has reserved for itself the right to resort to nuclear weapons in Europe rather than accept a conventional defeat there. Thus, the United States has already publicly discarded the notion of abiding by any rules of "limited war" if those rules should prove to mean a defeat for the United States. And there is certainly very little reason to suppose that the Soviet Union is any more willing to volunteer for defeat than the United States. That being the likely state of things, there seems little chance that a conventional war between nuclear powers could stay limited. And this means that a conventional war between nuclear powers must not even be begun, since it threatens the same holocaust that the limited use of nuclear weapons threatens. As a practical matter, this rule has up to now been followed by the statesmen of the nuclear world. Disregarding theoretical treatises on the possibility of "limited war" between nuclear powers, including "limited nuclear war," they have held back from any war; thus, in our thirty-six years of experience with nuclear weapons no two nuclear powers have ever entered into even conventional hostilities. The same cannot be said, of course, of hostilities between nuclear powers and non-nuclear powers, such as the Vietnam War or the Soviet-Afghanistan war. These remain possible—although, for reasons that I shall not go into here, they are not, it would seem, profitable.

It is often said that nuclear arms have made war obsolete, but this is a misunderstanding. Obsolescence occurs when a means to some end is superseded by a new and presumably better means—as when it was discovered that vehicles powered by internal-combustion engines were more efficient than vehicles pulled by horses at transporting people and goods from one place to another. But war has not been superseded by some better means to its end, which is to serve as the final arbiter of disputes among sovereign states. On the contrary, war has gone out of existence without leaving behind any means at all—whether superior or inferior—to that end. The more than three decades of jittery peace between the nuclear super-powers which the world has experienced since the invention of nuclear weapons is almost certainly the result of this lack. There is thus no need to "abolish war" among the nuclear powers; it is already gone. The choices don't include war any longer. They consist now of peace, on the one hand, and annihilation, on the other. And annihilation—or "assured destruction"—is as far from being war as peace is, and the sooner we recognize this the sooner we will be able to save our species from self-extermination.

When nuclear weapons were invented, it was as though a battlefield on which two armies had been fighting for as long as anyone could remember had suddenly been bisected in an earthquake by a huge chasm, so that if the armies tried to rush at one another in order to engage in battle they would plunge into this chasm instead, pulling their nations in with them. And it was as though, further, the generals of these armies, having spent their lifetimes fighting this war and hearing about their forebears' exploits in it, periodically forgot about the existence of the chasm, and therefore from time to time sent their armies into the field—only to discover that the chasm was still there.

The disabling of war is in itself something to be welcomed (although not if the price is extinction, or even the perpetual threat of extinction), but the system of sovereignty was bereft by it. The ultimate purpose of military forces in the system of sovereignty—the defense of one's nation by combating and defeating the attacking forces of the enemy—was nullified in a stroke, for there could be no defense against nuclear weapons. The "final arbiter" had been taken away, and nations, now living in terror of their annihilation but also terrified of being taken over by their enemies, were left to figure out some new means of securing their survival and of pursuing their aims in the world. In effect, the system of sovereignty faced a breakdown. The world now had to decide whether to reject sovereignty and "war" (which, suddenly, no longer was war) and institute global political arrangements that would arbitrate international disputes or to try to shore up sovereignty with the use or deployment of nuclear weapons. Lord Russell and a few other people favored the first course, but a larger number favored the second. Still others favored the first course in the abstract but turned out to be unwilling in practical terms to make the radical political changes that were called for. It was easy to say, as many did, that in a nuclear world mankind had to live in peace or perish; it was a far different matter to make actual political sacrifices that would permit the nuclear peril to be lifted. The present-day United Nations is the empty husk of those irresolute good intentions. But, whatever people said, or ineffectually hoped for, the world in fact chose the course of attempting to refashion the system of sovereignty to accommodate nuclear weapons.

The doctrine that resulted was the doctrine of nuclear deterrence: the forbidding political and intellectual product of our attempt to live simultaneously in the two worlds—the nuclear, scientific world and the pre-nuclear military and political one. Since the doctrine is the means by which the world now endeavors to escape its doom from moment to moment, it deserves our most searching examination. In its intellectual, emotional, and moral tone as well as in its content, the doctrine was something new. Not surprisingly, the people in charge of framing this doctrine and putting it into practice seem at times to suffer from double vision, as though at some moments they recognized that we live in a nuclear world, in which the life of the species is at stake, but at other times forgot this, and believed that wars could still be fought without the risk of self-extermination. It is a symptom of the schism between what Einstein called our "thinking" and the reality around us that when our strategists set out to think their "unthinkable" thoughts they feel obliged to quite deliberately leave the rest of their human equipment—their feelings, their moral sense, their humanity—behind. For the requirements of strategy in its present form force them to plan actions that from any recognizable moral point of view are indefensible. One strategic thinker, in a striking inversion of the usual understanding of ethical obligation, has said that an "iron will" is required if one is to recommend the slaughter of hundreds of millions of people in a nuclear attack—a point of view that is uncomfortably close to that of Heinrich Himmler, who told the commanders of the SS that in order to carry out the extermination of the Jews they had to be "superhumanly inhuman." In both statements, it is not obedience to our moral feelings but resistance to those feelings that is presented as our obligation, as though moral feeling were a siren call that it would be weak to give in to and that it is our duty to resist. Once the "strategic necessity" of planning the deaths of hundreds of millions of people is accepted, we begin to live in a world in which morality and action inhabit two separate, closed realms. All strategic sense becomes moral nonsense, and vice versa, and we are left with the choice of seeming to be either strategic or moral idiots. The feeling of unreality that present strategic thinking arouses is compounded by the fact, itself a unique feature of life in the nuclear world, that the strategist must incessantly plan for future attacks and counterattacks whose prevention is supposedly the planning's whole purpose. Strategic thinking thus refers to a reality that is supposed never to come into existence. Therefore, not only is morality deliberately divorced from "thinking" but planning is divorced from action. The result of all these novel mental operations is a fantastic intellectual construct— the body of strategic theory built up over more than thirty years— in which ratiocination, unrestrained either by moral feelings or by facts, has been permitted to run wild in a riot of pure theory. On this "thinking" almost no bounds are set, and the slaughter of whole populations and the extinction of man become all too "thinkable." But the divorce of thought from feeling, of strategy from morality, and of planning from action are all only manifestations of the more fundamental divorce between the pre-nuclear basis of our whole approach to political life and the reality of our nuclear world. The reason we cannot bear emotionally and morally to face the actions that we "think" about and plan and the reason the aim of all our strategic planning must be to prevent the actions we are planning to take are the same: the actions we have in mind, which risk the termination of our species, are irredeemably senseless. And as long as we continue to accept the underlying assumptions of this strategy we will be condemned to go on sketching "scenarios" for futures that must never be, while neglecting all planning for futures that *can* be, and that would permit us to be.

The central proposition of the deterrence doctrine—the piece of logic on which the world theoretically depends to see the sun rise tomorrow—is that a nuclear holocaust can best be prevented if each nuclear power, or bloc of powers, holds in readiness a nuclear force with which it "credibly" threatens to destroy the entire society of any attacker, even after suffering the worst possible "first strike" that the attacker can launch. Robert McNamara, who served as Secretary of Defense for seven years under Presidents Kennedy and Johnson, defined the policy, in his book "The Essence of Security," published in 1968, in the following terms: "Assured destruction is the very essence of the whole deterrence concept. We must possess an actual assured-destruction capability, and that capability also must be credible. The point is that a potential aggressor must believe that our assured-destruction capability is in fact actual, and that our will to use it in retaliation to an attack is in fact unwavering." Thus, deterrence "means the certainty of suicide to the aggressor, not merely to his military forces, but to his society as a whole." Let us picture what is going on here. There are two possible eventualities: success of the strategy or its failure. If it succeeds, both sides are frozen into inaction by fear of retaliation by the other side. If it fails, one side annihilates the other, and then the leaders of the second side annihilate the "society as a whole" of the attacker, and the earth as a whole suffers the consequences of a full-scale holocaust, which might include the extinction of man. In point of fact, neither the United States nor the Soviet Union has ever adopted the "mutual-assured-destruction" doctrine in pure form; other aims, such as attempting to reduce the damage of the adversary's nuclear attack and increasing the capacity for destroying the nuclear forces of the adversary, have been mixed in. Nevertheless, underlying these deviations the concept of deterring a first strike by preserving the capacity for a devastating second strike has remained constant. The strategists of deterrence have addressed the chief issue in any sane policy in a nuclear-armed world—the issue of survival—and have come up with this answer: Salvation from extinction by nuclear weapons is to be found in the nuclear weapons themselves. The possession of nuclear weapons by the great powers, it is believed, will prevent the use of nuclear weapons by those same powers. Or, to put it more accurately, the threat of their use by those powers will prevent their use. Or, in the words of Bernard Brodie, a pioneer in nuclear strategy, in "The Absolute Weapon: Atomic Power and World Order," a book published in 1946: "Thus far, the chief purpose of our military establishment has been to win wars. From now on its chief purpose must be to avert them. It can have almost no other useful purpose." Or, in the classic, broad formulation of Winston Churchill, in a speech to the House of Commons in 1955: "Safety will be the sturdy child of terror, and survival the twin brother of annihilation."

This doctrine, in its detailed as well as its more general formulations, is diagrammatic of the world's failure to come to terms with the nuclear predicament. In it, two irreconcilable purposes clash. The first purpose is to permit the survival of the species, and this is expressed in the doctrine's aim of frightening everybody into holding back from using nuclear weapons at all; the second purpose is to serve national ends, and this is expressed in the doctrine's permitting the defense of one's nation and its interests by threatening to use nuclear weapons. The strategists are pleased to call this clash of two opposing purposes in one doctrine a paradox, but in actuality it is a contradiction. We cannot both threaten ourselves with something and hope to avoid that same thing by making the threat—both intend to do something and intend not to do it. The head-on contradiction between these aims has set up a crosscurrent of tension within the policies of each superpower. The "safety" that Churchill mentions may be emphasized at one moment, and at the next moment it is the "terror" that comes to the fore. And since the deterrence doctrine pairs the safety and the terror, and makes the former depend on the latter, the world is never quite sure from day to day which one is in the ascendant—if, indeed, the distinction can be maintained in the first place. All that the world can know for certain is that at any moment the fireballs may arrive. I have said that we do not have two earths, one to blow up experimentally and the other to live on; nor do we have two souls, one for reacting to daily life and the other for reacting to the peril to all life. But neither do we have two wills, one with which we can intend to destroy our species and the other with which we can intend to save ourselves. Ultimately, we must all live together with one soul and one will on our one earth.

For all that, the adoption of the deterrence doctrine represented a partial recognition that the traditional military doctrine had become an anachronism—a doctrine that was suited well enough to the pre-nuclear world but lost all application and relevance when the first nuclear bomb flashed over the New Mexico desert. In assessing the advance made by deterrence, we must acknowledge how radically it departed from traditional military doctrine. Traditional military doctrine and nuclear doctrine are based on wholly different factual circumstances, each set of which corresponds to the technical realities of its period. Traditional military doctrine began, as I have suggested, with the premise that the amounts of force available to the belligerents were small enough to permit one side or the other to exhaust itself before both sides were annihilated. Nuclear doctrine, on the other hand, begins with the premise that the amounts of force are so great that both sides, and perhaps all mankind, will be annihilated before either side exhausts its forces. Like postulates in geometry, these two premises determine the entire systems of thought that follow, and no discussion of military strategy can make any sense unless one clearly specifies which premise one is starting from. But, as I pointed out at some length at the outset of these observations, there is no longer room for doubt that in our time the second premise is the correct one.

The chief virtue of the doctrine of nuclear deterrence is that it begins by accepting this basic fact of life in the nuclear world, and does so not only on the rhetorical plane but on the practical plane of strategic planning. Hence, it acknowledges that victory can no longer be obtained in a contest between two well-armed nuclear powers, such as the United States and the Soviet Union. Senator Barry Goldwater wrote a book, published in 1962, whose title was "Why Not Victory?" To this question the strategists of deterrence have a decisive answer: Because in the present-day, nuclear world "victory" is oblivion. From this recognition flows the conclusion, arrived at by Brodie in 1946, that the sole purpose of possessing nuclear strategic arms is not to win war but to prevent it. The adoption of the aim of preventing rather than winning war requires the adoption of other policies that fly in the face of military tradition. One is abandonment of the military defense of one's nation—of what used to be at the center of all military planning and was the most hallowed justification of the military calling. The policy of deterrence does not contemplate doing anything in defense of the homeland; it only promises that if the homeland is annihilated the aggressor's homeland will be annihilated, too. In fact, the policy goes further than this: it positively requires that each side leave its population open to attack, and make no serious effort to protect it. This requirement follows from the basic logic of deterrence, which is that safety is "the sturdy child of terror." According to this logic, the safety can be only as great as the terror is, and the terror therefore has to be kept relentless. If it were to be diminished—by, for example, building bomb shelters that protected some significant part of the population—then safety would be diminished, too, because the protected side might be tempted to launch a holocaust, in the belief that it could "win" the hostilities. That is why in nuclear strategy "destruction" must, perversely, be "assured," as though our aim were to destroy, and not to save, mankind.

In strategic terms, the requirement that the terror be perfected, and never allowed to deteriorate toward safety, translates into the requirement that the retaliatory force of both sides be guaranteed—first, by making sure that the retaliatory weapons cannot be destroyed in a first strike, and, second, by making sure that the society of the attacking power *can* be destroyed in the second strike. And since in this upside-down scheme of things the two sides will suffer equally no matter which one opens the hostilities, each side actually has an interest in maintaining its adversary's retaliatory forces as well as its own. For the most dangerous of all the configurations of forces is that in which one side appears to have the ability to destroy the nuclear forces of the other in a first strike. Then not only is the stronger side theoretically tempted to launch hostilities but—what is probably far more dangerous—the other side, fearful of completely losing its forces, might, in a crisis, feel compelled to launch the first strike itself. If on either side the population becomes relatively safe from attack or the retaliatory strike becomes vulnerable to attack, a temptation to launch a first strike is created, and "stability"—the leading virtue of any nuclear balance of power —is lost. As Thomas Schelling, the economist and noted nuclear theorist, has put it, in "The Strategy of Conflict," a book published in 1960, once instability is introduced on either side, both sides may reason as follows: "He, thinking I was about to kill him in self-defense, was about to kill me in self-defense, so I had to kill him in self-defense." Under deterrence, military "superiority" is therefore as dangerous to the side that possesses it as it is to the side that is supposedly threatened by it. (According to this logic, the United States should have heaved a sigh of relief when the Soviet Union reached nuclear parity with it, for then stability was achieved.) All these conclusions follow from the deterrence doctrine, yet they run so consistently counter to the far simpler, more familiar, and emotionally more comprehensible logic of traditional military thinking —not to mention instinct and plain common sense, which rebel against any such notion as "assuring" our own annihilation—that we should not be surprised when we find that the deterrence doctrine is constantly under challenge from traditional doctrine, no matter how glaringly at odds with the facts traditional doctrine may be.

The hard-won gains of deterrence, such as they are, are repeatedly threatened by a recrudescence of the old desire for victory, for national defense in the old sense, and for military superiority, even though every one of these goals not only would add nothing to our security but, if it should be pursued far enough, would undermine the precarious safety that the deterrence doctrine tries to provide.

If the virtue of the deterrence policy lies in its acceptance of the basic fact of life in the nuclear world—that a holocaust will bring annihilation to both sides, and possibly the extinction of man as well—its defect lies in the strategic construct that it erects on the foundation of that fact. For if we try to guarantee our safety by threatening ourselves with doom, then we have to mean the threat; but if we mean it, then we are actually planning to do, in some circumstance or other, that which we categorically must never do and are supposedly trying to prevent—namely, extinguish ourselves. This is the circularity at the core of the nuclear-deterrence doctrine; we seek to avoid our self-extinction by threatening to perform the act. According to this logic, it is almost as though if we stopped threatening ourselves with extinction, then extinction would occur. Brodie's formula can be reversed: if the aim of having nuclear forces is to avert annihilation (misnamed "war" by him), then we must cling for our lives to those same forces. Churchill's dictum can be reversed, too: If safety is the sturdy child of terror, then terror is equally the sturdy child of safety. But who is to guarantee which of the children will be born? And if survival is the twin brother of annihilation, then we must cultivate annihilation. But then we may *get* annihilation. By growing to actually rely on terror, we do more than tolerate its presence in our world: we place our trust in it. And while this is not quite to "love the bomb," as the saying goes, it decidedly is to place our faith in it, and to give it an all-important position in the very heart of our affairs. Under this doctrine, instead of getting rid of the bomb we build it ever more deeply into our lives.

The logical fault line in the doctrine runs straight through the center of its main strategic tenet—the proposition that safety is achieved by assuring that any nuclear aggressor will be annihilated in a retaliatory strike. For while the doctrine relies for its success on a nuclear-armed victim's resolve to launch the annihilating second strike, it can offer no sensible or sane justification for launching it in the event. In pre-nuclear military strategy, the deterrent effect of force was a useful by-product of the ability and willingness to wage and win wars. Deterrence was the shadow cast by force, or, in Clausewitz's metaphor, the credit that flowed from the ability to make the cash payment of the favorable decision by arms. The logic of pre-nuclear deterrence escaped circularity by each side's being frankly ready to wage war and try for victory if deterrence failed. Nuclear deterrence, however, supposedly aims solely at forestalling any use of force by either side, and has given up at the outset on a favorable decision by arms. The question, then, is: Of what object is nuclear deterrence the shadow? Of what cash payment is it the credit? The theoretical answer, of course, is: The retaliatory strike. Yet since in nuclear-deterrence theory the whole purpose of having a retaliatory capacity is to deter a first strike, one must ask what reason would remain to launch the retaliation once the first strike had actually arrived. Nuclear deterrence requires one to prepare for armed conflict not in order to "win" it if it breaks out but in order to prevent it from breaking out in the first place. But if armed conflict breaks out anyway, what does one do with one's forces then? In pre-nuclear times, the answer would have required no second thought: it would have been to strive for the decision by arms—for victory. Yet nuclear deterrence begins by assuming, correctly, that victory is impossible. Thus, the logic of the deterrence strategy is dissolved by the very event—the first strike—that it is meant to prevent. Once the action begins, the whole doctrine is self-cancelling. In sum, the doctrine is based on a monumental logical mistake: one cannot credibly deter a first strike with a second strike whose *raison d'être* dissolves the moment the first strike arrives. It follows that, as far as deterrence theory is concerned, there is no reason for either side not to launch a first strike.

What seems to be needed to repair the doctrine is a motive for retaliation—one that is not supplied by the doctrine itself and that lies outside its premises—but the only candidates are those belonging to traditional military doctrine; namely, some variation of victory. The adherents of nuclear victory—whatever that would be—have on occasion noted the logical fallacy on which deterrence is based, and stepped forward to propose their solution: a "nuclear-war-fighting" capacity. Thus, the answer they give to the question of what to do after the first strike arrives is: Fight and "win" a "nuclear war." But victory does not suddenly become possible simply because it offers a solution to the logical contradiction on which the mutual-assured-destruction doctrine rests. The facts remain obdurately what they are: an attack of several thousand megatons will annihilate any country on earth many times over, no matter what line of argument the strategists pursue; and a "nuclear exchange" will, if it is on a large scale, threaten the life of man. Indeed, if victory were really possible there would have been no need for a deterrence strategy to begin with, and traditional military strategy would have needed no revision. This "solution" is therefore worse than the error it sets out to remedy. It resolves the contradiction in the deterrence doctrine by denying the tremendous new reality that the doctrine was framed to deal with, and that all of us now have to deal with on virtually every level of our existence. Consequently, this "solution" could lead us to commit the ultimate folly of exterminating ourselves without even knowing what we were doing. Aiming at "victory," we would wind up extinct.

In the last analysis, there can be no credible threat without credible use—no shadow without an object, no credit without cash payment. But since use is the thing above all else that we don't want, because it means the end of all of us, we are naturally at a loss to find any rationale for it. To grasp the reality of the contradiction, we have only to picture the circumstances of leaders whose country has just been annihilated in a first strike. Now their country is on its way to becoming a radioactive desert, but the retaliatory nuclear force survives in its silos, bombers, and submarines. These leaders of nobody, living in underground shelters or in "doomsday" planes that could not land, would possess the means of national defense but no nation to defend. What rational purpose could they have in launching the retaliatory strike? Since there was no longer a nation, "national security" could not be the purpose. Nor could defense of other peoples be the purpose, since the retaliatory strike might be the action that would finally break the back of the ecosphere and extinguish the species. In these circumstances, it seems to me, it is really an open question whether the leaders would decide to retaliate or not.

This conclusion is not one that is likely to be breathed aloud by anyone in or near power in either the Soviet Union or the United States. Since deterrence depends fully as much on one's adversary's perception of one's "unwavering" will to retaliate as on one's technical ability to do it, an acknowledgment that retaliation is senseless would in a way amount to unilateral disarmament by verbal means. The doctrine of nuclear deterrence thus deters debate about itself, and this incidental "deterrence" may have been no small factor in the sharp limits placed on the definition of "respectable," so-called "realistic" thinking about nuclear strategy. Nevertheless, the contradiction at the heart of the doctrine has occasioned considerable indirect intellectual twisting and turning among the nuclear theorists, and the resulting recommendations lead one into byways of the maze of strategic theory which stand out as bizarre and frightening even for the catalogues of nuclear strategic "options." The commonest solution to the problem of the missing motive for retaliation is to suggest that the policymakers try to cultivate an appearance of unreason, for if one is insane one doesn't need to supply any motive for retaliating—one might do it simply out of madness. The nuclear theorist Herman Kahn, for example, suggests that "it might best deter the attack" by an "*appearance* of irrationally inexorable commitment." Kahn first wonders whether it might not be enough merely to "pretend" to be irrationally committed, but he concludes that a pretense of unreason is not reliable, and that one must "*really intend to do it.*" The prescription, then, which he calls the policy of "the rationality of irrationality," is to coolly resolve to be crazy. How statesmen are to go about this, Kahn does not say. Another solution, quite closely related, is to try to create either the appearance or the reality of being out of control. Uncontrol, like insanity, removes the need for a rational motive in retaliating, this time by arranging for the retaliation to occur "by accident." Thomas Schelling, addressing the general question "How can one commit himself in advance to an act that he would in fact prefer not to carry out in the event?," suggests the tactic either of pretending that the crucial decisions will be in part up to "chance" or of actually arranging things so that this is true, thus adding to Kahn's concept of reasoned insanity the planned accident. With this strategy in effect, he writes, "the brink is not . . . the sharp edge of a cliff, where one can stand firmly, look down, and decide whether or not to plunge." Rather, "the brink is a curved slope that one can stand on with some risk of slipping." Therefore, "brink-manship involves getting onto the slope where one may fall in spite of his own best efforts to save himself, dragging his adversary with him." That these astonishing remedies are no less consequential in the real world than the doctrinal illogicality they try to remedy is testified to by, among other things, a statement in the memoirs of President Richard Nixon's chief of staff H. R. Haldeman that Nixon believed in the "Madman Theory" of the Presidency, according to which the nation's foes would bow to the President's will if they believed that he had taken leave of his senses and was ready to risk a holocaust in order to secure some limited national gain. Whether or not Nixon had read the writings of Kahn and Schelling, he was following their counsel to the letter.

The recommendation of these tactics naturally raises the questions of whether, with the life of our species at stake, we want our nuclear decision-makers to be cultivating irrationality and uncontrol, and whether a slippery slope over the nuclear abyss is where we all want to be. But these questions, which I think must be answered with a resounding "no," come up only as a consequence of our reliance on "terror" to provide "safety," and on the threat of "annihilation" to provide "survival." For it is in an effort to strengthen and shore up the terror and make annihilation more certain that the strategists and statesmen are forced into these appalling postures. Their problem is to find a way of appearing "inexorably" resolved to do things that can never make any sense or ever be justified by any moral code, and irrationality and uncontrol fulfill the requirements for the very reason that they represent the abandonment of morality and sense. Adopted as policy, they lend credibility to actions that are—conveniently for strategic purposes, if not for the safety of mankind—immoral and insane.

It must be added that there is another extreme solution, which would entirely remove the defect in the doctrine of nuclear deterrence. This solution, described (but not recommended) by Kahn, would be to construct a literal doomsday machine, which would blow up the whole world as soon as an adversary engaged in some activity that had previously been defined as "unacceptable" by the machine's possessor. Kahn, who estimated in 1960 that a doomsday machine might be built for as little as ten billion dollars, points out that the machine would eliminate any doubt concerning the retaliatory strike by making it fully automatic. The retaliatory strike would still be senseless, but this senselessness would no longer cloud its "credibility," since the action would have been predetermined: the foundation would have been provided for a fully consistent policy of nuclear deterrence, under which nations would be deterred from launching nuclear attacks by the prearranged certainty that their own countries would perish in the ensuing global annihilation. But Kahn is also quick to point out a disadvantage of the doomsday machine which makes its construction immediately repugnant and intolerable to anyone who thinks about it: once it is in place, "there is no chance of human intervention, control, and final decision." And behind this objection, we may add, is an even simpler and more basic one: the chief reason we don't want a doomsday machine is that we don't want doom—not in any circumstances. Doom doesn't become any more acceptable because it comes about as someone's "final decision." And, of course, even though no enemy attack has been launched, in a moment of computer confusion the doomsday machine might make its own "final decision" to go off.

Because deterrence, on which we all now rely for whatever safety we have, is a psychological strategy, which aims at terrorizing the adversary into holding back from attacking us, it might seem that the discovery in one or the other command center of the logical absurdity of the policy would lead to the breakdown of the system—or, at least, to the abandonment of the doctrine. That this has not occurred is an indication that, even in the abstruse realm of nuclear doctrine, theory and practice, thought and reality are still different. In the real world, there are several stand-ins for the missing motive for the crucial retaliatory strike. The first stand-in is revenge, which, even though retaliation is not a rational action, might cause it to be carried out anyway. According to the emotional logic of revenge, the living act to right the wrong inflicted on the unjustly slain, who, being dead, cannot themselves realign the unbalanced scales of justice. Revenge is neither sensible nor constructive—especially not in a nuclear holocaust—but it is human, and the possibility that it would well up in the breasts of the leaders of a country that has just been effaced from the earth can by no means be ruled out by an aggressor; he has to consider that, even without any irrationality of the planned sort, a "rational" response to a nuclear attack can hardly be counted on. The second, and perhaps more important, stand-in for the missing motive is the irreducible unpredictability of events once the nuclear threshold is crossed. At this verge, with the survival of the species at stake, the human mind falters. The leaders of the nuclear powers have no choice, as they stare into McNamara's "vast unknown," but to assume that the stakes are total. Certainly there is no need for anyone to strain to appear irrational, as Kahn suggests, or out of control, as Schelling suggests: a world that has embarked on a holocaust is in its nature irrational and out of control.

Our experience of nuclear crises leads us to believe that when the leaders of nuclear powers are forced to contemplate the reality of a holocaust at close quarters they have looked on it in this light. That is, they have assumed that if limited nuclear war, or even conventional war between the superpowers, breaks out, a holocaust is the likely result. Michael Mandelbaum, in his history of nuclear strategy and experience, "The Nuclear Question," published in 1979, observes that when the Soviet and American leaders confronted one another in the Cuban missile crisis they discovered that the fearful nature of a holocaust, which during the days of the crisis partly emerged from abstraction and unreality to become almost palpable in people's emotions, strongly deterred them from inaugurating hostilities at no matter how minor a level. Brought face to face with the beast, both sides realized that "there was no way to fight a nuclear war." Thus, "in striving to avoid having to fight a nuclear war they took great care not to start a war of any kind, which they feared would become nuclear." This lesson of experience offered some complementary lessons. One was that although no one had decided to establish a doomsday machine, people had to act as though one were in place. They had to assume that one misstep could be the misstep that ended the world. The notion that there was a middle ground of "tactical" nuclear hostilities of a limited kind, or even of conventional hostilities, disappeared under the awful pressure of the crisis. The doorway to the "vast unknown" seemed always right at hand, and all the scenarios of "limited war" and the like tended to crumble.

A final "deterrent," which, although fallible, is both rational and human, but which goes unmentioned in deterrence theory, is the humanity of the leaders of the nuclear powers. History is crowded with ruthless, berserk actions, yet there are none that have attained the horror and insanity of a nuclear holocaust, and very few that have gone as far as the worst crime of which we do have experience—genocide. I believe that without indulging in wishful thinking we can grant that the present leaders of both the Soviet Union and the United States are considerably deterred from launching a nuclear holocaust by sheer aversion to the unspeakable act itself.

The inconsistencies that bedevil the doctrine of nuclear deterrence —the reliance upon a second strike that has no explicable purpose, the need to cultivate irrationality and uncontrol to remedy this and other defects, the reliance upon the logic of the doomsday machine combined with the failure to carry the logic through to its conclusion, and many others that might be mentioned—are all consequences of the larger, inherent inconsistency of reliance upon preparations for annihilation to prevent annihilation. The result of relying on this contradictory system for our survival is our present half-numb, half-terror-stricken world, in which growing mountains of nuclear weapons are supposed to improve the world's safety, and in which we do not know from one moment to the next whether we will survive or be exploded back into our original atoms. Reflecting on the frightful effects of this arrangement—effects that, even without a holocaust, corrupt our lives—we are led to wonder why it should be necessary to seek safety in terror, survival in annihilation, existence in nothingness, and to wonder why we shouldn't resort to the more straightforward measure of disarmament: of seeking survival by banning the instruments of death.

Even to put this question, however, is to reveal that in Churchill's and Brodie's formulations, which have been echoed with great regularity, in many versions, by the statesmen who have been in charge of the world's nuclear arsenals (President Kennedy, for example, said in his Inaugural Address, "Only when our arms are certain beyond doubt can we be certain beyond doubt that they will never be used"), an essential part of the truth is being left out. The missing element is the political aim of strategy. For the fact is that the nuclear powers do *not*, as the statesmen so often proclaim, possess nuclear weapons with the sole aim of preventing their use and so keeping the peace; they possess them also to defend national interests and aspirations—indeed, to perpetuate the whole system of sovereign states. But now, instead of relying on war for this enforcement, as nations did in pre-nuclear times, they rely on the threat of extinction. The proposition based on the aim of survival is that one prepares for extinction only in order to secure survival; however, the aim of holding on to the system of sovereignty introduces a much less reassuring, much less frequently voiced, and much less defensible proposition, which is that one prepares for extinction in order to protect national interests. This threat not only makes no sense in its own terms, since actual execution of the threat would eradicate any national interest in whose pursuit the hostilities were launched, but also undercuts the policy of deterrence, by continually propelling nations to threaten to bring about the holocaust whose avoidance is supposedly the policy's main justification. For while the aim of survival causes statesmen to declare regularly that no purpose could ever be served by a holocaust, and that the aim of nuclear policy can only be to prevent such insanity, the pursuit of national objectives forces them to declare in the next breath that they are unwaveringly resolved to perpetrate exactly this unjustifiable and insane action if some nation threatens a "vital interest" of theirs.

Thus, the peril of extinction is the price that the world pays not for "safety" or "survival" but for its insistence on continuing to divide itself up into sovereign nations. Without this insistence, there would be no need to threaten annihilation in order to escape annihilation, and the world could escape annihilation by disarming, as Russell, Einstein, and others recommended as early as the mid-nineteen-forties. Churchill's aphorism thus needs revision to read, "National sovereignty will be the sturdy child of terror and the twin brother of annihilation." This is less pithy and less palatable than the original, but it is the truth about our present nuclear arrangements. Or, to be exact, and to give those arrangements their due, the statement should read, "Safety will be the sturdy child of terror, and survival the twin brother of annihilation, *provided that nations respect one another's vital interests; otherwise, we end the world.*" But, no matter how one phrases it, the fact, which is rarely, if ever, mentioned either in the cold, abstract language of the theorists or in the ringing tones of the statesmen, is that the nuclear powers put a higher value on national sovereignty than they do on human survival, and that, while they would naturally prefer to have both, they are ultimately prepared to bring an end to mankind in their attempt to protect their own countries.

That we have let extinction replace war as the final protector of national interests is concealed to a certain extent by the fact that so far nuclear threats have been used, broadly speaking, for defensive purposes, to preserve rather than upset the status quo. For example, no one has attempted simply to conquer other countries through the threat or the use of nuclear weapons. Our reliance on extinction to thus freeze the world more or less in its present state is, in a sense, flushed out of hiding in times of crisis, when the status quo is challenged. At these moments—the Berlin crisis, the Cuban missile crisis, the American mining of Haiphong Harbor in 1972, the Soviet invasion of Afghanistan in 1979, among others— the world suddenly glimpses how far the superpowers are ready to go in pursuit of their interests. When calm returns, however, we are permitted to forget this ugly fact about the nuclear world, and to indulge ourselves again in the illusion that we possess nuclear arms solely in order to prevent their use.

As I have noted earlier, the crisis brought about by the Soviet invasion of Afghanistan serves to illustrate the contradictory pressures that operate on statesmen in any nuclear crisis. When the Soviet Union began the airlift of thousands of troops into Afghanistan, early in December of 1979, and, a few weeks later, oversaw the murder of the country's leader, President Hafizullah Amin (an extreme leftist who had fallen out of favor with Moscow), and installed its own man, Babrak Karmal, in his place, the American reaction was immediate and strong, but it involved neither the use nor the threat of force. President Carter sharply curtailed the sale of grain and certain other items to the Soviet Union, asked the United States Olympic Committee not to participate in the Olympics in Moscow in the summer of 1980 (the request was honored), and announced that he was asking the Senate to delay consideration of the SALT II treaty, which he and Brezhnev had already signed. The lack of military action, or even a threat of such action, against the Soviets in Afghanistan signalled that, while the American government was greatly disturbed by the invasion, it did not regard it as menacing the "vital interests" of the United States. The same could not be said, however, of a possible invasion of Afghanistan's neighbor Iran, which supplied oil in large quantities to the West, or of nearby Saudi Arabia, which has the largest oil reserves of any country in the world. The independence of these nations was indeed considered to be a vital interest of the United States, because the nations of the Western alliance and Japan had come to depend on Middle Eastern oil for the functioning of their economies; and it was a growing fear that the Soviet Union might next

211

threaten these countries that gave the crisis a nuclear dimension. The fact was that the United States was worried not so much about Afghanistan and its people as about Western oil supplies. And to counter that perceived peril the United States did resort to a military threat, which took the form of Carter's statement, in his State of the Union address, in January, that "an attempt by any outside force to gain control of the Persian Gulf region will be regarded as an assault on the vital interests of the United States of America," and that "such an assault will be repelled by any means necessary, including military force." And shortly afterward any ambiguity about the meaning of the threat was dispelled by the story in the *Times* concerning a Defense Department "study" (apparently leaked by the Administration) that found that in the event of a Soviet invasion of northern Iran the United States should consider the use of nuclear weapons. However, just as everyone knew that the Soviet Union had conventional superiority in the Persian Gulf, everyone also knew that the Soviet Union possessed nuclear weapons and would be perfectly capable of using them in retaliation if the United States used them first. No one could suppose that the Soviet Union would advance into Iran only to give up and go home once the United States had used nuclear weapons against its troops. Rather, it was thought, the Soviet Union would either hold off from such an invasion in the first place or have some plan in mind for responding to an American nuclear attack. Furthermore, it was clear to all observers that neither side could expect to "win" a nuclear "war" in the Middle East. Only after all the missiles were fired—not only at targets in the Middle East but at targets throughout the world—would any outcome be reached, but that outcome, of course, would be mutual annihilation. Since these elementary facts were well known to both sides, and had certainly been rehearsed countless times in "war games" and the like, both sides were well aware that President Carter in threatening to use "any means necessary" to defend the Persian Gulf was in effect invoking the ultimate sanction: the threat of pushing the world into a nuclear holocaust. I shall not deal here with the question of whether or not Carter was correct in his judgment that the Soviet Union was considering the conquest of the Persian Gulf countries, and thus needed to be deterred from doing so. I only wish to observe that in the present global political system a leader of a nuclear power who comes to believe that his nation's vital interests are being threatened by another nuclear power faces a pair of alternatives that never confronted any statesman of pre-nuclear times: he can acquiesce in the aggression—a policy that, if it were to be followed consistently, could leave his nation at the adversary's mercy—or he can threaten, as Carter did, to unleash a holocaust in which the life of mankind might be lost, his hope being, of course, that the threat alone will deter the enemy from its aggressive action.

We are left to wonder what Carter would have done if the Soviets had ignored his threat and invaded Iran or Saudi Arabia, just as we are left to wonder what any Soviet or American leaders would do if an "unacceptable" move against the "vital interests" of their countries ever actually materialized—if, for example, the Soviet Union invaded West Germany, or the NATO forces invaded East Germany. This is what the world had to ask itself during the Cuban missile crisis, and what it has to ask itself whenever the interests of the superpowers clash in any part of the world. (And the question also comes up now in Sino-Soviet disputes—as it did when the Chinese recently engaged in a border war against the Soviet-backed Vietnamese. The divide that defines "the brink" now runs between the Soviet Union and China as well as between the Soviet Union and the United States.) As in the case of the retaliatory strike in deterrence theory, we encounter the disparity between the supposed rationality of *threatening* the use of nuclear weapons and the irrationality of actually *using* them if the threat should fail. For while it arguably makes sense to *deter* the foe from some action with the threat of a holocaust, it can never make sense to *launch* the holocaust if the foe is not deterred, since there is no human purpose that can justify extinction. And yet the success of the deterrence doctrine depends on the credibility of the threat of this unjustifiable use. Would Carter—a dedicated Christian—have risked extinction in the attempt to hold on to Middle Eastern oil? When he made his threat, did he consider his obligation to all of mankind and to the numberless future generations of human beings? Would he have plunged the world into the "vast unknown"? And did Brezhnev consider those obligations when he jarred the peace of the world by sending his armies across Soviet borders to subjugate one of the earth's sovereign peoples? Would Brezhnev, who has stated that to launch a nuclear holocaust would be "suicide," commit that suicide if he believed that the West was about to gain control of Eastern Europe? Would Deng Xiaoping take that risk to keep hold of a piece of Inner Mongolia? Did Khrushchev weigh the importance of the earth and the human species when he sent into Cuba missiles capable of carrying nuclear warheads? And did Kennedy weigh the importance of those things when he blockaded Cuba and then, according to his brother, waited to find out whether events over which "he no longer had control" would lead the world into a holocaust? These are the questions that hang in the air over our nuclear world, leaving us perpetually uncertain whether the next moment may not be the world's last.

When one great power adopts a strategic theory, it becomes a doctrine; when two rival great powers adopt it, it becomes a system; and when those rivals more or less abide by the rules of the system, and even hold negotiations aimed at strengthening it (I am thinking of SALT), and are prepared to see new nations enter it as they develop the necessary technical equipment, the system can be described as entrenched. This is the point at which the system of deterrence has arrived today. In essence, it is, as we have seen, a system of sovereign nation-states presided over by a hedged, or qualified, doomsday machine, with which we hope to reap the deterrent benefits of the threat of doom without clearly committing ourselves to doom if deterrence should fail—as we know that it well may, especially with the number of nuclear powers in the world growing. The basic dictate of the system is that if in the opinion of any nuclear power any other nuclear power seriously breaks the rules, then all powers are to be annihilated. Since in a holocaust the consequences may be the same for the aggressor, its punisher, and bystanders, the distinction between friendly and hostile nuclear forces has lost most of its meaning, and the nuclear arsenals of the world are effectively combined by policy into one great arsenal, which is looked to by all powers equally for their "safety." By the same token, even conventionally armed nations have the potential of blowing the world up, for they may draw the superpowers into one of their wars. We can picture this system in simple form if we imagine it as a doomsday machine possessed jointly by all nuclear powers. It is as though a number of people, each one possessing certain valuables that the others want and, furthermore, think they have a right to, are grouped in a room around a single bomb that is large enough to kill them all if it goes off. Each person holds in his hands a switch with which he can detonate the bomb. Every once in a while, a new person enters, also holding a switch. These people constantly reassure one another that the purpose of the whole system is to frighten everyone into inaction and let everyone enjoy in peace the valuables he has, and that for anyone to pull the switch would be suicidal and insane. Yet whenever a dispute breaks out over which valuables rightfully belong to whom, those same people hotly declare that enjoyment of their valuables is more important to them than everyone's life, their own included, and declare their "unwavering" and "inexorable" determination to set off the bomb if they cannot have their way. To this description we must add that some of the people in the room are not quite sure that the system works the way they have been told it does, and suspect that if they are the ones to set off the bomb they may be spared and only the others killed.

Examined in theoretical terms, the deterrence system emerges as a monstrous hybrid, stuck halfway between what the political philosophers call a "state of nature," in which individuals live together without founding any central authority among them, and the so-called "civil state," in which such an authority has been founded. In the passage from the state of nature to the civil state, each individual surrenders his capacity for violence to the central authority, which then employs the gathered resources, according to a system of laws, in the service of the common good. In the

215

deterrence system, the individuals have combined their forces into a single force—the machine that will punish everyone with annihilation if anyone breaks the rules—but have failed to establish any central authority to preside over it. Thus, they have centralized the means of violence while leaving the decision-making decentralized —in effect, delegating to each member of the community a veto power over the continued survival of the species. It is no overstatement to say that if any society organized its affairs in this way, giving to each citizen the power to kill all the others, it would be regarded as deranged. (The system is even worse than anarchy, in which the evil that each person can do is at least limited by the limits of his own strength.) But, for some reason, when it comes to organizing the whole world, and providing for its survival, we regard such a system as a masterpiece of prudent statesmanship.

The dilemma of the nation that in order to protect its national sovereignty finds that it must put the survival of mankind at risk is a trap from which there is no escape as long as nations possess arsenals of nuclear weapons. The deterrence doctrine seeks to rationalize this state of affairs, but it fails, because at the crucial moment it requires nations to sacrifice mankind for their own interests—an absurdity as well as a crime beyond reckoning. Indeed, the deterrence doctrine actually almost *compels* the world to live perpetually on the brink of doom, for any nation that took a step or two back would put its interests and, ultimately, its independence at the mercy of the military forces of its adversaries. And although, for any number of reasons, an adversary might not press its advantage (as, for example, the United States did not right after the Second World War, when it possessed a monopoly on nuclear weapons), no nation has yet volunteered to put itself at this competitive disadvantage. It appears that the only way to escape from the trap is to change the system, and take away from nuclear weapons the responsibility for defending nations. But unless one supposes that, in a global spread of quietism, nations and people in general are going to give up the pursuit of their interests and their ideals and become wholly inactive, this separation can be achieved only if a new way—a nonviolent way—of making and guaranteeing these decisions is found.

In the decades since nuclear arms first appeared in the world, the doctrine of nuclear deterrence has commanded the sincere respect and adherence of many people of good will—especially when they found themselves arguing, as they so often did, with the adherents of traditional military doctrine, who even today, in the face of extinction itself, go on arguing for "military superiority," and the like. And if one once accepts the existence of the doomsday machine, then deterrence theory, however flawed, does offer the hope of certain benefits, the main one being a degree of "stability." Therefore, the perpetual struggle of its adherents against the sheer lunacy of "fighting a nuclear war" is a creditable one. But the fundamental truth about the doctrine and about its role in the wider political—and, it must be added, biological—scheme of things also has to be recognized. For the doctrine's central claim—that it deploys nuclear weapons only in order to prevent their use—is simply not true. Actually, it deploys them to protect national sovereignty, and if this aim were not present they could be quickly dismantled. The doctrine, then, has been the intellectual screen behind which the doomsday machine was built. And its deceptive claim that only by building nuclear weapons can we save ourselves from nuclear weapons lent the doomsday machine a veneer of reason and of respectability—almost of benevolence—that it should never have been given. For to build this machine at all was a mistake of the hugest proportions ever known—without question the greatest ever made by our species. The only conceivable worse mistake would be to put the machine to use. Now deterrence, having rationalized the construction of the machine, weds us to it, and, at best, offers us, if we are lucky, a slightly extended term of residence on earth before the inevitable human or mechanical mistake occurs and we are annihilated.

Yet the deterrence policy in itself is clearly not the deepest source of our difficulty. Rather, as we have seen, it is only a piece of repair work on the immeasurably more deeply entrenched system of national sovereignty. People do not want deterrence for its own sake; indeed, they hardly know what it is, and tend to shun the whole subject. They want the national sovereignty that deterrence promises to preserve. National sovereignty lies at the very core of the political issues that the peril of extinction forces upon us. Sovereignty is the "reality" that the "realists" counsel us to accept as inevitable, referring to any alternative as "unrealistic" or "utopian." If the argument about nuclear weapons is to be conducted in good faith, then just as those who favor the deterrence policy (not to speak of traditional military doctrine) must in all honesty admit that their scheme contemplates the extinction of man in the name of protecting national sovereignty, so must those who favor complete nuclear and conventional disarmament, as I do, admit that their recommendation is inconsistent with national sovereignty; to pretend otherwise would be to evade the political question that is central to the nuclear predicament. The terms of the deal that the world has now struck with itself must be made clear. On the one side stand human life and the terrestrial creation. On the other side stands a particular organization of human life— the system of independent, sovereign nation-states. Our choice so far has been to preserve that political organization of human life at the cost of risking all human life. We are told that "realism" compels us to preserve the system of sovereignty. But that political realism is not biological realism; it is biological nihilism—and for that reason is, of course, political nihilism, too. Indeed, it is nihilism in every conceivable sense of that word. We are told that it is human fate— perhaps even "a law of human nature"—that, in obedience, perhaps, to some "territorial imperative," or to some dark and ineluctable truth in the bottom of our souls, we must preserve sovereignty and always settle our differences with violence. If this is our fate, then it is our fate to die. But must we embrace nihilism? Must we die? Is self-extermination a law of our nature? Is there nothing we can do? I do not believe so. Indeed, if we admit the reality of the basic terms of the nuclear predicament—that present levels of global armament are great enough to possibly extinguish the species if a holocaust should occur; that in extinction every human purpose would be lost; that because once the species has been extinguished there will be no second chance, and the game will be over for all time; that therefore this possibility must be dealt with morally and politically as though it were a certainty; and that either by accident or by design a holocaust can occur at any second—then, whatever political views we may hold on other matters, we are driven almost inescapably to take action to rid the world of nuclear arms. Just as we have chosen to make nuclear weapons, we can choose to unmake them. Just as we have chosen to live in the system of sovereign states, we can choose to live in some other system. To do so would, of course, be unprecedented, and in many ways frightening, even truly perilous, but it is by no means impossible. Our present system and the institutions that make it up are the debris of history. They have become inimical to life, and must be swept away. They constitute a noose around the neck of mankind, threatening to choke off the human future, but we can cut the noose and break free. To suppose otherwise would be to set up a false, fictitious fate, molded out of our own weaknesses and our own alterable decisions. We are indeed fated by our acquisition of the basic knowledge of physics to live for the rest of time with the knowledge of how to destroy ourselves. But we are not for that reason fated to destroy ourselves. We can choose to live.

In this book, I have not sought to define a political solution to the nuclear predicament—either to embark on the full-scale reëxamination of the foundations of political thought which must be undertaken if the world's political institutions are to be made consonant with the global reality in which they operate or to work out the practical steps by which mankind, acting for the first time in history as a single entity, can reorganize its political life. I have left to others those awesome, urgent tasks, which, imposed on us by history, constitute the political work of our age. Rather, I have attempted to examine the physical extent, the human significance, and the practical dimensions of the nuclear predicament in which the whole world now finds itself. This predicament is a sort of cage that has quietly grown up around the earth, imprisoning every person on it, and the demanding terms of the predicament—its durability, its global political sweep, its human totality—constitute the bars of that cage. However, if a description of the predicament, which is the greatest that mankind has ever faced, cannot in itself reveal to us how we can escape, it can, I believe, acquaint us with the magnitude and shape of the task that we have to address ourselves to. And it can summon us to action.

To begin a summary with the matter of war: By effectively removing the limits on human access to the forces of nature, the invention of nuclear weapons ruined war, which depended for its results, and therefore for its usefulness, on the exhaustion of the forces of one of the adversaries. War depended, above all, on the weakness of human powers, and when human powers came to exceed human and other earthly endurance—when man as master of nature grew mightier than man as a vulnerable, mortal part of nature—war was ruined. Since war was the means by which violence was fashioned into an instrument that was useful in political affairs, the ruin of war by nuclear weapons has brought about a divorce between violence and politics. I submit that this divorce, being based on irreversible progress in scientific knowledge, not only is final but must ultimately extend across the full range of political affairs, and that the task facing the species is to shape a world politics that does not rely on violence. This task falls into two parts—two aims. The first is to save the world from extinction by eliminating nuclear weapons from the earth. Just recently, on the occasion of his retirement, Admiral Hyman Rickover, who devoted a good part of his life to overseeing the development and construction of nuclear-powered, nuclear-missile-bearing submarines for the United States Navy, told a congressional committee that in his belief mankind was going to destroy itself with nuclear arms. He also said of his part in the nuclear buildup that he was "not proud" of it, and added that he would like to "sink" the ships that he had poured so much of his life into. And, indeed, what everyone is now called on to do is to sink all the ships, and also ground all the planes, and fill in all the missile silos, and dismantle all the warheads. The second aim, which alone can provide a sure foundation for the first, is to create a political means by which the world can arrive at the decisions that sovereign states previously arrived at through war. These two aims, which correspond to the aims mentioned earlier of preserving the existence of life and pursuing the various ends of life, are intimately connected. If, on the one hand, disarmament is not accompanied by a political solution, then every clash of will between nations will tempt them to pick up the instruments of violence again, and so lead the world back toward extinction. If, on the other hand, a political solution is not accompanied by complete disarmament, then the political decisions that are made will not be binding, for they will be subject to challenge by force. And if, as in our present world, there is neither a political solution nor disarmament, then the world will be held perpetually at the edge of doom, and every clash between nuclear powers will threaten to push it over the edge.

The significance of the first aim—disarmament—which, without being paradoxical, we can describe as a "strategic" aim, can be clarified if we extend to its logical conclusion the reasoning that underlies the doctrine of deterrence. At present, the world relies on nuclear weapons both to prevent the use of nuclear weapons and to regulate the behavior of nations; but let us go a step—a very large step—further, and suppose, for a moment, that the world had established a political means of making international decisions and thus had no further need for nuclear or any other weapons. In order for such a thing to happen, we may ask, would the doctrine of deterrence and the fears on which it is based have to evaporate in the warmth of global good will? They would not. On the contrary, fear of extinction would have to increase, and permeate life at a deeper level: until it was great enough to inspire the complete rearrangement of world politics. Indeed, only when the world has given up violence does Churchill's dictum that safety is the sturdy child of terror actually become true. (At present, as we have seen, it is not safety but sovereignty that is the sturdy child of terror.) Under the current deterrence doctrine, one might say, safety is only the frail, anemic child of terror, and the reason is precisely that the terror is not yet robust enough to produce a sturdy offspring. For we still deny it, look away from it, and fail to let it reach deep enough into our lives and determine our actions. If we felt the peril for what it is—an urgent threat to our whole human substance—we would let it become the organizing principle of our global collective existence: the foundation on which the world was built. Fear would no longer dictate particular decisions, such as whether or not the Soviet Union might place missiles in Cuba; rather, it would be a moving force behind the establishment of a new system by which every decision was made. And, having dictated the foundation of the system, it would stand guard over it forever after, guaranteeing that the species did not slide back toward anarchy and doom.

This development would be the logical final goal of the doctrine of nuclear deterrence. In the pre-nuclear world, the threat of war, backed up by the frequent practice of war, served as a deterrent to aggression. Today, the threat of extinction, unsupported, for obvious reasons, by practice but backed up by the existence of nuclear arms and the threat to use them, serves as the ultimate deterrent. Thus, in today's system the actual weapons have already retired halfway from their traditional military role. They are "psychological" weapons, whose purpose is not to be employed but to maintain a permanent state of mind—terror—in the adversary. Their target is someone's mind, and their end, if the system works, is to rust into powder in their silos. And our generals are already psychological soldiers—masters of the war game and of the computer terminal but not, fortunately, of the battlefield. In this cerebral world, strategy confronts strategy and scenario battles scenario, the better to keep any of them from ever actually unfolding. But we need to carry this trend further. We need to make the weapons *wholly* cerebral—not things that sit in a silo ready to be fired but merely a thought in our minds. We need to destroy them. Only then will the logical fallacy now at the heart of the deterrence doctrine be removed, for only then will the fear of extinction by nuclear arms be used for the sole purpose of preventing extinction, and not also for the pursuit of national political aims. In a perfected nuclear deterrence, the knowledge in a disarmed world that re-armament potentially means extinction would become the deter-rent. Now, however, it would be not that each nuclear-armed country would deter its nuclear-armed adversary but that aware-ness of the peril of extinction would deter all mankind from reëm-barking on nuclear armament. All human beings would join in a defensive alliance, with nuclear weapons as their common enemy. But since that enemy could spring only from our own midst, deterrer and deterred would be one. We thus arrive at the basic strategic principle of life in a world in which the nuclear predica-ment has been resolved: *Knowledge is the deterrent.* The nuclear peril was born out of knowledge, and it must abide in knowledge. The knowledge in question would be, in the first place, the un-losable scientific knowledge that enables us to build the weapons and condemns us to live forever in a nuclear world. This knowledge is the inexpungible minimum presence that the nuclear peril will always have in the life of the world, no matter what measures we adopt. In the second place, the knowledge would be the full emo-tional, intellectual, spiritual, and visceral understanding of the meaning of extinction—above all, the meaning of the unborn genera-tions to the living. Because extinction is the end of mankind, it can never be anything more than "knowledge" for us; we can never "experience" extinction. It is *this* knowledge—this horror at a mur-derous action taken against generations yet unborn, which exerts pressure at the center of our existence, and which is the whole reality of extinction insofar as it is given to us to experience it—that must become the deterrent.

In a disarmed world, we would not have eliminated the peril of human extinction from the human scene—it is not in our power to do so—but we would at least have pitted our whole strength against it. The inconsistency of threatening to perpetrate extinction in order to escape extinction would be removed. The nuclei of atoms would still contain vast energy, and we would still know how to extinguish ourselves by releasing that energy in chain reactions, but we would not be lifting a finger to do it. There would be no complicity in mass murder, no billions of dollars spent on the machinery of annihilation, no preparations to snuff out the future generations, no hair-raising lunges toward the abyss.

The "realistic" school of political thinking, on which the present system of deterrence is based, teaches that men, on the whole, pursue their own interests and act according to a law of fear. The "idealistic" school looks on the human ability to show regard for others as fundamental, and is based on what Gandhi called the law of love. (Whereas the difference between traditional military thinking and nuclear strategic thinking lies in the different factual premises that they start from, the difference between the "realistic" and the "idealistic" schools of political philosophy lies in different judgments regarding human nature.) Historically, a belief in the necessity of violence has been the hallmark of the credo of the "realist"; however, if one consistently and thoroughly applies the law of fear in nuclear times one is driven not to rely on violence but to banish it altogether. This comes about as the result not of any idealistic assumption but of a rigorous application to our times of the strictly "military" logic of traditional war. For today the only way to achieve genuine national defense for any nation is for all nations to give up violence together. However, if we had begun with Gandhi's law of love we would have arrived at exactly the same arrangement. For to one who believed in nonviolence in a pre-nuclear setting the peril of extinction obviously adds one more reason—and a tremendous one, transcending all others—for giving up violence. Moreover, in at least one respect the law of love proves to fit the facts of this peril better than the law of fear. The law of fear relies on the love of self. Through deterrence—in which anyone's pursuit of self-interest at the expense of others will touch off general ruin that will destroy him, too—this self-love is made use of to protect everyone. However, self-love—a narrow, though intense, love—cannot, as we have seen, extend its protection to the future generations, or even get them in view. They still do not have any selves whose fear of death could be pooled in the common fund of fear, and yet their lives are at stake in extinction. The deterrence doctrine is a transaction that is limited to living people

—it leaves out of account the helpless, speechless unborn (while we can launch a first strike against them, they have no forces with which to retaliate)—and yet the fate of the future generations is at the heart of extinction, for their cancellation is what extinction is. Their lives are at stake, but their vote is not counted. Love, however, can reach them—can enable them to be. Love, a spiritual energy that the human heart can pit against the physical energy released from the heart of matter, can create, cherish, and safeguard what extinction would destroy and shut up in nothingness. But in fact there is no need, at least on the practical level, to choose between the law of fear and the law of love, because ultimately they lead to the same destination. It is no more realistic than it is idealistic to destroy the world.

In supposing for a moment that the world had found a political means of making international decisions, I made a very large supposition indeed—one that encompasses something close to the whole work of resolving the nuclear predicament, for, once a political solution has been found, disarmament becomes a merely technical matter, which should present no special difficulties. And yet simply to recognize that the task is at bottom political, and that only a political solution can prepare the way for full disarmament and real safety for the species, is in itself important. The recognition calls attention to the fact that disarmament in isolation from political change cannot proceed very far. It alerts us to the fact that when someone proposes, as President Carter did in his Inaugural Address, to aim at ridding the world of nuclear weapons, there is an immense obstacle that has to be faced and surmounted. For the world, in freeing itself of one burden, the peril of extinction, must inevitably shoulder another: it must assume full responsibility for settling human differences peacefully. Morever, this recognition forces us to acknowledge that nuclear disarmament cannot occur if conventional arms are left in place, since as long as nations defend themselves with arms of any kind they will be fully sovereign, and as long as they are fully sovereign they will be at liberty to build nuclear weapons if they so choose. And if we assume that wars do break out and some nations find themselves facing defeat in the conventional arena, then the reappearance of nuclear arms, which would prevent such defeat, becomes a strong likelihood. What nation, once having entrusted its fortunes to the force of arms, would permit itself to be conquered by an enemy when the means of driving him back, perhaps with a mere threat, was on hand? And how safe can the world be while nations threaten one another's existence with violence and retain for themselves the sovereign right to build whatever weapons they choose to build? This vision of an international life that in the military sphere is restricted to the pre-nuclear world while in the scientific realm it is in the nuclear world is, in fact, thoroughly implausible. If we are serious about nuclear disarmament—the minimum technical requirement for real safety from extinction—then we must accept conventional disarmament as well, and this means disarmament not just of nuclear powers but of all powers, for the present nuclear powers are hardly likely to throw away their conventional arms while non-nuclear powers hold on to theirs. But if we accept both nuclear and conventional disarmament, then we are speaking of revolutionizing the politics of the earth. The goals of the political revolution are defined by those of the nuclear revolution. We must lay down our arms, relinquish sovereignty, and found a political system for the peaceful settlement of international disputes.

The task we face is to find a means of political action that will permit human beings to pursue any end for the rest of time. We are asked to replace the mechanism by which political decisions, whatever they may be, are reached. In sum, the task is nothing less than to reinvent politics: to reinvent the world. However, extinction will not wait for us to reinvent the world. Evolution was slow to produce us, but our extinction will be swift; it will literally be over before we know it. We have to match swiftness with swiftness. Because everything we do and everything we are is in jeopardy, and because the peril is immediate and unremitting, every person is the right person to act and every moment is the right moment to begin, starting with the present moment. For nothing underscores our common humanity as strongly as the peril of extinction does; in fact, on a practical and political plane it establishes that common humanity. The purpose of action, though, is not to replace life with politics. The point is not to turn life into a scene of protest; life is the point.

Whatever the eventual shape of a world that has been re-invented for the sake of survival, the first, urgent, immediate step, which requires no deep thought or long reflection, is for each person to make known, visibly and unmistakably, his desire that the species survive. Extinction, being in its nature outside human experience, is invisible, but we, by rebelling against it, can indirectly make it visible. No one will ever witness extinction, so we must bear witness to it before the fact. And the place for the rebellion to start is in our daily lives. We can each perform a turnabout right where we are—let our daily business drop from our hands for a while, so that we can turn our attention to securing the foundation of all life, out of which our daily business grows and in which it finds its justification. This disruption of our lives will be a preventive disruption, for we will be hoping through the temporary suspension of our daily life to ward off the eternal suspension of it in extinction. And this turnabout in the first instance can be as simple as a phone call to a friend, a meeting in the community.

However, even as the first steps are taken, the broad ultimate requirements of survival must be recognized and stated clearly. If they are not, we might sink into self-deception, imagining that inadequate measures would suffice to save us. I would suggest that the ultimate requirements are in essence the two that I have mentioned: global disarmament, both nuclear and conventional, and the invention of political means by which the world can peacefully settle the issues that throughout history it has settled by war. Thus, the first steps and the ultimate requirements are clear. If a busload of people is speeding down a mountainside toward a cliff, the passengers do not convene a seminar to investigate the nature of their predicament; they see to it that the driver applies the brakes. Therefore, at a minimum, a freeze on the further deployment of nuclear weapons, participated in both by countries that now have them and by countries that do not yet have them, is called for. Even better would be a reduction in nuclear arms—for example, by cutting the arsenals of the superpowers in half, as George Kennan suggested recently. Simultaneously with disarmament, political steps of many kinds could be taken. For example, talks could be started among the nuclear powers with the aim of making sure that the world did not simply blunder into extinction by mistake; technical and political arrangements could be drawn up to reduce the likelihood of mechanical mistakes and misjudgments of the other side's intentions or actions in a time of crisis, and these would somewhat increase the world's security while the predicament was being tackled at a more fundamental level. For both superpowers—and, indeed, for all other powers—avoiding extinction is a common interest than which none can be greater. And since the existence of a common interest is the best foundation for negotiation, negotiations should have some chance of success. However, the existence of negotiations to reduce the nuclear peril would provide no reason for abandoning the pursuit of other things that one believed in, even those which might be at variance with the beliefs of one's negotiating partner. Thus, to give one contemporary example, there is no need, or excuse, for the United States not to take strong measures to oppose Soviet-sponsored repression in Poland just because it is engaged in disarmament talks with the Soviet Union. The world will not end if we suspend shipments of wheat to the Soviet Union. On the other hand, to break off those talks in an effort to help the Poles, who will be as extinct as anyone else if a holocaust comes about, would be self-defeating. To seek to "punish" the other side by breaking off those negotiations would be in reality self-punishment. All the limited aims of negotiation can be pursued in the short term without danger if only the ultimate goal is kept unswervingly in mind. But ordinary citizens must insist that all these things be done, or they will not be.

If action should be concerted, as it eventually must be, in a common political endeavor, reaching across national boundaries, then, just as the aim of the endeavor would be to hold the gates of life open to the future generations, so its method would be to hold its own gates open to every living person. But it should be borne in mind that even if every person in the world were to enlist, the endeavor would include only an infinitesimal fraction of the people of the dead and the unborn generations, and so it would need to act with the circumspection and modesty of a small minority. From its mission to preserve all generations, it would not seek to derive any rights to dictate to the generations on hand. It would not bend or break the rules of conduct essential to a decent political life, for it would recognize that once one started breaking rules in the name of survival no rule would go unbroken. Intellectually and philosophically, it would carry the principle of tolerance to the utmost extreme. It would attempt to be as open to new thoughts and feelings as it would be to the new generations that would think those thoughts and feel those feelings. Its underlying supposition about creeds and ideologies would be that whereas without mankind none can exist, with mankind all can exist. For while the events that might trigger a holocaust would probably be political, the consequences would be deeper than any politics or political aims, bringing ruin to the hopes and plans of capitalists and socialists, rightists and leftists, conservatives and liberals alike. Having as the source of its strength only the spontaneously offered support of the people of the earth, it would, in turn, respect each person's will, which is to say his liberty. Eventually, the popular will that it marshalled might be deployed as a check on the power of whatever political institutions were invented to replace war.

Since the goal would be a nonviolent world, the actions of this endeavor would be nonviolent. What Gandhi once said of the spirit of nonviolent action in general would be especially important to the spirit of these particular actions: "In the dictionary of nonviolent action, there is no such thing as an 'external enemy.'" With the world itself at stake, all differences would by definition be "internal" differences, to be resolved on the basis of respect for those with whom one disagreed. If our aim is to save humanity, we must respect the humanity of every person. For who would be the enemy? Certainly not the world's political leaders, who, though they now menace the earth with nuclear weapons, do so only with our permission, and even at our bidding. At least, this is true for the democracies. We do not know what the peoples of the totalitarian states, including the people of the Soviet Union, may want. They are locked in silence by their government. In these circumstances, public opinion in the free countries would have to represent public opinion in all countries, and would have to bring its pressure to bear, as best it could, on all governments.

At present, most of us do nothing. We look away. We remain calm. We are silent. We take refuge in the hope that the holocaust won't happen, and turn back to our individual concerns. We deny the truth that is all around us. Indifferent to the future of our kind, we grow indifferent to one another. We drift apart. We grow cold. We drowse our way toward the end of the world. But if once we shook off our lethargy and fatigue and began to act, the climate would change. Just as inertia produces despair—a despair often so deep that it does not even know itself as despair—arousal and action would give us access to hope, and life would start to mend: not just life in its entirety but daily life, every individual life. At that point, we would begin to withdraw from our role as both the victims and the perpetrators of mass murder. We would no longer be the destroyers of mankind but, rather, the gateway through which the future generations would enter the world. Then the passion and will that we need to save ourselves would flood into our lives. Then the walls of indifference, inertia, and coldness that now isolate each of us from others, and all of us from the past and future generations, would melt, like snow in spring. E. M. Forster told us, "Only connect!" Let us connect. Auden told us, "We must love one another or die." Let us love one another—in the present and across the divides of death and birth. Christ said, "I come not to judge the world but to save the world." Let us, also, not judge the world but save the world. By restoring our severed links with life, we will restore our own lives. Instead of stopping the course of time and cutting off the human future, we would make it possible for the future generations to be born. Their inestimable gift to us, passed back from the future into the present, would be the wholeness and meaning of life.

The Choice

Two paths lie before us. One leads to death, the other to life. If we choose the first path—if we numbly refuse to acknowledge the nearness of extinction, all the while increasing our preparations to bring it about—then we in effect become the allies of death, and in everything we do our attachment to life will weaken: our vision, blinded to the abyss that has opened at our feet, will dim and grow confused; our will, discouraged by the thought of trying to build on such a precarious foundation anything that is meant to last, will slacken; and we will sink into stupefaction, as though we were gradually weaning ourselves from life in preparation for the end. On the other hand, if we reject our doom, and bend our efforts toward survival—if we arouse ourselves to the peril and act to forestall it, making ourselves the allies of life—then the anesthetic fog will lift: our vision, no longer straining not to see the obvious, will sharpen; our will, finding secure ground to build on, will be restored; and we will take full and clear possession of life again. One day—and it is hard to believe that it will not be soon—we will make our choice. Either we will sink into the final coma and end it all or, as I trust and believe, we will awaken to the truth of our peril, a truth as great as life itself, and, like a person who has swallowed a lethal poison but shakes off his stupor at the last moment and vomits the poison up, we will break through the layers of our denials, put aside our fainthearted excuses, and rise up to cleanse the earth of nuclear weapons.

INDEX

Index

unborn, the, *see* generations, future
uncertainty:
  and extinction as possibility, 76–7,
    94–5
  and holocaust calculations, 25,
    72–8 *passim*, 207
  and knowledge of earth, 76–8
  principle (of W. Heisenberg), 76
  in scientific research, 104–5
"Unforgettable Fire," by survivors
  of Hiroshima, 38–9, 42
United Nations, 194
United States:
  nuclear attack on, 55–9
  nuclear capabilities of, 31, 54
  nuclear conflict with Soviet Union,
    27, 71–2, 191, 192
  Persian Gulf policy, 29–30, 211–13
  and precipitation of nuclear
    hostilities, 28–30, 211–14
  see also superpowers; *and depart-*
    ments and programs of the
    federal government under their
    own names, e.g. Dept. of
    Agriculture
"unthinkable":
  deputized to think tanks, 149
  extinction as, 128, 138–9, 139–43,
    186
  holocaust as, 4, 8, 32, 141
  moral sense separated from, 195
  radical evil as, 146
uranium, 13, 14
Urbach, Frederick, 85
U.S.S.R., *see* Soviet Union

value, *see* worth
vegetation, *see* plants
"victory" in nuclear conflict, 159–60,
  190, 199, 202, 203
violence:
  abandoned by all nations, 224
  capacity for, centralized, 215–16
  as innate, in mankind, 185, 218
  and politics, 220
  war as outcome of, 191, 220

war:
  Clausewitz on, 188, 189, 190, 191,
    202

  as means of settling disputes,
    159–60, 186–7, 188, 193
  and nuclear weapons, 189–93, 220
  and scientific knowledge, 106
  and sovereignty, system of, 186–7,
    189–93
war, limited, 31–2, 33, 66, 192, 207–8
war, nuclear, *see* holocaust, nuclear;
  hostilities, nuclear; strategy,
  nuclear; war, limited
weak-force reactions, 9, 11; *see also*
  radiation, nuclear
weapons, nuclear:
  countries armed with, 72, 108, 214
  denial of, *see* denial of nuclear
    peril
  destructive effects of: extent of,
    37; global primary, 19–21; local
    primary, 17–19, 22; on ozone
    layer, 75, 81–2; secondary (or
    indirect), 19, 23; *see also* blast
    wave; electromagnetic pulse;
    fallout, radioactive; fire(s);
    mass; fireball; radiation, nuclear;
    thermal pulse
  and first-strike strategy, 27–8,
    202–4 *passim*
  governmental secrecy about, 101,
    107, 149
  limitation of, *see* disarmament
    efforts; nonproliferation
  manufacture of, 99–100
  opposition to, *see* anti-nuclear
    movements; disarmament efforts
  proliferation of, 54, 94, 107, 148,
    149–50, 183–4, 209
  psychological effects of, 8
  and sovereignty, 187
  and war (traditional forms), 189–
    93, 220
  yield (explosive) of, 20, 46, 54–5
  see also bomb(s)
Whitehead, Alfred North, 101
wind:
  in nuclear attacks on U.S., 48, 49,
    57
  whirlwind at Hiroshima, 37
Woodwell, George M., 63, 64
worth:
  of mankind, 124–30, 153
  standards of, 124

244

A Note on the Type

The text of this book was set in Caledonia, a Lintoype face designed by W. A. Dwiggins. It belongs to the family of printing types called "modern faces" by printers—a term used to mark the change in style of type letters that occurred about 1800. Caledonia borders on the general design of Scotch Modern, but is more freely drawn than that letter.

Composed, printed, and bound by
American Book–Stratford Press, Saddle Brook, New Jersey.